Free Exercise of Religion and the United States Constitution

The United States is extremely diverse religiously and, not infrequently, individuals sincerely contend that they are unable to act in accord with law as a matter of conscience. The First Amendment to the United States Constitution protects the free exercise of religion and the United States Supreme Court has issued many decisions exploring the depth and breadth of those protections. This book addresses the Court's free exercise jurisprudence, discussing what counts as religion and the protections that have been afforded to a variety of religious practices. Regrettably, the Court has not offered a principled and consistent account of which religious practices are protected or even how to decide whether a particular practice is protected, which has resulted in similar cases being treated dissimilarly. Further, the Court's free exercise jurisprudence has been used to provide guidance in interpreting federal statutory protections, which is making matters even more chaotic.

This book attempts to clarify what the Court has said in the hopes that it will contribute to the development of a more consistent and principled jurisprudence that respects the rights of the religious and the non-religious.

Mark Strasser is Trustees Professor of Law at Capital University Law School in Columbus, Ohio. His previous books include *Religion, Education and the State: An Unprincipled Doctrine in Search of Moorings* (2011), *Same-Sex Unions Across the United States* (2011), *On Same-Sex Marriage, Civil Unions, and the Rule of Law: Constitutional Interpretation at the Crossroads* (2002), *The Challenge of Same-Sex Marriage: Federalist Principles and Constitutional Protections* (1999), *Legally Wed: Same-Sex Marriage and the Constitution* (1997), *Agency, Free Will, and Moral Responsibility* (1992), *The Moral Philosophy of John Stuart Mill: Toward Modifications of Contemporary Utilitarianism* (1991), and *Francis Hutcheson's Moral Theory: Its Form and Utility* (1990).

ICLARS Series on Law and Religion

Series Editors:
Silvio Ferrari, University of Milan, Italy, Russell Sandberg, Cardiff University, UK, Pieter Coertzen, University of Stellenbosch, South Africa, W. Cole Durham, Jr., Brigham Young University, USA, and Tahir Mahmood, Amity International University, India

The *ICLARS Series on Law and Religion* is a new series designed to provide a forum for the rapidly expanding field of research in law and religion. The series is published in association with the International Consortium for Law and Religion Studies, an international network of scholars and experts of law and religion founded in 2007 with the aim of providing a place where information, data and opinions can easily be exchanged among members and made available to the broader scientific community. The series aims to become a primary source for students and scholars while presenting authors with a valuable means to reach a wide and growing readership.

Other titles in this series:

Islam, Law and the Modern State: (Re)imagining Liberal Theory in Muslim Contexts
Arif A. Jamal, National University of Singapore, Singapore

Religious Freedom and the Australian Constitution: Origins and Future
Luke Beck, Western Sydney University, Australia

Law and International Religious Freedom: The Rise and Decline of the American Model
Pasquale Annicchino, European University Institute, Italy

Proportionality, Equality Laws, and Religion: Conflicts in England, Canada, and the USA
Megan Pearson, University of Southampton, UK

Islam and Women's Income
Farah Deeba Chowdhury, Queen's University, Canada

Blasphemy, Islam and the State
Stewart Fenwick, University of Melbourne, Australia

Religions and Constitutional Transitions in the Muslim Mediterranean
Edited by Alessandro Ferrari, University of Insubria, Italy and James Toronto, Brigham Young University, USA

Religion, Pluralism, and Reconciling Difference
W. Cole Durham, Jr. and Donlu Thayer, both at Brigham Young University, USA

Religion and Equality
Edited by W. Cole Durham, Jr. and Donlu Thayer, both at Brigham Young University, USA

www.routledge.com/ICLARS-Series-on-Law-and-Religion/book-series/ICLARS

Free Exercise of Religion and the United States Constitution
The Supreme Court's Challenge

Mark P. Strasser

LONDON AND NEW YORK

First published 2018 by Routledge

2 Park Square, Milton Park, Abingdon, Oxfordshire OX14 4RN
52 Vanderbilt Avenue, New York, NY 10017

Routledge is an imprint of the Taylor & Francis Group, an informa business

First issued in paperback 2019

Copyright © 2018 Mark P. Strasser

The right of Mark P. Strasser to be identified as author of this work has been asserted by him in accordance with sections 77 and 78 of the Copyright, Designs and Patents Act 1988.

All rights reserved. No part of this book may be reprinted or reproduced or utilised in any form or by any electronic, mechanical, or other means, now known or hereafter invented, including photocopying and recording, or in any information storage or retrieval system, without permission in writing from the publishers.

Notice:
Product or corporate names may be trademarks or registered trademarks, and are used only for identification and explanation without intent to infringe.

British Library Cataloguing-in-Publication Data
A catalogue record for this book is available from the British Library

Library of Congress Cataloging-in-Publication Data
Names: Strasser, Mark Philip, 1955-, author.
Title: Free exercise of religion and the United States Constitution : the Supreme Court's challenge / Mark P. Strasser.
Description: New York : Routledge, 2018. |
Series: ICLARS series on law and religion | Includes bibliographical references and index.
Identifiers: LCCN 2017046179 | ISBN 9780815366898 (hardback)
Subjects: LCSH: Freedom of religion—United States. |
Church and state—United States. | United States. Supreme Court.
Classification: LCC KF4783 .S76 2018 | DDC 342.7308/52—dc23
LC record available at https://lccn.loc.gov/2017046179

ISBN: 978-0-8153-6689-8 (hbk)
ISBN: 978-0-367-89358-3 (pbk)

Typeset in Galliard
by Keystroke, Neville Lodge, Tettenhall, Wolverhampton

To George, Emma, and Nathan

Contents

Acknowledgments ix

Introduction 1

1 **Free exercise and the definition of religion** 5
   Limiting what counts as religion and what free exercise protects 5
      Setting the stage 6
      Modern free exercise 9
      Echoes of nineteenth-century ambivalence? 10
      The Court refuses to classify certain very unusual beliefs as non-religious 11
      Special treatment for religion? 13
      Conflicts between religious and civil requirements 15
   Is it necessary to define religion? 18
      Why define religion? 18
      The breadth of what counts as religion 18
      Sincerity 19
   Conclusion 20

2 **Institutional autonomy and the ministerial exception** 26
   Institutional protections 26
      Areas of competence 27
      Religious determinations and neutral principles 30
   Conclusion 37

3 **Fighting wars and claims of conscience** 40
   Pacifists, benefits, and burdens 40
      Immigration and naturalization 41
      University military instruction 43
      Who qualifies for conscientious objector status? 45
   Conclusion 53

4 **Early modern free exercise** 57
   Fulfilling religious obligations in society 57
      Modern free exercise jurisprudence 57
      Distributing religious tracts 59

Sunday closing laws 60
Employees who cannot work on their Sabbath 63
Decisions about schooling 65
Refusing to make war weapons 67
Conclusion 68

5 Free exercise becomes (more) chaotic — 72

On government rules and religious exemptions 72
Social Security 72
Other labor limitations 76
AFDC benefits 78
Subsequent change of religion 82
Sacred ground 82
Idiosyncratic beliefs 84
Sales and use taxes 84
Conclusion 85

6 The *Smith* revolution — 90

Smith *and its aftermath* 90
The free exercise revolution 90
Targeting religion 96
RFRA and the states 97
RLUIPA and the Establishment Clause 99
RFRA and the federal government 100
Conclusion 101

7 Corporate conscience — 106

On corporate consciences and substantial burdens 106
Corporate conscience exemptions 106
Beard length 119
Conclusion 119

8 Lower courts and the protection of religion — 125

State and federal protection of religion and the lower courts 125
Substantial burdens 126
What is religious? 128
State RFRAs 135
Conclusion 138

Bibliography 148
Index 155

Acknowledgments

I have discussed these and related subjects in various law reviews.

"Neutrality, Accommodation, and Conscience Clause Legislation," *Alabama Civil Rights & Civil Liberties Law Review* 8:197–238 (2017)
"Narrow Tailoring, Compelling Interests, and Free Exercise: On ACA, RFRA and Predictability," *University of Louisville Law Review* 53:467–508 (2016)
"*Hobby Lobby*, RFRA, and Family Burdens," *Boston University Public Interest Law Journal* 25:239–64 (2016)
"Free Exercise and Substantial Burdens Under Federal Law," *Nebraska Law Review* 94:633–84 (2016)
"Free Exercise and the Definition of Religion: Confusion in the Federal Courts," *Houston Law Review* 53:909–37 (2016)
"Definitions, Religion, and Free Exercise Guarantees," *Tulsa Law Review* 51:1–38 (2015)
"Old Wine, Old Bottles, and Not Very New Corks: On State RFRAs and Free Exercise Jurisprudence," *Saint Louis University Public Law Review* 34:335–66 (2015)
"The Protection of Conscience: On ACA, RFRA and Free Exercise Guarantees," *Tennessee Law Review* 82:345–404 (2015)
"*Hosanna-Tabor*, the Ministerial Exception, and Judicial Competence," *Elon Law Review* 6:151–71 (2014)
"Innocents Beware: On Religion Clause Jurisprudence and the Negligent Retention or Hiring of Clergy," *William and Mary Bill of Rights Journal* 22:177–210 (2013)
"Making the Anomalous Even More Anomalous: On Hosanna-Tabor, the Ministerial Exception, and the Constitution," *Virginia Journal of Social Policy & the Law* 19:400–49 (2012)
"When Churches Divide: On Neutrality, Deference, and Unpredictability," *Hamline Law Review* 32:427–75 (2009)
"The Protection and Alienation of Religious Minorities: On the Evolution of the Endorsement Test," *Michigan State Law Review* 2008:667–724 (2008)
"Preaching, Fundraising, and the Constitution: On Proselytizing and the First Amendment," *Denver University Law Review* 85:405–41 (2007)

Introduction

The United States is extremely diverse religiously with adherents of many well-established and less well-established religions from all over the world. Individuals within the various faith traditions vary greatly with respect to their beliefs about which religious practices are obligatory, optional, or forbidden. In addition, many individuals identify as religious or spiritual but do not self-identify as being affiliated with an organized religious group.

As has always been true, some individuals are guided by their religious beliefs with respect to all aspects of life, whereas others are guided only with respect to certain practices or, perhaps, what to do on certain days of the year. With so many different beliefs about what religion requires, permits, and prohibits, conflicts among individuals and between individuals and the state are inevitable.

The law permits individuals to make a variety of important religious decisions for themselves—individuals can choose to perform or refrain from performing a variety of activities as a matter of conscience. For example, individuals may choose to consume or refrain from consuming certain foods or beverages for religious reasons. Further, the law may accommodate certain religious beliefs and practices, for example, excuse religious pacifists from having to take up arms in defense of their country. That said, however, the law does regulate certain aspects of life, and those laws may conflict with religious dictates. The focus here is on the degree to which the state must exempt individuals because of their religious beliefs and practices.

The First Amendment to the United States Constitution protects the free exercise of religion. Many individuals claim that the constitutional guarantees contained in that amendment preclude the state from adversely affecting those who refuse to act in ways that violate their religious convictions. Whether the First Amendment in fact provides protection in a particular case will depend upon a variety of factors including whether the asserted beliefs are sincerely held and the relative importance of the implicated state and individual interests.

The United States Supreme Court has addressed the strength and reach of First Amendment free exercise guarantees in numerous cases. Regrettably, those decisions have been rather inconsistent with respect to what those guarantees protect or even what test should be used to determine whether a particular practice is protected. Indeed, the Court has sent mixed messages about what counts as a religion for First Amendment purposes.

The Court's contradictory signals on these matters are becoming increasingly problematic. Not only is there a wider range of religious views represented in the United States, but there is increased balkanization in the country and an increasing lack of consensus with respect to a variety of issues. More and more individuals are claiming that they should not be forced to act in ways that contravene their consciences, and this simply is not the time for the Court to make matters more rather than less muddled.

Some jurists and commentators suggest that one of the Court's opinions in particular—*Employment Division v. Smith*—was wrongly decided. There is merit in the criticisms that the *Smith* Court did not accurately represent the Court's previous decisions and that the very standard announced by the *Smith* Court arguably required that a religious exemption be granted in that particular case. Yet, those criticizing the decision often do not recognize some of its strengths. The *Smith* Court rightly recognized that previous decisions often purportedly involved the application of one standard but in reality involved the application of a far weaker standard. The *Smith* Court was also correct that the Court's claiming to apply one standard but in reality applying another standard threatened to undermined constitutional jurisprudence more generally.

Courts and commentators debate how much protection should be afforded to free exercise. Such a determination might take into account a number of factors including historical practices, the developing jurisprudence, and the changing demographics of the country. But whatever approach is adopted must be applied consistently and must be viewed as principled.

Too many commentators wrongly suggest that the decisions prior to *Smith* were rather protective of free exercise. On the contrary, not only were the preceding decisions not protective of free exercise as a general matter, but they were chaotic and unprincipled. Worse still, the Court claimed at the time to be offering a consistent jurisprudence, offering specious distinctions to justify incompatible results. Those wishing to return to the pre-*Smith* mode of analysis are advocating (perhaps unknowingly) a return to chaos.

When individuals seek to return to the pre-*Smith* case law, they likely mean returning to certain earlier decisions but ignoring other decisions that impliedly represent a much different understanding of the strength and reach of free exercise protections (even though the Court was allegedly applying the same standard in all of the cases). Yet, returning to some cases (and ignoring others) does not restore the past jurisprudence but instead creates a new one, which would not only impliedly overrule some of those past decisions but might also prevent the Court from choosing to protect certain practices while refusing to exempt others. Such an approach would have the benefit of being more principled but would also have certain costs in the eyes of some commentators, e.g., because favored religious beliefs and practices could not so readily be privileged over disfavored ones. At least some of those demanding a return to the Court's previous approach would likely complain bitterly both about what that approach would protect and what it would not.

Chapter 1 discusses the evolving jurisprudence with respect to what counts as religion and what free exercise guarantees protect. The Court has emphasized the importance of the distinction between religion and non-religion, noting that free exercise guarantees are not triggered unless the former practices are at issue. But the Court has offered mixed messages about what counts as religious, suggesting some criteria but then rejecting them in subsequent opinions. The Court has consistently suggested that not all beliefs count as religious, but has not been forthcoming with respect to criteria that might usefully distinguish the religious from the non-religious. Judging from what the Court has refused to classify as non-religious, the Constitution incorporates a very inclusive approach to what counts as religion for First Amendment purposes.

Free exercise protections apply to religious institutions as well as individuals. The Court has decided several cases involving challenges to church leadership or ownership of church property, and has suggested that civil courts cannot decide theological matters but can address disputes involving religious parties if applying neutral principles of law. But the permissibility of civil courts deciding religious disputes in light of neutral legal principles itself incorporates an exception—the law cannot force a religious institution to unwillingly accept someone as a minister. The ministerial exception requires further clarification both as to who counts as a minister and as to the contexts in which the civil law is precluded from pressuring a religious entity to accept or reject someone as a member of the clergy. However, as Chapter 2 illustrates, the Court recently suggested that it may eschew the more balanced approach of the previous jurisprudence in favor of a robust immunity for religious institutions that is neither in accord with the past jurisprudence nor good public policy.

Much of the Court's free exercise jurisprudence involves the rights of individuals rather than religious institutions. Even when an individual's beliefs qualify as religious, a separate question involves the conditions under which the state must grant exemptions because of religious beliefs. Chapter 3 discusses how the Court has handled a classic problem for the State—what if anything should be done with those individuals who refuse to serve in the military out of sincere religious convictions? The Court's cases tended to involve interpretations of federal statutes rather than the First Amendment, although the Court's statutory interpretations were informed by the existing constitutional limitations. While some commentators argue that the Court's conscientious objector jurisprudence provides support for the contention that free exercise guarantees are rather robust, a closer examination of what the Court has said and done reveals that Congress may but need not offer robust protections of free exercise. This means that the constitutional protections of conscience are actually much less robust than many commentators seem to think.

It might seem unfair to judge a nation's commitment to the protection of conscience in light of how it treats those who refuse to serve in the military, precisely because the security of the nation is such an important interest. Even those who strongly value the protection of conscience might nonetheless believe that conscientious objections should be overridden when the fate of the nation is at risk. Chapter 4 examines some of the earlier cases in modern free exercise jurisprudence where the security of the nation did not hang in the balance. The Court offered an inconsistent account of free exercise, varying not only in the relative robustness of the protections but also in the standard to be used in cases where free exercise protections were at issue. Members of the Court were aware that their decisions seemed inconsistent and that the distinctions offered seemed specious rather than plausible. Regrettably, no member of the Court could offer an overarching principle or approach that plausibly accounted for the Court's decisions.

One way to read these earlier cases in modern free exercise jurisprudence is to suggest that the Court made some missteps initially but then settled upon a consistent approach. As Chapter 5 illustrates, such a reading of the jurisprudence involves a fundamental misunderstanding. The Court continued in its inconsistent approach, sometimes affirming one standard offering robust guarantees and at other times affirming a different standard with very weak protections for free exercise. The Court would offer one test and rationale in one case and then ignore or expressly reject that test and rationale in another, making the jurisprudence chaotic and providing no guidance to lower courts or anyone else.

Recognizing that the jurisprudence was in disarray, the Court announced a new approach in *Employment Division v. Smith*. Chapter 6 discusses some of the merits and demerits of that decision. The Court was correct that its past case law was inconsistent with respect to (1) the strength of the guarantees, (2) which test was applicable, and (3) how the relevant test should be applied. However, rather than announce that it was adopting a new standard and justifying that standard in light of constitutional principles and public policy, the *Smith* Court instead suggested that its new approach reflected what the Court had been doing all along. But this implausible account of the past jurisprudence resulted in a backlash against both the holding and the methodology. Further, matters were not helped when the test announced by the *Smith* Court arguably yielded a different result in the very case used as a vehicle for announcing the new test. Congress's reaction to *Smith* was swift and extremely critical, resulting in the passage of two different laws—the Religious Freedom Restoration Act (RFRA) and, later, the Religious Land Use and Institutionalized Persons Act (RLUIPA)—to restore what had been allegedly taken away.

Smith has never been overruled. Chapter 7 discusses how the Court has interpreted and applied RFRA and RLUIPA. Regrettably, the Court has offered interpretations of those statutes that neither capture congressional intent nor provide a sustainable approach to free exercise. Instead, the lower courts will have to ignore or radically rework what the Court has said if only because the Court has offered contradictory messages about what the statutory free exercise guarantees protect. Ironically, the pre-*Smith* jurisprudence may be restored through federal statutes, not in affording strong protection of free exercise but in offering inconsistent protection with implausible justifications and rationales.

While the United States Supreme Court has not decided many cases involving RFRA and RLUIPA, there nonetheless has been much litigation involving these statutes in the lower courts. Further, after RFRA was struck down as applied to the states, various state legislatures adopted their own Religious Freedom Restoration Acts. The courts have had many opportunities to address some of the important issues raised by these statutes and have reached very different interpretations of the meanings of key terms and the relative strengths of the protections offered. The Court has offered too little helpful guidance to lower courts wrestling with these issues, even when the lower courts have adopted approaches in clear conflict with the spirit of what the United States Supreme Court has said. Chapter 8 discusses some of the approaches lower courts have taken when interpreting RFRA, RLUIPA, or their own state RFRAs. These interpretations have been less forgiving about what constitutes religion or what constitutes a substantial burden on religious practice than the Court has been. But the Court has not taken the opportunity to provide clear and consistent guidance to the lower courts on these issues. On the contrary, the Court has already started to incorporate its inconsistent and unprincipled approach to free exercise into the jurisprudence interpreting federal statutory protections of religion, which bodes poorly for consistent application of federal protections of religion, especially when nontraditional religious practices are at issue. Both the religious and the non-religious should be alarmed by the current approach to the legal protection of religious practice, especially because it seems to signal an even more chaotic approach in the future.

1 Free exercise and the definition of religion

The First Amendment to the United States Constitution protects the free exercise of religion, and non-religious practices do not receive those same protections. Regrettably, there has been no consensus about the appropriate criteria for determining what counts as religious—sometimes, the implicit criteria focus on the kind of beliefs, sometimes on the strength of the beliefs or on the role that they play in an individual's life, and sometimes on the sincerity of the beliefs. What qualifies as religious under one of these criteria might not qualify as religious under another, which means that whether particular practices will be protected under free exercise guarantees may depend upon which of these criteria are used or emphasized.

The lack of determinate criteria might not seem particularly problematic if only because the Court could simply announce the relevant criteria in one or more cases. Yet, the difficulty is not so easily resolved because the Court has suggested that it is beyond the competence of courts in almost all cases to determine what qualifies as religious. The Court's articulated positions virtually guarantee an incoherent jurisprudence by sending contradictory signals with respect to what counts as religion and who is authorized to make that determination.

This chapter traces the Court's wavering approaches to free exercise guarantees, noting some of the areas in which the Court continues to send mixed messages—the Court has both affirmed and rejected that religious practices are afforded special protection under free exercise guarantees and has been utterly inconsistent with respect to whether courts can decide which beliefs qualify as religious or what criteria would be appropriate when making such a determination. While some of the Court's articulated positions are simply impossible to reconcile, many of the Court's seemingly inconsistent assertions are reconcilable, although in a way that doubtless will strike many as involving an uncomfortable compromise.

Limiting what counts as religion and what free exercise protects

The First Amendment to the United States Constitution protects the free exercise of religion, although it nowhere specifies what counts as religion. So, too, the United States Supreme Court has never specified how to distinguish the religious from the non-religious, although it has offered comments over the years that at least suggest an approach. In the earlier years, the Court was neither particularly clear about what counted as religion nor about whether free exercise rights were strong or, instead, rather weak.

Setting the stage

Over 140 years ago, the United States Supreme Court seemed to suggest that free exercise rights have robust protection. In *Watson v. Jones*, the Court explained that

> the full and free right to entertain any religious belief, to practice any religious principle, and to teach any religious doctrine which does not violate the laws of morality and property, and which does not infringe personal rights, is conceded to all.[1]

This full and free right sounds rather robust, although a closer examination of the comment reveals that that the promised protection may not be so strong after all.

As an initial point, the Court's statement must be interpreted. Consider the qualifier "which does not violate the laws of morality and property, and which does not infringe personal rights." That limitation might seem to apply only to the right to "teach any doctrine," which would suggest that the right to "practice any principle" is unqualified. But such an interpretation does not seem plausible—it would be most surprising if there were a limitation on teaching but not on practice, if only because what one does is a way of teaching by example.

If the qualifications involving morality, property and the rights of others apply to religious rights more generally, then the strength and breadth of those protections will depend upon how broadly those exceptions are construed. The Court may be suggesting that free exercise is protected as long as one's practices do not harm other persons or property, which seems relatively protective. Or, the Court may be suggesting that the state can prohibit any religious practice thought to contravene conventional morality. If that is the Court's meaning and if it is believed immoral to ingest alcoholic beverages, for example, then communion can be prohibited without offending constitutional guarantees. Precisely because conventional morality might prohibit more than what harms other persons or property, this latter interpretation does not suggest that free exercise guarantees are particularly strong.

In *Reynolds v. United States*,[2] the Court examined the degree to which free exercise rights were protected, at least with respect to whether the Constitution afforded protection to polygamy. The Court explained that the First Amendment prohibits Congress from interference with religious liberty, but then noted that the question at hand was, "[W]hat is the religious freedom which has been guaranteed[?]"[3]

When discussing the First Amendment's free exercise guarantees, the Court distinguished between belief and practice in a way that would be repeated in the subsequent case law. "Laws are made for the government of actions, and while they cannot interfere with mere religious belief and opinions, they may with practices."[4] Thus, religious beliefs as such are immune from regulation, although the same cannot be said of religious practices. For example, suppose that a particular religious group believes in human sacrifice. A state is not barred from criminalizing such activity even assuming that the individual to be sacrificed is a volunteer.

The *Reynolds* Court reasoned that Congress has the power to prohibit polygamy in federal territories as a general matter, and then examined whether an exception must be recognized for those whose practice of polygamy involves a religious exercise. Contrary to the *Watson* opinion issued just seven years earlier, which might be taken to suggest that the Constitution's free exercise guarantees are robust, the *Reynolds* opinion suggested that religious practices do not receive any special protection from the Constitution. Any other view would allegedly have anomalous implications because those in plural marriages for secular reasons could be prosecuted, whereas those in such marriages for religious reasons could not. The Court feared that permitting individuals to be immune from the operation of that law because of their religious belief "would be to make the professed doctrines of religious belief superior to the law of the land, and in effect to permit every citizen to become a law unto himself."[5]

The Court's fear that protecting religious exercise would make each citizen a law unto himself or herself was unwarranted for a few different reasons. First, the individual might be required to establish the sincerity of the religious belief at issue before an exemption could be afforded. Many individuals would have much difficulty in establishing that their sincere religious beliefs require that they be exempted from a variety of laws, so the worry that recognition of free exercise rights would invite anarchy is overstated. Second, the importance of the implicated state interest would determine whether even sincere religious practices could be prohibited—the state's interest in the preservation of human life presumably justifies the prevention of human sacrifice, sincere religious beliefs notwithstanding. Third, the Court *might* try to limit which "religious" beliefs and practices counted for purposes of federal constitutional guarantees, although such an approach has its own problems.

There is some difficulty in interpreting *Reynolds*, precisely because the Court did not rest its upholding the polygamy ban on the alleged great dangers of polygamy. That is not to say that the Court treated the "odious"[6] practice of polygamy lightly, having mentioned that the punishment for it in England was death. Nonetheless, if it is anomalous to punish certain lawbreakers but to refrain from punishing other lawbreakers who have religious compunctions about following the law at issue, then that anomalousness is also present in cases involving matters other than polygamy.

In *Davis v. Beason*, the Court explained its view of the dangers of bigamy and polygamy, which "tend to destroy the purity of the marriage relation, to disturb the peace of families, to degrade woman, and to debase man."[7] The practice of polygamy was condemned in no uncertain terms, because "[f]ew crimes are more pernicious to the best interests of society, and receive more general or more deserved punishment."[8] Affording an exemption to those who practiced polygamy out of religious belief would "shock the moral judgment of the community."[9] The danger posed by polygamy was allegedly so great that the *Davis* Court seemed to reject the belief/action dichotomy discussed in *Reynolds* a little over a decade earlier, explaining that calling "advocacy [of polygamy] a tenet of religion [and thus protected] is to offend the common sense of mankind."[10]

Here, the Court's meaning was not immediately clear. The *Davis* Court might have been suggesting that because engaging in polygamy was a crime, advocating that individuals enter into polygamous relationships was also a crime.

> If they [bigamy and polygamy] are crimes, then to teach, advise, and counsel their practice is to aid in their commission, and such teaching and counseling are themselves criminal, and proper subjects of punishment, as aiding and abetting crime are in all other cases.[11]

If teaching religious doctrine counts as an act rather than a belief (and thus is subject to prohibition), then the belief/act distinction has either been rejected or at least modified in an important way. The *Reynolds* Court suggested that the Constitution protects the belief that polygamy is appropriate or that God approves of polygamy as long as one does not act on that belief by entering into a polygamous relationship, whereas the *Davis* Court suggested either that the belief/action distinction is not viable or that the prohibited activity includes not only entering into a polygamous relationship but also teaching that polygamy is viewed positively by one's religion.

A different explanation of why advocacy of polygamy could not be considered a religious tenet was that the Court (may have) rejected that the Church of Latter Day Saints was really a religion. The Court explained that "religion" is sometimes confused with "cultus,"[12] suggesting that polygamy may not be entitled to free exercise protection because not qualifying as a *religious* exercise. This interpretation of the *Davis* opinion does not undercut the robustness of free exercise protections but instead limits the range of belief systems that qualify for free exercise of religion protections.

Basically, the Court offered two explanations for its rejection of protection for polygamy, one suggesting that polygamy did not even count as a religious practice and the other suggesting that polygamy was not protected even if it was a religious practice, because the First Amendment does not offer "protection against legislation for the punishment of acts inimical to the peace, good order, and morals of society."[13] If the First Amendment is not intended to immunize behavior inimical to the public welfare, then it will be important to determine which acts are sufficiently dangerous that they should fall out of the ambit of that amendment's protections.

The Court believed that a good indicator of what was inimical to the good order of society was whether a particular practice had been criminalized—"free . . . exercise of religion . . . must be subordinate to the criminal laws of the country, passed with reference to actions regarded by general consent as properly the subjects of punitive legislation."[14] But such an interpretation of free exercise guarantees suggests that they are not very robust. States might criminalize matters ranging from activities that pose great danger to life and limb to activities that pose no apparent harm to anyone. The very fact that something had been criminalized would be enough to exempt it from free exercise protections.

Suppose that a particular sect believed that individuals should have sexual relations outside of marriage, perhaps because the sect did not believe in marriage. Would such individuals be immune from prosecution under fornication statutes? The *Davis* Court explained that if such a sect were to "find its way into this country, swift punishment would follow the carrying into effect of its doctrines, and no heed would be given to the pretense that, as religious beliefs, their supporters could be protected in their exercise by the constitution of the United States."[15] Again, the *Davis* Court seemed to be offering two differing rationales, one focusing on religious practices that might be thought immoral and the other focusing on practices that should not be considered religious. Because practices involving sexual relations between unmarried parties were "recognized . . . as proper matters for prohibitory legislation,"[16] the Court rejected that the "punitive power of the government for [such] acts . . . must be suspended in order that the tenets of a religious sect encouraging crime may be carried out without hindrance."[17] Thus, the Court suggested, such religious practices cannot be permitted because they are contrary to societal welfare. Yet, by talking about the *pretense* that non-marital relations must be protected based on religious beliefs, the Court might instead have been suggesting that such beliefs and practices do not count as religious.

The *Davis* Court offered ambiguous rationales in other parts of the opinion as well.

> Whilst legislation for the establishment of a religion is forbidden, and its free exercise permitted, it does not follow that everything which may be so called can be tolerated. Crime is not the less odious because sanctioned by what any particular sect may designate as "religion."[18]

Here, too, the Court offers two different rationales, one suggesting that merely because certain views are called or designated as religious does not make them so and the other suggesting that even if particular practices are religious, they may nonetheless be odious and subject to punishment.

Perhaps there was no need to choose between the two rationales, because a practice such as human sacrifice would be sufficiently pernicious that it could be regulated whether or not religiously required. Nonetheless, there were clear costs associated with the Court's failure to make clear what it was arguing. If indeed the practices described did not count as religious, then there was no need to undermine the strength of free exercise protections because they had not even been triggered. If these practices did count as religious but were so odious that they could not be countenanced notwithstanding their triggering free exercise guarantees, then there was no need to suggest that criminal laws as a general matter could be enforced against those practicing their religion. Instead, such enforcement might be appropriate when compelling state interests were at stake but not when merely legitimate but not compelling state interests were implicated.

Modern free exercise

Many commentators suggest that modern free exercise jurisprudence begins with *Cantwell v. Connecticut*.[19] The case involved a challenge to the convictions of the Cantwells—Newton, Jesse, and Russell—for soliciting funds without the required certificate and for breach of the peace. The Cantwells were Jehovah's Witnesses who went from house to house attempting to distribute religious pamphlets and books in exchange for donations.

The *Cantwell* Court explained: "Freedom of conscience and freedom to adhere to such religious organization or form of worship as the individual may choose cannot be restricted by law."[20] Echoing a distinction offered in *Reynolds*, the Court distinguished between the "freedom to believe and [the] freedom to act."[21] The freedom to believe is "absolute,"[22] although "[c]onduct remains subject to regulation for the protection of society."[23] As support for the proposition that the state can reach religious conduct, the Court cited both *Reynolds* and *Davis*, although the Court nowhere intimated that the *Reynolds* and *Davis* Courts disagreed even implicitly about whether the action/belief distinction was good law.

When suggesting that the state can regulate religious activity under certain conditions, the *Cantwell* Court nonetheless warned that the fact that the "the power to regulate must be so exercised as not, in attaining a permissible end, unduly to infringe the protected freedom."[24] One of the questions at hand involved who had the power to determine whether the activity in question was religious. The Connecticut statute read:

> No person shall solicit money, services, subscriptions or any valuable thing for any alleged religious, charitable or philanthropic cause, from other than a member of the organization for whose benefit such person is soliciting or within the county in which such person or organization is located unless such cause shall have been approved by the secretary of the public welfare council.[25]

The *Cantwell* Court reasoned that the Connecticut law

> requires an application to the secretary of the public welfare council of the State; . . . [who] is empowered to determine whether the cause is a religious one, and . . . the issue of a certificate depends upon his affirmative action.[26]

10 *Free exercise and the definition of religion*

If the secretary found that the cause was not religious, then solicitation for it would be a crime. But criminalizing an important means of raising money would greatly disincentivize the use of that means, which might adversely impact the ability of the group to survive. The Court noted that

> to condition the solicitation of aid for the perpetuation of religious views or systems upon a license, the grant of which rests in the exercise of a determination by state authority as to what is a religious cause, is to lay a forbidden burden upon the exercise of liberty protected by the Constitution.[27]

The state interest supporting the legislation was the prevention of fraud. While not "intend[ing] even remotely to imply that, under the cloak of religion, persons may, with impunity, commit frauds upon the public,"[28] the Court nonetheless suggested that the fate of a religion could not be based on a state official's "appraisal of facts, . . . exercise of judgment, and . . . formation of an opinion"[29] with respect to whether certain beliefs constituted a religion.

It is simply unclear whether the *Cantwell* Court was suggesting that state officials as a general matter must refrain from deciding which groups are religious. If so, then state courts would have much difficulty in rejecting that a group's claimed religious beliefs were in fact religious, although courts might still determine whether the beliefs in question were sincerely held.

Assuming that the Constitution permits courts to distinguish between religious and non-religious beliefs, an important issue involves the appropriate criterion for making that determination. The Court has repeatedly admitted the difficulty posed in distinguishing between the religious and non-religious, has provided no clear criteria in light of which such a determination should be made, but nonetheless continues to assert that the distinction is of constitutional consequence.

Echoes of nineteenth-century ambivalence?

Murdock v. Pennsylvania,[30] decided in 1943, illustrates that the Court's ambivalence in the nineteenth century about whether to treat polygamy as a religious practice continued into the twentieth century. At issue in *Murdock* was whether Jehovah's Witnesses could be forced to buy a license to sell religious literature. The issue presented differed from what had been decided in *Cantwell*, because the state official was not trying to determine which groups were religious. Nonetheless, this state law would impose a financial burden on poor groups seeking to distribute their religious tracts. The petitioners had not purchased a license and had nonetheless gone door to door distributing religious literature and asking for donations.

When evaluating the constitutionality of the ordinance, the Court noted that the "hand distribution of religious tracts is an age-old form of missionary evangelism—as old as the history of printing presses."[31] Distribution of religious tracts by hand involved a combination of preaching and of distributing religious literature, and thus "occup[ied] the same high estate under the First Amendment as do worship in the churches and preaching from the pulpits, [which meant that it had] . . . the same claim to protection as the more orthodox and conventional exercises of religion."[32] The Court had no difficulty in classifying the Witnesses' activity as religious and entitled to First Amendment protection, echoing one of the worries articulated in *Cantwell*, namely, that the state must not be permitted to prevent poor religious groups from engaging in free exercise. Were the tax upheld, then "[s]preading religious beliefs in this ancient and honorable manner would . . . be denied the needy."[33]

Lest its meaning be misunderstood, the Court expressly rejected that "any conduct can be made a religious rite and by the zeal of the practitioners swept into the First Amendment."[34] The Court explained that *Reynolds* and *Davis* "denied any such claim to the practice of polygamy and bigamy."[35] Presumably, this meant that polygamy did not even fall under the First Amendment (could not be swept into that amendment), although the Court might merely have been suggesting that such practices, even if religious, would not be protected under the First Amendment. Thus, when noting that "[o]ther claims may well arise which deserve the same fate,"[36] the Court did not explain whether those envisioned practices would not even trigger First Amendment analysis or whether, instead, the First Amendment analysis would be applied but would be unavailing to save the practice. The *Murdock* Court clearly envisioned that some types of religious conduct could be regulated, noting that the way in which certain evangelistic actions are "practiced at times gives rise to special problems with which the police power of the states is competent to deal."[37]

That certain practices might fall within the First Amendment but be subject to regulation "merely illustrates that the rights with which [the Court had been] . . . dealing are not absolutes."[38] Thus, as had been true in previous cases, the *Murdock* Court's analysis was ambiguous with respect to whether there were some unspecified criteria by which to determine which practices were religious or whether, instead, the Court was only suggesting that certain religious practices are not protected by the Free Exercise Clause.

The Court refuses to classify certain very unusual beliefs as non-religious

In *United States v. Ballard*,[39] the Court had a golden opportunity to illustrate that certain beliefs do not qualify as religious, even if the Court was unprepared at that time to offer the criteria in light of which such decisions should be made. At issue were the claims of those in the "I Am" movement. One of the beliefs of those in the movement was that certain individuals "had, by reason of supernatural attainments, the power to heal persons of ailments and diseases and to make well persons afflicted with any diseases, injuries, or ailments."[40] These "designated persons had the ability and power to cure persons of those diseases normally classified as curable and also of diseases which are ordinarily classified by the medical profession as being incurable diseases."[41] Not only did these individuals claim to have such powers, but they claimed to have exercised them. Allegedly, "the three designated persons had in fact cured . . . hundreds of persons afflicted with diseases and ailments."[42] The Ballards publicly represented that they had these powers, and members of the public would send money, presumably in the hopes that the power to cure the incurable would be used. The Ballards were charged with fraud.

A fraud conviction requires that false representations have been made. However, the *Ballard* Court explained that courts cannot judge which religious beliefs are true and which false. The First Amendment "embraces the right to maintain theories of life and of death and of the hereafter which are rank heresy to followers of the orthodox faiths."[43] The Founders had been aware of the varied religious views that people might have, and "[t]hey fashioned a charter of government which envisaged the widest possible toleration of conflicting views."[44] While "[t]he religious views espoused by respondents [the Ballards] might seem incredible, if not preposterous, to most people,"[45] the Court reasoned that "if those doctrines are subject to trial before a jury charged with finding their truth or falsity, then the same can be done with the religious beliefs of any sect."[46]

Chief Justice Harlan Stone dissented, denying that "the constitutional guaranty of freedom of religion affords immunity from criminal prosecution for the fraudulent procurement of money by false statements as to one's religious experiences, more than it renders polygamy or libel immune from criminal prosecution."[47] For example, if the individuals had claimed to have cured hundreds of people, then it was open to the government to try to show that no people had ever been cured.

Perhaps the claims of effecting cures could have been shown to be false, for example, if the Ballards had claimed to have gone to San Francisco and cured hundreds and it could be shown that the Ballards had never even visited California. Of course, fraud would have been more difficult to establish if particular individuals believed themselves to have been cured after having had contact with one of the Ballards.

The approach adopted by the *Ballard* Court is important, a least in part, because of its refusal to classify the contested beliefs as non-religious. While sympathetic to the *Cantwell* Court's denial that "under the cloak of religion, persons may, with impunity, commit frauds upon the public,"[48] the *Ballard* Court nonetheless held that the Constitution precludes the trier of fact from finding that certain beliefs were "cloaked"[49] as religious, that is, were falsely represented as religious. The Court was silent as to how a fraud conviction could withstand constitutional review if an essential element of the crime involved the falsity of religious beliefs.

As a general matter, an individual can be convicted of fraud only if he made an intentional misrepresentation of a fact or state of affairs with the purpose of inducing someone to surrender something of value. For example, an individual might induce someone to give him money for a particular charitable purpose but then might use the money for his own enrichment as he had intended all along. But the jury trying the Ballards was precluded from evaluating the truth or falsity of the Ballards' underlying religious beliefs, which might be taken to mean that the jury was precluded from finding that there had been a false statement regarding the Ballards' power to effect cures.

Suppose that the Ballards in fact had the power to cure people but, unfortunately, were unaware that they indeed had that power. Their claims to having the power would be insincere (because they did not believe that they had such a power), but *ex hypothesi* the underlying representation of their power would have been true rather than false. It is not fraud to insincerely assert the truth.

After affirming the trial court's jury instructions directing jury members to assess the Ballards' sincerity but not the underlying truth or falsity of the religious beliefs, the Court remanded the case to the circuit court to address some remaining issues. On remand, the Ninth Circuit affirmed the conviction. That decision was appealed and the Supreme Court reversed, because of the "intentional and systematic exclusion of women"[50] from the jury pool. That exclusion was contrary to California law, which was the applicable law for the federal courts in California. The United States Supreme Court dismissed the indictment, which had been tainted by the illegal, purposeful exclusion of women, although the Court acknowledged that the Ballards might again be tried and convicted.

Justice Robert Jackson suggested in his concurrence that if the applicable statute required not only insincerity but, in addition, that the underlying assertion be provably false, then the fraud conviction could not stand. The majority apparently had a different view, expecting that the government would re-indict the Ballards.

The majority nowhere stated how the finding of insincerity could itself suffice for a finding of fraud, given the requirement that there be a knowingly false assertion made to induce someone to surrender something of value. Nonetheless, the dispute between Justice Jackson and the majority *might* be understood in the following way:

Justice Jackson viewed the requisite false assertion as the claim that the Ballards "had, by reason of supernatural attainments, the power to heal persons of ailments and diseases and to make well persons afflicted with any diseases, injuries, or ailments."[51] Because that was a religious belief and the jury was precluded from finding it false, a necessary element of fraud (a false representation of a fact or state of affairs) was missing. However, the majority may instead have been focusing on the Ballards' assertion that they would attempt to cure individuals who donated money. If it could be shown that the Ballards had no intention of doing anything (perhaps there were incriminating statements to that effect), then *perhaps* it could be shown that there was both a false assertion (that the Ballards would *attempt* to cure donors) and the requisite insincerity (if there was evidence that the Ballards knew when making the promise that they had no intention of doing anything to cure those who had donated money).

Even Justice Jackson did not want to foreclose fraud prosecutions as a general matter, "for example, if one represents that funds are being used to construct a church when in fact they are being used for personal purposes."[52] Nonetheless, Justice Jackson wanted to foreclose such prosecutions where the allegedly false assertion was itself a religious belief.

One of the unexplored difficulties raised by *Ballard* involves the potential missteps that jury members might take when attempting to make the requisite sincerity assessment. At the very least, careful jury instructions would have to be offered. Otherwise, the sincerity test might simply be another way of asking the jury about the plausibility of the beliefs—jury members might say that they could not find that the defendant sincerely believed something that they themselves found incredible. The Court was sensitive to the possibility that an unsympathetic jury might well find certain beliefs false, and the same attitude might make a jury less sympathetic to the claim that anyone could sincerely hold such views.

Special treatment for religion?

Just as the nineteenth-century ambivalence about whether polygamy was a religious rather than a non-religious practice was also present in the twentieth-century case law, the nineteenth-century ambivalence about whether the Constitution afforded religious practice special treatment was also present in the twentieth-century case law. *Everson v. Board of Education*[53] is a good example. At issue was the authorization of reimbursement to parents of transportation costs to parochial schools. The appellant, a taxpayer, claimed that this expenditure was "an establishment of religion."[54] The Court disagreed.

While the focus of the decision was on whether the reimbursement program violated Establishment Clause guarantees, the Court also addressed free exercise protections, noting that "other language of the [First] [A]mendment commands that New Jersey cannot hamper its citizens in the free exercise of their own religion."[55] The way that the Court spelled out those protections was worthy of note, because the Court reasoned that the state was constitutionally precluded from "exclud[ing] individual Catholics, Lutherans, Mohammedans, Baptists, Jews, Methodists, *Non-believers*, Presbyterians, or the members of any other faith, because of their faith, *or lack of it*, from receiving the benefits of public welfare legislation."[56] Here, the Court implied that free exercise guarantees were not reserved for those professing a religion, because they also applied to "Non-believers" and to those lacking faith. Perhaps the Court had in mind some of the difficulties associated with determining what counts as a religion.

In *Torcaso v. Watkins*,[57] the Court examined the constitutionality of a religious test for employment—the appellant was denied a commission as a notary public because he would not affirm his belief in God's existence. The Court held that "[t]his Maryland religious test for public office unconstitutionally invades the appellant's freedom of belief and religion and therefore cannot be enforced against him."[58]

Torcaso can be interpreted in a number of ways. Insofar as the state is seeking to privilege certain religious beliefs over others, the requirement implicates Establishment Clause guarantees. In addition, requiring an individual to assert something contrary to faith implicates free exercise concerns.

Insofar as the focus is on free exercise, one way to understand the Court's decision is that the state cannot privilege religion over non-religion, although a different way to understand the decision is that the State cannot privilege theocentric religions over non-theocentric religions. In a footnote, the Court noted several "religions in this country which do not teach what would generally be considered a belief in the existence of God."[59]

Arguably, the Maryland requirement at issue in *Torcaso* violated both establishment and free exercise guarantees, and at least one question involves how to distinguish between the requirements of each. The Court in *Engel v. Vitale*[60] provided a partial answer.

Engel involved an official prayer to start the school day. The prayer at issue—"Almighty God, we acknowledge our dependence upon Thee, and we beg Thy blessings upon us, our parents, our teachers and our Country"[61]—was struck down as a violation of the Establishment Clause.

The Court distinguished between establishment and free exercise by noting:

> The Establishment Clause, unlike the Free Exercise Clause, does not depend upon any showing of direct governmental compulsion and is violated by the enactment of laws which establish an official religion whether those laws operate directly to coerce nonobserving individuals or not.[62]

Here, the Court implied that free exercise guarantees may be violated when "laws operate directly to coerce non-observing individuals."[63] At least one question raised by such a distinction is whether the coercion of non-observant individuals itself violates free exercise guarantees (regardless of what those individuals actually believe) or whether such coercion is a violation only because the coercion contravenes religious beliefs that the (non-observant) individual has. If the former view accurately captures the relevant protections, then free exercise guarantees preclude an individual from being coerced to do or say something religious even if the individual has no religious beliefs of her own. However, if the latter is accurate, then free exercise guarantees preclude an individual from being coerced to do or say something religious only if the individual has religious beliefs of her own that would be contravened if the person were to succumb to the coercion.

Consider *School District of Abington Township v. Schempp*,[64] which involved the constitutionality of prayers beginning the school day. Pennsylvania law required that Bible verses be read every day, although children would be excused with a written note from their parents. The Schempps, Unitarians, challenged the law. While Edward Schempp had considered having his children excused, he believed that their leaving the classroom during these readings would put them at a disadvantage.

The Court struck down the state law on Establishment Clause grounds, but made numerous points about free exercise protections while doing so. For example, the Court noted that the Free Exercise Clause "recognizes the value of religious training, teaching and observance and, more particularly, the right of every person to freely choose his own course with reference thereto, free of any compulsion from the state."[65] Echoing analyses previously offered in the case law, the Court explained that "it is necessary in a free exercise case for one to show the coercive effect of the enactment as it operates against him in the practice of his religion."[66] The *Schempp* comment suggests that free exercise guarantees are implicated only if an individual is coerced to do something that violates his religious beliefs.

Yet, the *Schempp* Court's understanding of what counted as religion seemed rather broad—one of the questions presented was whether prohibiting Bible-reading would create a "religion of secularism" in the schools.[67] The Court agreed that it was impermissible to "establish a 'religion of secularism' in the sense of affirmatively opposing or showing hostility to religion, thus 'preferring those who believe in no religion over those who do believe,'"[68] although the Court rejected that its ruling had that impermissible effect.

In his concurrence, Justice William Brennan noted that "the line which separates the secular from the sectarian in American life is elusive."[69] Explaining that "our religious composition makes us a vastly more diverse people than were our forefathers,"[70] he pointed out that

> [t]oday the Nation is far more heterogeneous religiously, including as it does substantial minorities not only of Catholics and Jews but as well of those who worship according to no version of the Bible and those who worship no God at all.[71]

Here, Justice Brennan included among the religious "those who worship no God at all,"[72] citing to *Torcaso*'s discussion of "those religions founded on different beliefs,"[73] those beliefs not predicated on the existence of God or, perhaps, beliefs predicated on the non-existence of God.

The Court's comments about a religion of secularism as well as Justice Brennan's comments about religions founded on different beliefs suggest that religion is being construed rather broadly. These comments also suggest that when determining whether something counts as religious, the Court's focus may not be on the contents of the beliefs but on something else, for example, the role played by the beliefs in the person's life.

Conflicts between religious and civil requirements

While members of the Court have rejected that individuals must have particular views about God in order to qualify as having a religion, the Court nonetheless continues to distinguish between religious and non-religious beliefs. Consider *Wisconsin v. Yoder*[74] in which the Court suggested that individuals might receive an exemption for religious reasons that would not otherwise be available to them.

Yoder involved a Wisconsin law requiring students to remain in school until they reached age 16. Jonas Yoder, Wallace Miller, and Adin Yutzy, who were Amish, did not want their children, ages 14 and 15, to attend public school past the eighth grade. Yoder *et al.* were tried and fined for failure to comply with the compulsory schooling law. They argued that having their children attend those schools would violate their religious beliefs—indeed, the respondents "believed that by sending their children to high school, they would not only expose themselves to the danger of the censure of the church community, but . . . also endanger their own salvation and that of their children."[75]

These Amish parents believed that high school would undermine the values that they sought to impart to their children. "The high school tends to emphasize intellectual and scientific accomplishments, self-distinction, competitiveness, worldly success, and social life with other students."[76] In contrast, "Amish society emphasizes informal learning-through-doing; a life of 'goodness,' rather than a life of intellect; wisdom, rather than technical knowledge, community welfare, rather than competition; and separation from, rather than integration with, contemporary worldly society."[77]

The *Yoder* Court reasoned that "a State's interest in universal education . . . is not totally free from a balancing process when it impinges on fundamental rights and interests, such as those specifically protected by the Free Exercise Clause of the First Amendment."[78] In order for the Wisconsin statute to be upheld,

> it must appear either that the State does not deny the free exercise of religious belief by its requirement, or that there is a state interest of sufficient magnitude to override the interest claiming protection under the Free Exercise Clause.[79]

Yoder discussed the negative "impact that compulsory high school attendance could have on the continued survival of Amish communities as they exist in the United States today,"[80] although more had to be shown than that the Amish children might be influenced by "teachers who are not of the Amish faith—and may even be hostile to it."[81] In addition, it was necessary to show the *religious* basis of the threatened way of life. "A way of life, however virtuous and admirable, may not be interposed as a barrier to reasonable state regulation of education if it is based on purely secular considerations."[82] The *Yoder* Court explained that "to have the protection of the Religion Clauses, the claims must be rooted in religious belief."[83]

If the Religion Clauses only afford protection to claims "rooted in religious belief,"[84] then it will be necessary to distinguish among kinds of beliefs. While acknowledging that "a determination of what is a 'religious' belief or practice entitled to constitutional protection may present a most delicate question,"[85] the *Yoder* Court nonetheless reasoned that "the very concept of ordered liberty precludes allowing every person to make his own standards on matters of conduct in which society as a whole has important interests."[86] For example,

> if the Amish asserted their claims because of their subjective evaluation and rejection of the contemporary secular values accepted by the majority, much as Thoreau rejected the social values of his time and isolated himself at Walden Pond, their claims would not rest on a religious basis.[87]

The Court announced that "Thoreau's choice was philosophical and personal rather than religious, and such belief does not rise to the demands of the Religion Clauses."[88]

Regrettably, the Court did not explain what made Henry David Thoreau's choice philosophical and personal. It was not clear, for example, whether the Court believed Thoreau's beliefs failed to "play the role of a religion and function as a religion in . . . [his] life."[89] Instead, the Court explained what sufficed about the Amish beliefs to entitle them to protection—"the traditional way of life of the Amish is not merely a matter of personal preference, but one of deep religious conviction, shared by an organized group, and intimately related to daily living."[90]

By contrasting Thoreau's personal (idiosyncratic?) preferences with those shared by an organized group, *Yoder* raises whether actions must be based on *shared* values in order to trigger free exercise guarantees. That question was addressed in *Thomas v. Review Board of the Indiana Employment Security Division*.[91]

At issue was the denial of a claim by Eddie Thomas for unemployment compensation. Thomas, a Jehovah's Witness, worked at a roll foundry making sheet metal for industrial use. When the foundry closed, he was transferred to another department making tank turrets.

Because he could not make war weapons as a matter of conscience, he checked to see if there was a different position within the company that he could occupy that would not contravene his beliefs. But none were available, and he quit his job rather than violate his religious convictions.

His application for unemployment benefits was denied, allegedly because "the belief was more 'personal philosophical choice' than religious belief."[92] One of the factors contributing to the judgment that Thomas's reasons were more personal than religious was that a friend of his, also a Jehovah's Witness, had told him that it was "'scripturally' acceptable"[93] to make the turrets. Thomas disagreed with that interpretation, "conclud[ing] that his friend's view was based upon a less strict reading of Witnesses' principles than his own."[94] The *Thomas* Court noted that it is not unusual for members of the same faith tradition to have differing understandings of their religious obligations, believing "the judicial process . . . singularly ill equipped to resolve such differences in relation to the Religion Clauses."[95] While conceding that it is possible to "imagine an asserted claim so bizarre, so clearly nonreligious in motivation, as not to be entitled to protection under the Free Exercise Clause,"[96] the Court emphasized that "the guarantee of free exercise is not limited to beliefs which are shared by all of the members of a religious sect."[97]

Once it was established that Thomas's refusal to work implicated free exercise guarantees, the state had to establish that its interests were sufficiently compelling and the means chosen sufficiently closely tailored to justify its infringement of Thomas's religious liberty. The Court rejected the state's suggestion that "the number of people who find themselves in the predicament of choosing between benefits and religious beliefs is large enough to create 'widespread unemployment,' or even to seriously affect unemployment."[98]

While the *Thomas* Court reiterated that "[o]nly beliefs rooted in religion are protected by the Free Exercise Clause, which, by its terms, gives special protection to the exercise of religion,"[99] the interpretation of what would not count as religious—"an asserted claim so bizarre, so clearly nonreligious in motivation, as not to be entitled to protection under the Free Exercise Clause"[100]—seems rather forgiving. After reiterating that the "determination of what is a 'religious' belief or practice is more often than not a difficult and delicate task,"[101] the Court explained the approach the courts should *not* take—

> the resolution of that question is not to turn upon a judicial perception of the particular belief or practice in question; religious beliefs need not be acceptable, logical, consistent, or comprehensible to others in order to merit First Amendment protection.[102]

In *Thomas*, the Court refused to take sides when individuals of a particular sect disagreed about the content of particular religious obligations. Suppose, however, that an individual does not identify with a particular sect but nonetheless claims particular benefits by virtue of free exercise protections. *Frazee v. Illinois Department of Employment Security*[103] involved an individual's sincere refusal to work based on his "personal professed religious belief."[104] However, William Frazee did not belong to a particular sect and was not a member of a particular church. Basically, he identified as a Christian and believed that it was religiously inappropriate to work on Sunday. The *Frazee* Court noted that in the previous unemployment decisions involving claims of free exercise infringement, the claimant had been a member of a religious sect. However, those decisions had not been predicated on sect membership. Instead, the "judgments in those cases rested on the fact that each of the claimants had a sincere belief that religion required him or her to refrain from the work in question."[105] Further, the Court had never suggested that "unless a claimant belongs to a sect that forbids what his job requires, his belief, however sincere, must be deemed a purely personal preference rather than a religious belief."[106]

The *Frazee* Court reiterated its appreciation of the difficulty in "distinguishing between religious and secular convictions and in determining whether a professed belief is sincerely held."[107] Nonetheless, such determinations are important, because "[o]nly beliefs rooted in religion are protected by the Free Exercise Clause,"[108] and "[p]urely secular views" do not suffice.[109] Further, "[s]tates are clearly entitled to assure themselves that there is an ample predicate for invoking the Free Exercise Clause"[110] and "membership in an organized religious denomination, especially one with a specific tenet forbidding members to work on Sunday, would simplify the problem of identifying sincerely held religious beliefs."[111] The Court nonetheless expressly "reject[ed] the notion that to claim the protection of the Free Exercise Clause, one must be responding to the commands of a particular religious organization."[112]

Because denying Frazee benefits triggered free exercise guarantees, the state was required to show that it had a sufficiently compelling interest to justify the imposition of a burden. The Court suggested that while "there may exist state interests sufficiently compelling to override a legitimate claim to the free exercise of religion,"[113] no such interests had been asserted in the instant case.

Is it necessary to define religion?

The United States Supreme Court has suggested that religion must be construed rather broadly. While repeatedly insisting that free exercise guarantees are only triggered by religious (as opposed to non-religious) practices, the Court has not explained how to distinguish between religion and non-religion. There are various ways to understand the Court's approach, although a synthesis of several of the points made in the case law makes clear the direction that should be taken when outlining the prevailing approach.

Why define religion?

Some commentators suggest that there is no need to define religion for free exercise purposes—instead, we should look at the commonalities among paradigmatic religions, which will provide all that is needed.[114] Certainly, we would expect paradigmatic religious practices to be included within those beliefs and practices potentially triggering free exercise protections, and focusing on paradigmatic beliefs and practices might provide a useful guide in some respects. Nonetheless, such an approach has its drawbacks, if only because it assumes agreement about which sets of beliefs are paradigmatically religious.[115] If that assumption is not warranted,[116] then the approach will lose much of its usefulness and may in effect give judges free rein to decide whether a particular set of beliefs qualifies as religious.[117]

Suppose that there was agreement about which beliefs or features were paradigmatically religious. Even so, that might be much less helpful than might originally be thought, because religion for free exercise purposes might be much broader than the definition of religion for other purposes.

The breadth of what counts as religion

The Court's apparent willingness to construe religion broadly for free exercise purposes implies that judges should give the benefit of the doubt to assertions that particular beliefs are religious. Yet, telling judges that they must give the benefit of the doubt to such assertions will not provide sufficient guidance unless much more is said about the kinds of beliefs that might qualify.

While the current jurisprudence countenances a much broader definition of religion than it once did, the Court nonetheless believes that what counts as religion for free exercise purposes is not unlimited. Religion is expressly afforded special treatment in the First Amendment and the protections contained therein would seem to do little work if religion could not be differentiated from non-religion. The Court has explained that the beliefs in question must not merely be "philosophical,"[118] although the Court has not spelled out how to distinguish the philosophical from the non-philosophical.

Some commentators suggest that the Court's exclusion of the philosophical indicates that religious beliefs must be based on faith rather than reason,[119] although that would seem to reject Catholicism as a religion[120] and would seem to limit philosophy too severely as well, which need not be reason-based. Further, such an explanation does not capture the tone of the Court's jurisprudence. For example, the *Thomas* Court explained that beliefs do not need to be logical, consistent, or comprehensible to qualify as religious. Yet, in suggesting that, the Court was not implying that religious beliefs *could not* be based on reason.

Some commentators suggest that the proper way to understand the content protected by free exercise guarantees is that "any concern deemed ultimate [must] be protected."[121] But such a standard requires someone, for example, the believer or a court, to decide whether the beliefs at issue are sufficiently important to meet that standard. But permitting a court to decide whether a belief is sufficiently important would seem no more appropriate than having a court decide which religious beliefs are true. Further, such a standard would be both too narrow and too broad—purely secular beliefs might be matters of ultimate concern and thus protected, and paradigmatic religious beliefs might not be viewed as of ultimate concern by the believer, herself, and thus would seem not to qualify.

Nor does the ultimate concern approach capture the Court's jurisprudence—the definition of religion adopted for free exercise purposes has not excluded what would normally be thought of as religious beliefs even where there has been no showing that the believer viewed the beliefs as implicating matters of ultimate concern. A more plausible interpretation of the jurisprudence is that whatever degree of commitment is represented by a variety of believers is the requisite level of commitment, which means that beliefs would not have to be of ultimate or even great concern to qualify—instead, a "meaningful belief"[122] suffices.

Sincerity

The Court has repeatedly affirmed that states are permitted to judge the sincerity of belief. However, at least two points might be made about such a criterion. The sincerity that must be shown is simply that the individual holds the belief. Beliefs do not have to form a consistent and coherent creed in order to be considered religious and protected. As the *Thomas* Court explained: "religious beliefs need not be acceptable, logical, consistent, or comprehensible to others in order to merit First Amendment protection."[123]

Further, it is important to prevent the trier of fact from imputing insincerity because the underlying belief does not seem credible. While the Court has suggested that "bizarre" beliefs may not "be entitled to protection under the Free Exercise Clause,"[124] the degree to which beliefs must be bizarre in order to be unprotected is rather high, as is illustrated by the protection accorded to the beliefs at issue in *Ballard*.

One issue is whether an individual sincerely believes something; another is why she believes it. The Court has suggested that some beliefs are "so clearly nonreligious in motivation, as not to be entitled to protection under the Free Exercise Clause."[125] However, the mere presence of a compelling non-religious reason does not establish that the individual's motivation is in fact non-religious. For example, the Ballards had a compelling non-religious reason for their beliefs, because many individuals would send money in the hopes that the Ballards would exercise their alleged supernatural powers to cure illnesses that were (otherwise) incurable. But that pecuniary benefit did not render the Ballards' beliefs non-religious.

Conclusion

The Court has offered some very broad parameters about what counts as religion. The views cannot be "purely secular,"[126] which means that the views cannot be purely non-religious. However, that does not provide much of a limitation until it is clear what would count as purely secular, which is more difficult to determine than might be supposed. If secular humanism is considered a religion for free exercise purposes,[127] then it will be necessary to establish the respects in which secular humanism is not purely secular, for example, by suggesting that it incorporates a particular set of moral values or beliefs about transcendent issues,[128] or, perhaps, because there are certified counselors analogous to members of the clergy[129] or weekly meetings.[130]

The *Yoder* Court suggested that religious beliefs cannot simply be "subjective"[131] or "merely a matter of personal preference."[132] The Amish beliefs were protected because they were "of deep religious conviction, shared by an organized group, and intimately related to daily living."[133] But the *Yoder* Court was not thereby setting out the necessary conditions for triggering free exercise guarantees, as was made clear in *Frazee* almost two decades later.

The *Frazee* Court held that a "personal professed religious belief"[134] qualified for free exercise protection. When again affirming that "[o]nly beliefs rooted in religion are protected by the Free Exercise Clause"[135] and "[p]urely secular views" do not suffice,[136] the *Frazee* Court was not suggesting that purely personal views could not be entitled to protection—the Court expressly rejected that "one must be responding to the commands of a particular religious organization"[137] to trigger free exercise guarantees. So, too, the *Gillette* Court explained that "while the objection must have roots in conscience and personality that are 'religious' in nature, this requirement has never been construed to elevate conventional piety or religiosity of any kind above the imperatives of a personal faith."[138]

When the *Frazee* Court stated that "States are clearly entitled to assure themselves that there is an ample predicate for invoking the Free Exercise Clause,"[139] the Court presumably meant that states can consider the individual's sincerity of belief, the importance of the belief to the individual so that it is not a mere personal preference, and the content of the belief to assure that it is not utterly bizarre. In addition, the State can assure itself that the beliefs involve some moral rather than merely descriptive elements and that the commitment to that normative view is not a mere preference but involves more "deeply held moral, ethical, or religious beliefs."[140] Nonetheless, religion for constitutional purposes includes a whole host of beliefs that would not qualify as religious using a more conventional definition of that term.

The definition of religion for constitutional purposes will be both heartening and disheartening to individuals on each side of the Culture Wars. Religion is privileged over non-religion (which should cheer traditionalists), although that definition is broad enough to include a great variety of minority and nontraditional views (which should cheer nontraditionalists). Courts can look at the content of religious beliefs when assessing whether beliefs and practices are protected. However, that assessment cannot involve a determination of truth or falsity, and is quite limited in the kinds of judgments that can be offered—whether the belief is utterly bizarre or whether the belief is purely secular.

Much of the jurisprudence attempts to steer courts away from the wrong path in a case involving free exercise—they are not to judge religious beliefs in terms of consistency or plausibility. As long as the beliefs are sincerely held, have some normative element, and do not seem to involve a mere personal preference, they are the kind of beliefs that can trigger free exercise guarantees. A separate question involves the strength of protections that free exercise guarantees afford, although any analysis of those protections must take into account the utter breadth of beliefs and practices that would thereby be covered.

When discussing free exercise guarantees, the Court has made clear that *religious* beliefs must be at issue. In some of the cases in which the Court upheld state prohibitions burdening practices claimed to be religious, the Court cast doubt on whether the practices were in fact religious, which would have meant that the Court upholding the prohibition would not thereby have spoken to the strength of free exercise guarantees. But the Court has also suggested that free exercise guarantees do not immunize practices that have been criminalized, which does limit the force of those guarantees. It is precisely because the Court has sent mixed messages that the Court's understanding of both religion and free exercise have been difficult to discern—the Court sometimes upholds prohibitions by suggesting that the practices at issue are not really religious but at the same time hints that the prohibitions would probably be constitutional even if the practices were religious. Those reading the opinions are left to wonder whether the Court is qualifying what counts as religious or is qualifying the strength of free exercise guarantees or both.

The Court has also sent mixed messages when striking down laws as violations of free exercise guarantees. While repeatedly suggesting that some beliefs do not qualify as religious, the Court has offered very few examples of beliefs that would not qualify and has not explained which features in particular make the non-qualifying beliefs secular and not subject to protection. Those seeking to understand the relevant doctrine by examining what the Court has said and done have not had great success in producing a consistent and coherent doctrine.

Notes

1 *Watson v. Jones*, 80 U.S. 679, 728 (1871).
2 *Reynolds v. United States*, 98 U.S. 145 (1878).
3 *Id.* at 162.
4 *Id.* at 166.
5 *Id.* at 167.
6 *Id.* at 164.
7 *Davis v. Beason*, 133 U.S. 333, 341 (1890), *abrogated by Romer v. Evans*, 517 U.S. 620 (1996).
8 *Id.*
9 *Id.*
10 *Id.* at 342.
11 *Id.*
12 *Id.*
13 *Id.*
14 *Id.* at 342–43.
15 *Id.* at 343.
16 *Id.*
17 *Id.*
18 *Id.* at 345.

19 See Mark E. Chopko and Michael F. Moses, "Freedom to Be A Church: Confronting Challenges to the Right of Church Autonomy," *Georgetown Journal of Law & Public Policy* 3:387–452 (2005), p. 400 ("[T]he Court decided what is often cited as its first modern free exercise case, *Cantwell v. Connecticut*."); Edward J. Eberle, "Roger Williams' Gift: Religious Freedom in America," *Roger Williams University Law Review* 4:425–86 (1999), p. 428 n. 4 ("In the modern era, the Supreme Court began interpretation of the Free Exercise Clause in *Cantwell v. Connecticut*, 310 U.S. 296 (1940)."); Andy G. Olree, "The Continuing Threshold Test for Free Exercise Claims," *William & Mary Bill of Rights Journal* 17:103–56 (2008), p. 109 n. 33 ("*Cantwell* is often treated as the beginning of modern free exercise law.").
20 *Cantwell v. Connecticut*, 310 U.S. 296, 303 (1940).
21 *Id.*
22 *Id.*
23 *Id.* at 304.
24 *Id.*
25 *Id.* at 301–02.
26 *Id.* at 305.
27 *Id.* at 307.
28 *Id.* at 306.
29 *Id.* at 305.
30 *Murdock v. Pennsylvania*, 319 U.S. 105 (1943).
31 *Id.* at 108.
32 *Id.* at 113.
33 *Id.* at 112.
34 *Id.* at 109.
35 *Id.* at 110.
36 *Id.*
37 *Id.* (citing *Cox v. New Hampshire*, 312 U.S. 569 (1941) and *Chaplinsky v. New Hampshire*, 315 U.S. 568 (1942)).
38 *Id.* (citing *Schneider v. New Jersey*, 308 U.S. 147, 160, 161 (1938)).
39 *United States v. Ballard*, 322 U.S. 78 (1944).
40 *Id.* at 80.
41 *Id.*
42 *Id.*
43 *Id.* at 86.
44 *Id.* at 87.
45 *Id.*
46 *Id.*
47 *Id.* at 88–89 (Stone, C.J. dissenting).
48 *Cantwell*, 310 U.S. at 306.
49 *Id.*
50 *Ballard v. United States*, 329 U.S. 187, 190 (1946).
51 See *Ballard*, 322 U.S. at 80.
52 *Id.* at 95 (Jackson, J., dissenting).
53 *Everson v. Board of Education*, 330 U.S. 1 (1947).
54 *Id.* at 8.
55 *Id.* at 16.
56 *Id.* (emphasis added).
57 *Torcaso v. Watkins*, 367 U.S. 488 (1961).
58 *Id.* at 496.
59 *Id.* at 495 n.11.
60 *Engel v. Vitale*, 370 U.S. 421 (1962).
61 *Id.* at 422.
62 *Id.* at 430.
63 *Id.*
64 *School District of Abington Township v. Schempp*, 374 U.S. 203 (1963).
65 *Id.* at 222.
66 *Id.* at 223.

67 *See id.* at 225.
68 *See id.* (citing *Zorach v. Clauson*, 343 U.S., 306, 314 (1952)).
69 *Id.* at 231 (Brennan, J., concurring).
70 *Schempp*, 374 U.S. at 240 (Brennan, J., concurring).
71 *Id.* (Brennan, J., concurring).
72 *Id.* (Brennan, J., concurring).
73 *Torcaso*, 367 U.S. at 495.
74 *Wisconsin v. Yoder*, 406 U.S. 205 (1972).
75 *Id.* at 209.
76 *Id.* at 211.
77 *Id.*
78 *Id.* at 214.
79 *Id.*
80 *Id.* at 209.
81 *Id.* at 211.
82 *Id.* at 215.
83 *Id.*
84 *Id.*
85 *Id.*
86 *Id.* at 215–16.
87 *Id.* at 216.
88 *Id.*
89 *Welsh v. United States*, 398 U.S. 333, 339 (1970).
90 *Yoder*, 406 U.S. at 216.
91 *Thomas v. Review Board of the Indiana Employment Security Division*, 450 U.S. 707 (1981).
92 *Id.* at 713 (citing *Thomas v. Review Board*, 391 N.E.2d 1127, 1131 (Indiana 1979), *reversed* 450 U.S. 707 (1981)).
93 *Id.* at 715.
94 *Id.* at 711.
95 *Id.* at 715
96 *Id.*
97 *Thomas*, 450 U.S. at 708.
98 *Id.* at 719.
99 *See id.* at 713 (citing *Sherbert v. Verner*, 374 U.S. 398 (1963); *Yoder*, 406 U.S. at 215–16).
100 *Id.* at 715.
101 *See id.* at 714.
102 *See id.*
103 *Frazee v. Illinois Department of Employment Security*, 489 U.S. 829 (1989).
104 *Id.* at 831 (citing *Frazee v. Department of Employment Security*, 512 N.E.2d 789, 790 (Illinois Appellate 1987), reversed 489 U.S. 829 (1989)).
105 *Id.* at 833.
106 *Id.*
107 *Id.*
108 *Id.* (citing *Thomas*, 450 U.S. at 713).
109 *Frazee*, 489 U.S. at 833 (citing *United States v. Seeger*, 380 U.S. 163 (1965); *Yoder*, 406 U.S. at 215–16).
110 *Id.*
111 *Id.* at 834.
112 *Id.*
113 *Id.* at 835.
114 See George C. Freeman III, "The Misguided Search for the Constitutional Definition of 'Religion,'" *Georgetown Law Journal* 71:1519–65 (1983), p. 1565 ("There simply is no essence of religion, no single feature or set of features that all religions have in common and this distinguishes religion form everything else. There is only a focus, coupled with a set of paradigmatic features. These, without more, however, are enough.").
115 Some commentators suggest that one differentiating feature between religion and non-religion is that the former imposes certain kinds of requirements on individuals and imposes

certain kinds of penalties on those who do not fulfill their obligations. See Chad Flanders, "The Possibility of a Secular First Amendment," *Quinnipiac Law Review* 26:257–303 (2008), p. 289 ("[R]eligion requires obedience to a higher authority; in other words, religion shows believers (and people in general) that they are accountable to a non-temporal judge, and that there may be extra-temporal consequences to their actions."). However, such a view would doubtless be quite controversial depending upon how the criteria for the non-temporal judge and the extra-temporal consequences were spelled out.

116 See Mason Blake Binkley, "A Loss for Words: 'Religion' in the First Amendment," *University of Detroit Mercy Law Review* 88:185–234 (2010), p. 210 ("[T]he approach unrealistically presupposes broad agreement on a set of paradigmatic features of religion.").

117 Eduardo Penalver, "The Concept of Religion," *Yale Law Journal* 107:791–822 (1997), p. 816 ("The . . . definitions by analogy . . . would do nothing to constrain the decision-making processes of individual judges. They would leave each judge completely free to determine whether or not a belief system is a religion according to the presence or absence of any single characteristic (or combination of characteristics) the judge chooses.").

118 *Yoder*, 406 U.S. at 216.

119 See Andrew W. Austin, "Faith and the Constitutional Definition of Religion," *Cumberland Law Review* 22:1–47 (1992), p. 33 ("Religious beliefs are non-rational; they cannot be proven or demonstrated by their adherents because they are not based upon reason, but are based upon what might be referred to as intuition or faith.").

120 Cf. Book Note, "Religion and *Roe*: The Politics of Exclusion," *Harvard Law Review* 108:495–500 (1994), p. 496 (reviewing Elizabeth Mensch and Alan Freeman, *The Politics of Virtue: Is Abortion Debatable?* (1993)) ("Catholicism's natural law tradition emphasizes an 'objective natural order' revealed to our 'careful human reason.'").

121 See Note, "Toward a Constitutional Definition of Religion," *Harvard Law Review* 91:1056–89 (1978), pp. 1075–76; see also Michael Rhea, "Denying and Defining Religion under the First Amendment: Waldorf Education as a Lens for Advocating a Broad Definitional Approach," *Louisiana Law Review* 72:1095–127 (2012), pp. 1105–06 ("[T]he test does not examine the content of the belief at issue but instead aims to determine whether a belief is subjectively identifiable in the eyes of an adherent as an ultimate, gravely significant concern.").

122 *United States v. Seeger*, 380 U.S. 163, 174 (1965).

123 *Thomas*, 450 U.S. at 714.

124 *Id.* at 715.

125 *Id.*

126 *Yoder*, 406 U.S. at 215.

127 See *Torcaso*, 367 U.S. at 495 n. 11 ("Among religions in this country which do not teach what would generally be considered a belief in the existence of God are Buddhism, Taoism, Ethical Culture, Secular Humanism and others."); *Grove v. Mead School District Number 354*, 753 F.2d 1528, 1534 (9th Cir. 1985) ("Secular humanism may be a religion.").

128 See *Smith v. Board of School Commissioners of Mobile County*, 655 F. Supp. 939, 982 (S.D. Alabama), *reversed on other grounds*, 827 F.2d 684 (11th Cir. 1987) ("A statement that there is no transcendent or supernatural reality is a religious statement. A statement that there is no scientific proof of supernatural or transcendent reality is irrelevant and non-sensical, because inquiry into the fundamental nature of man and reality itself may not be confined solely within the sphere of physical, tangible, observable science.").

129 *Id.* at 970 ("The American Humanist Association certifies humanist counselors who enjoy the legal status of ordained priests, pastors, and rabbis.").

130 See *Kalka v. Hawk*, 215 F.3d 90, 99 (D.C. Cir. 2000) ("[A]n organization of Secular Humanists sought a tax exemption on the ground that they used their property 'solely and exclusively for religious worship.' Despite the group's non-theistic beliefs, the court determined that the activities of the Fellowship of Humanity, which included weekly Sunday meetings, were analogous to the activities of theistic churches and thus entitled to an exemption.") (citing *Fellowship of Humanity v. County of Alameda*, 315 P.2d 394, 409 (California Appellate 1957)).

131 *Yoder*, 406 U.S. at 216.

132 *Id.*

133 *Id.*
134 *Frazee*, 489 U.S. at 831 (citing *Frazee*, 512 N.E.2d at 790).
135 *Id.* at 833 (citing *Thomas*, 450 U.S. at 714).
136 *Id.* (citing *United States v. Seeger*, 380 U.S. 163 (1965); *Yoder*, 406 U.S. at 215–16).
137 *Id.* at 834.
138 *Gillette v. United States*, 401 U.S. 437, 454 (1971).
139 *Frazee*, 489 U.S. at 833.
140 *Id.* at 844.

2 Institutional autonomy and the ministerial exception

Free exercise protections are afforded to religious institutions as well as to individuals. The Court has explained the Constitution's free exercise protections for religious institutions in a few different cases in which church leadership or property ownership were at issue. While the Court has consistently held that the First Amendment protects religious institutions, the contours of those protections have been much less consistent than the Court or many commentators have been willing to admit.

Cases involving religious institutions may implicate a host of thorny issues. There may be disputes about theological matters, and courts are poorly equipped to make those kinds of determinations. But a court's refusing to hear a case at all because of a lack of competence with respect to the resolution of doctrinal matters may not be an option because, for example, some decision must be made about who owns property. Historically, the Court has tried to offer a nuanced approach to the kinds of cases and issues that civil courts may decide, although some of those nuances may have been underappreciated by the Court in its most recent decision on these matters.

This chapter discusses the Court's evolving approach to the kinds of decisions that civil courts may make when the parties before it include a religious institution. Historically, the Court drew lines with respect to the issues courts may decide, and then redrew those lines, sometimes *sub silentio*. The Court's focus has been on developing an approach that will permit civil courts to make some decisions involving religious institutions without forcing those courts to make decisions beyond their competence. Recently, the Court may have exaggerated the degree to which civil courts are precluded from deciding matters involving religious institutions, ignoring the past jurisprudence while claiming to apply it, although the contours of the current jurisprudence will only become clearer when the Court decides more cases involving religious institutions.

Institutional protections

Historically, challenges arose in a variety of contexts. A local church breaking away from a hierarchical church might claim ownership of church buildings and property. Or, two factions within a church might each claim to represent the true church and thus be entitled to the church property. Or, church personnel might challenge employment decisions made by the church, alleging that the church had violated antidiscrimination protections. Each of these kinds of cases requires a careful balancing so that courts will not go beyond their areas of competence but will nonetheless be able to decide issues well within their ken, even if one of the parties happens to be a religious institution.

Areas of competence

The Supreme Court has long recognized that civil courts are not competent to decide religious matters, for example, which of two competing groups in a church has the correct doctrinal understanding. This position was illustrated in *Watson v. Jones*,[1] which involved a schism within a church where two distinct bodies each claimed to represent the church. A large faction in the local church represented the pro-slavery group, whereas a smaller faction and the hierarchical church represented the anti-slavery group. The *Watson* Court upheld the power of church courts to determine their own religious beliefs:

> [T]he rule of action which should govern the civil courts ... is, that, whenever the questions of discipline, or of faith, or ecclesiastical rule, custom, or law have been decided by the highest of these church judicatories to which the matter has been carried, the legal tribunals must accept such decisions as final, and as binding on them, in their application to the case before them.[2]

While the Court was specifying that deference was owed to religious courts on certain matters, the *Watson* Court was not thereby endorsing an absolute rule of deference. To see why, it is helpful to consider different types of possible church disputes:

(1) A dispute between parties involving property that by the express terms of a will has been "devoted to the teaching, support, or spread of some specific form of religious doctrine or belief."[3]
(2) A dispute involving church property where the congregation "is strictly independent of other ecclesiastical associations, and so far as church government is concerned, owes no fealty or obligation to any higher authority."[4]
(3) A property dispute where the local religious congregation is "but a subordinate member of some general church organization in which there are superior ecclesiastical tribunals."[5]

With respect to the first kind of case, the *Watson* Court was confident that there would be clear cases in which civil courts could decide whether a religious organization had complied with the terms of a will. For example, suppose that someone had dedicated a house of worship "to the sole and exclusive use of those who believe in the doctrine of the Holy Trinity, and plac[ed] it under the control of a congregation which at the time holds the same belief."[6] Suppose further that there had been a change in the composition and beliefs of the congregation over time. The Court suggested that the law could "prevent that property from being used as a means of support and dissemination of the Unitarian doctrine, and as a place of Unitarian worship."[7] Admittedly, the task in such a case might be "delicate" and "difficult."[8] Nonetheless, "when the doctrine to be taught or the form of worship to be used is definitely and clearly laid down," courts are not only permitted but required "to inquire whether the party accused of violating the trust is holding or teaching a different doctrine, or using a form of worship which is so far variant as to defeat the declared objects of the trust."[9]

In some cases, courts are required to enforce the provisions of a will against an independent church. The doctrinal views of the congregation might have changed over time and the question might be whether those changes involved beliefs antithetical to the testator. The *Watson* Court reasoned that it is

> not in the power of the majority of ... [a] congregation, however preponderant, by reason of a change of views on religious subjects, to carry the property so confided to them to the support of new and conflicting doctrine.[10]

Further, this constraint is not confined to independent churches. Even if a particular church is part of a hierarchical organization, the *Watson* Court suggested that the church would not be permitted to keep property in support of a doctrine that substantially conflicted with the conditions that had been clearly laid down in a will.[11]

The *Watson* Court offered an additional hypothetical involving a dispute within an independent church, suggesting that the right to use the property at issue should be "determined by the ordinary principles which govern voluntary associations."[12] If a congregation abided by the principle of majority rule, then a minority who separated themselves from the church and refused to accept the authority of the majority could "claim no rights in the property from the fact that they had once been members of the church or congregation."[13]

It is no surprise that the *Watson* Court described the civil court's task in certain cases as difficult and delicate, because the civil court might be left to determine whether the evolution of doctrine had been sufficiently great to require the return of property. Such a decision would itself require a court to make a theological determination, because judgments about which doctrinal changes were substantial rather than minor would themselves be the kinds of judgments precluded under a very deferential approach.[14]

In many cases, reasonable courts might disagree about whether a particular change in doctrine was substantial. That kind of judgment might require careful calibration by a court, which might require an understanding and appreciation of a variety of doctrinal changes so that the court could appreciate which changes were substantial and which not. But there are great potential difficulties when courts are asked to make a decision about what constitutes a *substantial* deviation, even if those courts are informed about some of the past doctrinal developments.

The *Watson* Court's hypothetical involving civil enforcement of majority rule anticipated *Bouldin v. Alexander*.[15] There, the Court was asked to decide which of two rival factions represented the church. One faction, a small minority, had attempted to replace the trustees and remove the majority of the congregation from membership at a non-regularly scheduled set of meetings.[16] The Court held that the minority's actions were without force, finding that "[i]n a congregational church, the majority, if they adhere to the organization and to the doctrines, represent the church. An expulsion of the majority by a minority is a void act."[17] By adding the proviso "if they adhere . . . to the doctrines,"[18] the Court again seemed to be countenancing the possibility that a civil court would determine whether the majority had indeed adhered to the prevailing religious doctrine and thus was entitled to determine the future of the church.

The *Bouldin* decision resulted in the removal of the pastor, because he was in the minority that had attempted to remove the majority from the congregation. While that removal was not a result of a civil court's conclusion that the pastor's doctrinal approach was in error, the Court nonetheless approved of the use of neutral principles to cause a change in (although some would say a clarification of) church leadership. *Bouldin* suggests that civil courts can have a profound effect on who will lead a church, providing that the courts are applying secular rather than religious principles.

In *Gonzalez v. Roman Catholic Archbishop of Manila*,[19] the Court reaffirmed the requirement that civil courts defer to church authorities on religious matters, stating that "[i]n the absence of fraud, collusion, or arbitrariness, the decisions of the proper church tribunals on matters purely ecclesiastical, although affecting civil rights, are accepted in litigation before the secular courts as conclusive."[20] However, the *Gonzalez* Court left open the question of what would happen if a plaintiff could establish "fraud, collusion, or arbitrariness"[21] and, further, seemed to undermine or ignore *Watson* with respect to how wills should be treated when designating the use of an estate.

At issue in *Gonzalez* was (1) whether a particular individual had the right to be appointed chaplain, and (2) whether he was entitled to the monies accrued by virtue of the position having been vacant for a period of time. After a bequest established the chaplaincy, the conditions for appointment to it were modified by the church. The petitioner could not meet the new requirements, and an important issue was whether those new requirements should be applied to chaplaincy appointments. Rather than address whether the new requirements substantially deviated from the previous requirements (which was the approach the *Watson* Court suggested), the *Gonzalez* Court reasoned that neither the

> foundress, nor the church authorities, can have intended that the perpetual chaplaincy created in 1820 should, in respect to the qualifications of an incumbent, be forever administered according to the canons of the church which happened to be in force at that date.[22]

The Court seemed not to appreciate that such a position undercut the *Watson* example of an individual who had dedicated a building for those who believed in the Holy Trinity, since one would infer from *Gonzalez* that a testator should expect that even basic doctrine would and should change over time, and thus that conditions imposed in a will limiting the use of monies might well not be enforceable if the bequest had been made to a religious institution and its use had been made contingent on basic doctrine not substantially changing over time.

The Court's willingness to defer to church authorities about church matters was put to the test in *Kedroff v. St. Nicholas Cathedral of Russian Orthodox Church in North America*.[23] At issue was the right to the use and occupancy of a cathedral in New York City, which depended upon who was the head of the American churches religiously affiliated with the Russian Orthodox Church. Two different individuals claimed that title: Leonty, the Metropolitan of All America and Canada, the Archbishop of New York, who was elected by a sobor of the American churches; and Fedchenkoff, who based his right by virtue of his appointment by the Supreme Church Authority of the Russian Orthodox Church as the Archbishop of the Archdiocese of North America and the Aleutian Islands.

After offering a brief history of the relationship between the churches, the *Kedroff* Court noted that "the Russian Orthodox Church was, until the Russian Revolution, an hierarchical church with unquestioned paramount jurisdiction in the governing body in Russia over the American Metropolitanate,"[24] and that neither "the Sacred Synod [nor] the succeeding Patriarchs relinquished that authority or recognized the autonomy of the American church."[25] The Court then examined a New York state law that sought

> to transfer the control of the New York churches of the Russian Orthodox religion from the central governing hierarchy of the Russian Orthodox Church, the Patriarch of Moscow and the Holy Synod, to the governing authorities of the Russian Church in America, a church organization limited to the diocese of North America and the Aleutian Islands.[26]

This, the Court suggested, the state could not do.

The *Kedroff* Court appreciated that the state's goal was to protect rather than undermine religion. The New York Court of Appeals had taken judicial notice of events indicating that "the Russian Government exercised control over the central church authorities and that the American church acted to protect its pulpits and faith from such influences."[27] The New York high court accepted that "the Legislature's reasonable belief in such conditions justified the State in enacting a law to free the American group from infiltration of such atheistic or subversive influences."[28] Basically, the New York Court of Appeals agreed with the New York Legislature that the American diocese "would most faithfully carry out the purposes of the religious trust."[29]

Yet, it was not for the New York Court of Appeals to decide which church would most faithfully uphold Church doctrine and practice. Basically, all that had to be shown was that the Russian Orthodox Church had had administrative control over the American diocese and that such control had never been relinquished.[30] As support for that position, the *Kedroff* Court cited *Watson* in glowing terms:

> The opinion radiates . . . a spirit of freedom for religious organizations, an independence from secular control or manipulation—in short, power to decide for themselves, free from state interference, matters of church government as well as those of faith and doctrine. Freedom to select the clergy, where no improper methods of choice are proven, we think, must now be said to have federal constitutional protection as a part of the free exercise of religion against state interference.[31]

The *Kedroff* Court did not announce that the civil courts have no role in adjudicating property disputes between religious parties.[32] On the contrary, there are times "when civil courts must draw lines between the responsibilities of church and state for the disposition or use of property."[33] However, the Court warned that "when the property right follows as an incident from decisions of the church custom or law on ecclesiastical issues, the church rule controls."[34] Basically, the *Kedroff* Court suggested that the civil courts have a limited role to play when adjudicating property disputes between religious parties, and that role does not include the ability to determine which entity remains true to religious doctrine.

Religious determinations and neutral principles

Kedroff's deferential stance with respect to civil court determinations of religious doctrine was reaffirmed in *Presbyterian Church in the United States v. Mary Elizabeth Blue Hull Memorial Presbyterian Church*.[35] At issue was a Georgia law permitting a jury to decide whether a hierarchical general church departed from the tenets of faith as a way of deciding whether the local or national church would be entitled to particular property.

The challenge to the law arose in the following context. Two churches had withdrawn from a hierarchical church because of their disagreement with some of the church's positions, e.g., the ordaining of women as ministers and ruling elders. When reconciliation was found to be impossible, the national church took over the local churches' property until new leadership for those churches could be found.

The local churches filed suit to prevent the general church from trespassing on the property in question, the local churches having title to their respective properties. The jury was asked to determine whether

> the actions of the general church "amount to a fundamental or substantial abandonment of the original tenets and doctrines of the (general church), so that the new tenets and doctrines are utterly variant from the purposes for which the (general church) was founded."[36]

The jury found for the local churches.

The *Presbyterian Church* Court began its analysis by suggesting that "the State has a legitimate interest in resolving property disputes, and that a civil court is a proper forum for that resolution."[37] However, there are special constitutional concerns when there is a religious doctrinal dispute. While suggesting that neutral principles can be applied without violating constitutional guarantees, the Court cautioned that the Constitution will not permit church property disputes to turn on a civil court's resolution of a controversy involving religious doctrine. Thus, it could not be left up to a jury (or a judge for that matter) to decide whether there had been a substantial deviation from prior doctrine. The Court cited *Watson* for the proposition that courts cannot decide ecclesiastical questions, but did not discuss the *Watson* hypothetical involving the individual who left his estate to support the teaching of particular doctrine. Instead, the *Presbyterian Church* Court made clear that courts do not have the expertise to decide ecclesiastical matters. Further, precisely because courts cannot decide such matters, religious organizations should structure their property arrangements so as not to require courts to resolve religious disputes.

The *Presbyterian Church* Court offered a sensible approach to balancing the competing constitutional interests. The Court reaffirmed that the state cannot decide doctrinal matters, but also protected the state's interest in resolving property disputes. Further, the Court provided an inducement for religious institutions to make very clear in secular terms who owns what in the event of a dissolution or disaffiliation.[38] That way, courts will be less likely to be asked to decide matters beyond their competence.

In *Jones v. Wolf*,[39] the Court offered further discussion of the neutral-principles-of-law approach. At issue was a schism between a local and national church, and the question at hand was whether the property dispute could be decided based on neutral principles of law or whether instead the court had to defer to the decision of the authoritative tribunal of the hierarchical church as to who owned the property.

The Vineville Presbyterian Church was a member of the Augusta-Macon Presbytery of the Presbyterian Church in the United States ("PCUS"). However, at a meeting of the Church, a majority of the congregation voted to separate from PCUS. They informed PCUS of their action and then affiliated with another denomination, the Presbyterian Church in America. The Presbytery appointed a commission to investigate, eventually deciding that the minority faction constituted the "true Congregation of Vineville Presbyterian Church."[40]

Representatives of the minority sought to establish their right to the exclusive use and possession of the property. The trial court found for the majority using Georgia's neutral-principles-of-law approach, and was affirmed on appeal by the Georgia Supreme Court. In reviewing the Georgia Supreme Court's decision, the United States Supreme Court noted that: (1) the deeds conveyed the property to the local church, (2) neither the state's implied trust statutes nor the Vineville Church corporate charter indicated that the national organization had an interest in the property, and (3) the relevant provisions concerning property in the Book of Church Order (the PCUS Constitution) did not include any language suggesting a trust in favor of the Church.

The Court thereby illustrated how a neutral-principles-of-law approach might be used to determine whether a local or denominational church retained property when the local church split off from the denominational one. While civil courts must "defer to the resolution of issues of religious doctrine or polity by the highest court of a hierarchical church organization,"[41] they are permitted to use neutral principles of law as long as they can do so without treading on forbidden territory. Here, the civil court did not exceed its competence when rejecting the religious tribunal's resolution of a civil matter.

It is fair to suggest that the Court's recommended approach may be difficult to apply in some cases because there may be disagreement about what counts as a religious interpretation, and thus should not be second-guessed by a civil court, and what counts as an interpretation of secular law, and thus might be second-guessed by a civil court in light of neutral, secular principles. That said, however, while there may be difficulties in determining which language is religious and which is secular, there might also be difficulties in refusing to make such a determination and instead deferring to a religious tribunal. Deference to a religious tribunal's resolution of a secular matter would involve deferring to the court with less competence to decide that issue. Further, complete deference could result in a very unjust outcome, and the Constitution does not require the state to turn a blind eye to injustice merely because the alleged perpetrator is a religious institution.

Use of the neutral-principles approach will sometimes result in a local church being adjudicated the owner of disputed property and, at other times, the denomination will be adjudicated the owner. The Court noted that under the "neutral-principles approach, the outcome of a church property dispute is not foreordained."[42] Of course, there are ways that a hierarchical church can have its interests protected. For example, any time prior to the occurrence of a dispute, "the faction loyal to the hierarchical church . . . can modify the deeds or the corporate charter to include a right of reversion or trust in favor of the general church."[43] Or, the "constitution of the general church can be made to recite an express trust in favor of the denominational church."[44] Were these steps taken, the courts would "be bound to give effect to the result indicated by the parties, provided it is embodied in some legally cognizable form."[45]

Yet, the Court's suggested safeguards might not prove as protective as the Court envisioned. Suppose, for example, that the constitution of a general church had been modified to recite an express trust in favor of the hierarchical church. A separate question would be whether local churches that had affiliated *prior* to the change would be bound by that amendment or, instead, would have to manifest their acceptance of the amendment to the constitution by ratifying it.

At least with respect to the cases involving religious property disputes, the Court has articulated a few different principles. As a general matter, the civil courts cannot decide theological questions, although the Court *may* have created an exception to that rule. In particular kinds of cases involving legal instruments, the civil courts can and must determine whether there has been substantial compliance with the terms of the instrument. This *might* mean that in certain cases the civil courts can perform the difficult and delicate task of deciding whether a particular theological position (as determined by religious authorities) substantially deviates from the express terms incorporated in a document. That said, however, after *Presbyterian Church*, the Court might suggest that civil courts are precluded from deciding whether there has been a substantial deviation in doctrine. Just as civil courts are not competent to decide which theological position is true, it might also be argued that civil courts are not competent to decide whether a doctrinal deviation is substantial rather than minor. If this is the proper interpretation, then courts can appropriately decide whether a testator's wishes have been followed with respect to non-doctrinal matters but courts cannot make judgments about whether the testator's wishes with respect to doctrinal matters have been honored. This limitation would not merely be due to a presumption that the testator would expect that doctrine might change (the testator might expressly deny that he was willing to countenance doctrinal changes), but because the court would not be competent to make judgments about whether the doctrine had changed substantially.

While courts cannot make judgments about doctrinal matters, they can apply neutral principles of law when resolving church property disputes without violating constitutional guarantees. Application of these neutral principles might have profound effects on who owns a church or on who will lead a church.

The Court has left open what should be done in cases involving fraud or collusion and has suggested that even the choice of clergy may not be immune from scrutiny where "improper methods of choice are proven."[46] This presumably is an application of the neutral-principles approach. The question would not be whether the methods were improper as a matter of religious law, since that would be beyond the competence of the civil court. Instead, the question would be whether something improper in terms of secular rules had occurred, for example, whether majority rule had been ignored in a congregation that had specified that majority rule would be the method of decision-making.

In *Serbian Eastern Orthodox Diocese for United States of America and Canada v. Milivojevich*,[47] the Court reversed the Illinois Supreme Court's determination that a particular religious organization had violated its own procedures and constitutional guarantees. While the then-existing case law had left an opening for civil courts to decide religious matters in cases "challenging decisions of ecclesiastical tribunals as products of 'fraud, collusion, or arbitrariness,'"[48] the *Milivojevich* Court clarified that there is "no 'arbitrariness' exception— in the sense of an inquiry whether the decisions of the highest ecclesiastical tribunal of a hierarchical church complied with church laws and regulations."[49] Instead, "civil courts are bound to accept the decisions of the highest judicatories of a religious organization of hierarchical polity on matters of discipline, faith, internal organization, or ecclesiastical rule, custom, or law."[50] Thus, the *Milivojevich* Court rejected that a civil court could in effect reverse or overrule an "arbitrary" decision of a religious tribunal, which is what the Illinois Supreme Court had done. However, the *Milivojevich* Court left open "whether or not there is room for 'marginal civil court review' under the narrow rubrics of 'fraud' or 'collusion' when church tribunals act in bad faith for secular purposes."[51]

It is important not to overstate the *Milivojevich* holding. The Court struck down the Illinois Supreme Court's rejection of an interpretation of religious law offered by religious authorities, where the Illinois court had instead substituted its own interpretation of religious law. Civil courts simply do not have the expertise to second-guess religious authorities about the proper interpretation of religious belief and practice. Such a prohibition does not preclude civil courts from second-guessing religious authorities about whether civil law has been violated. On the contrary, the jurisprudence established by *Wolf*, *Milivojevich*, and the various cases discussed above is that that civil courts must not decide religious issues but can decide civil issues, even in cases involving religious parties.

Milivojevich reinforced two distinct prongs of the jurisprudence: (1) civil courts are not to dictate the authoritative interpretation of religious beliefs, customs, or policies, and (2) civil courts are not to determine who should lead religious groups. However, the *Milivojevich* Court did not overrule the *Gonzalez* exceptions entirely; instead, the Court merely rejected the arbitrariness exception in particular, thereby leaving open whether the exceptions for fraud or collusion still had force.

Not only did the *Milivojevich* Court expressly refuse to discuss the possibility that a church tribunal might act fraudulently or be in collusion with someone else, but another point about *Milivojevich* also bears emphasis. The Court precluded civil courts from second-guessing whether religious courts were acting arbitrarily, but a different question not even addressed in *Milivojevich* is whether civil courts are also precluded from examining the acts of other religious figures, e.g., religious leaders, for evidence of arbitrariness, fraud, or collusion. Thus, one interpretation of *Milivojevich* is that it precluded a civil court from second-guessing the actions of its religious counterpart for arbitrariness, which leaves open the court's ability to second-guess religious tribunal decisions based on fraud or collusion and, in addition, the actions of non-tribunal religious authorities for arbitrariness, as well as fraud or collusion.

The Court has not had occasion to address these matters. Perhaps the Court would say that the Constitution does not permit civil courts to review the actions of religious authorities as a general matter for arbitrariness, because that would require those courts to make judgments about what was reasonable rather than arbitrary in light of religious custom and practice. Even if that is so, however, the Court has never rejected the appropriateness of civil courts reviewing actions involving fraud or collusion. Further, the Court never suggested in the jurisprudence that civil courts were somehow not competent to apply neutral civil laws merely because one of the parties was a religious institution. The Court's approach on these matters *may* have changed recently, although it will be necessary to see subsequent decisions to determine whether the Court has in fact effected a major change in the jurisprudence.

In *Hosanna-Tabor Evangelical Lutheran Church & School v. Equal Employment Opportunity Commission*,[52] the Court held that the First Amendment incorporates the ministerial exception and, further, found that the plaintiff, Cheryl Perich, could not press her claim because she fell within that exception. Someone reading the *Hosanna-Tabor* opinion might assume that the constitutional issues were rather straightforward. Possibly sympathetic facts notwithstanding, the Constitution does not permit the state to intrude upon something so central to religious autonomy as who will speak for a religious institution on matters of doctrine. Yet such a reading of the jurisprudence is inaccurate: the *Hosanna-Tabor* Court failed to focus on some of the salient facts in the case itself and also failed to focus on what the Court previously said and did in various cases involving religious entities. While the Constitution imposes some restrictions on civil courts with respect to the kinds of matters that can be addressed when a religious institution is one of the parties, those restrictions are not nearly as robust as one might have inferred from the *Hosanna-Tabor* opinion.

Cheryl Perich, who taught kindergarten and fourth grade, alleged that her employer, the Hosanna-Tabor Evangelical Lutheran Church and School, improperly fired her in violation of the Americans with Disabilities Act (ADA).[53] The Hosanna-Tabor Church "argued that the suit was barred by the First Amendment because the claims at issue concerned the employment relationship between a religious institution and one of its ministers."[54]

The Hosanna-Tabor school employed two kinds of teachers, "lay" or "contract" teachers on the one hand and "called" teachers on the other. Lay teachers were hired for one-year renewable terms, whereas called teachers, who were approved by the congregation, were hired on an open-ended basis. To be "called," one had to satisfy certain academic requirements. Perich started out as a lay teacher but, after meeting the relevant requirements, later became a "called" teacher.

Perich's duties were the same whether her employment status was "lay" or "called." She taught a variety of secular classes—math, language arts, social studies, science, gym, art, and music. She also taught a religion class for 30 minutes four days per week and attended chapel service with her students. She led chapel service twice a year.

The school expected all teachers to act as Christian role models. Nonetheless, Perich taught the secular subjects using textbooks commonly used in public schools and she introduced religious topics into the secular studies extremely rarely. Further, the Hosanna-Tabor school did not require teachers to be "called" or even Lutheran, and all teachers, whether or not Lutheran, had the same responsibilities, including teaching religion classes and leading chapel service.

Perich became ill and had to take a medical leave of absence at the beginning of the school year. She was eventually diagnosed with narcolepsy. When she was ready to return during the spring semester, she was told that her replacement had been given a one-year contract.

The congregation was told that Perich would likely be unable to return during the current school year *or the next*, even though that contention was not supported by Perich or her doctor and even though Perich had already informed the church that she would be ready to come back that spring. Eventually, the congregation voted to rescind Perich's call, and Perich filed a charge of discrimination and retaliation with the Equal Employment Opportunity Commission (EEOC). The EEOC filed a complaint against the Hosanna-Tabor Church in district court and the case eventually went to the United States Supreme Court.

The *Hosanna-Tabor* Court explained that the relevant case law clearly established that "it is impermissible for the government to contradict a church's determination of who can act as its ministers."[55] Forcing "a church to accept or retain an unwanted minister, or punishing a church for failing to do so, intrudes upon more than a mere employment decision."[56] In addition, such an imposition "interferes with the internal governance of the church, depriving the church of control over the selection of those who will personify its beliefs."[57]

There are a few reasons that such a pronouncement was misleading when made in the context of the case before the Court. The cases the Supreme Court has previously decided involved individuals who were leading a church, not individuals who were schoolteachers. While it might be argued that the deference to be given to churches about who would lead them should also apply to individuals who teach classes in their schools, the existing jurisprudence simply did not address the deference owed in cases involving people in Perich's position.

In any event, the existing jurisprudence was hardly as deferential as the *Hosanna-Tabor* Court implied. While the civil courts are not to decide ecclesiastical matters, they are permitted to use neutral principles of law to resolve church disputes. Indeed, where improper means have been used, courts have been permitted to issue rulings that would result in a change in church leadership. Although there is a rule of deference, that deference is qualitatively different from what the *Hosanna-Tabor* Court implied was contained in the relevant jurisprudence.

Deference is required to "the decisions of the proper church tribunals on matters purely ecclesiastical,"[58] absent fraud or collusion. By the same token, the freedom to select the clergy has constitutional protection as long as "no improper methods of choice are proven."[59] The Court has neither spelled out the conditions under which proof of fraud or collusion permits civil courts to interfere in clergy selection decisions nor has it discussed what kinds of improper methods would remove the federal constitutional protections for decisions about clergy.

The *Hosanna-Tabor* Court noted the *Kedroff* qualification requiring that "no improper methods of choice are proven,"[60] but seemed not to appreciate that this exception might have been triggered in the very case before the Court—the process by which the congregation came to rescind Perich's call might have been improper. Was the congregation having been misled about Perich's availability for work constitutionally significant? That is unclear. Even if the congregation had been misled, would that constitute the improper methods in hiring and firing to which the Court referred in prior decisions? That, too, is unclear. But the *Hosanna-Tabor* Court referring to a qualification of the ministerial exception existing in the past jurisprudence but then failing to apply or even discuss that qualification will mean that courts attempting to apply the relevant jurisprudence will not know whether the *Hosanna-Tabor* Court has reaffirmed or, instead, overruled the existence of this limitation on the ministerial exception.

One of the difficulties presented in Perich's case was figuring out whether she was a minister for purposes of the ministerial exception. Consider the functions she performed. Her job responsibilities, including religious teaching, were no different from those of the lay teacher, who did not need to have any specialized training and did not have to be a member of the denomination. Hosanna-Tabor's willingness to have Perich's employment duties performed by lay teachers who might not even be Lutheran undercut the plausibility of its claim that Perich qualified as a minister. The *Hosanna-Tabor* Court disagreed, holding that she was a minister for purposes of the exception after adopting a very fact-specific approach and finding that

> [i]n light of these considerations—the formal title given Perich by the Church, the substance reflected in that title, her own use of that title, and the important religious functions she performed for the Church—we conclude that Perich was a minister covered by the ministerial exception.[61]

Regrettably, the Court's failure to discuss how much these different factors should be weighed almost guarantees confusion in the lower courts and might result in surprising conclusions.

If Perich qualified as a minister based in large part on the functions she performed and some of the individuals who performed those functions were not even members of the denomination, then it would seem that individuals who were not even members of the Church might nonetheless be deemed ministers. Arguably, the *Hosanna-Tabor* approach might result in an individual's being classified as a minister even though she was not even a member of that faith tradition. At the very least, this is a surprising result that may indicate that the Court's suggested approach needs fine-tuning.

A further difficulty that will likely result from the *Hosanna-Tabor* opinion is that courts will now sometimes become deeply immersed in fact-intensive examinations to determine whether an individual challenging church employment practices is indeed a minister for purposes of the exception, which might require courts to make decisions beyond their competence. For example, courts might not only be asked to decide whether those preaching or teaching are ministers, but also whether those handling sacred objects or, perhaps, those performing functions on church grounds are ministers for constitutional purposes. After *Hosanna-Tabor*, it is simply unclear whether those providing janitorial or landscaping services should qualify as ministers or even how to make that assessment.

The *Hosanna-Tabor* Court discussed the constitutional harms that might occur were a church forced to employ a minister whom that church did not wish to employ. Those harms were not limited to those that might arise from the wrong person preaching from the pulpit or imparting to impressionable students an incorrect representation of church doctrine, but included other harms as well that could not simply be avoided by refusing to afford a particular individual pulpit or classroom access. According to the *Hosanna-Tabor* Court, the ministerial exception when successfully invoked precludes a civil court from making a determination that a religious institution violated civil law with respect to a minister working there, at least insofar as the person's conditions of employment were concerned.

Here, the Court was expanding the limitations previously recognized. While the existing jurisprudence had established that civil courts could not make a determination that a church had chosen the wrong leader, e.g., because that leader allegedly had a mistaken doctrinal view or because the church had not followed its own bylaws or traditions in the selection, the Court had never suggested that a civil court would be precluded from finding that a church had not acted in accord with civil laws when hiring or firing someone.

The *Hosanna-Tabor* Court suggested that a damage award to Perich was precluded because such an award would mean that the Church had made a mistake. That same rationale might be employed to preclude an award against a church that had refused to fire a minister who was known to harm innocent individuals, because such an award would also be predicated on a determination that a church had made a mistake with respect to its decision to retain a particular minister. The issue of whether churches can be held liable for their reckless or negligent supervision or retention of clergy has arisen in several jurisdictions and the courts have been unable to reach a consensus about how such cases should be handled. The dicta in *Hosanna-Tabor* is likely to make the jurisprudence more muddled rather than less, which is especially unfortunate given recent scandals involving alleged molestations and cover-ups that are claimed to have resulted in further victimization.

Conclusion

Prior to *Hosanna-Tabor*, a few issues seemed relatively clear. Civil courts were not to substitute their own judgment for that of religious tribunals with respect to the contents of religious doctrines or practices. However, civil courts could apply neutral laws to religious institutions as long as they did not thereby exceed their own areas of competence.

If the Constitution really immunizes Church decisions regarding who will minister to the faithful, then the exception might be thought to immunize a great deal when a minister is involved. The cases involving the ministerial exception tend to involve an individual who is suing the church for wrongful treatment, e.g., sex or race discrimination in the employment context. But suppose that the individual suing the church is not himself a minister for purposes of the exception but is suing the church because a clergyman employed by the church has wronged him or her. Permitting that suit to go forward might undermine the church's ability to "select and control who will minister to the faithful"[62] and thus might be thought to be precluded by the Religion Clauses. If, indeed, the "church must be free to choose those who will guide it on its way,"[63] churches might be given very expansive immunity with respect to their leaders. Further, if churches are given very broad discretion with respect to who counts as a minister, then religious institutions would seem to have been afforded very broad immunity with respect to a much broader category of individuals, and might thereby be permitted to evade responsibility for the wrongful acts of employees who the institution knew or should have known would act wrongly.

The *Hosanna-Tabor* Court claimed to be applying the existing jurisprudence when holding that a minister of the church could neither sue for reinstatement nor for damages when she had allegedly been discriminated against in violation of civil law. But in these kinds of cases the lower courts are not being asked to interpret religious doctrine but instead to decide the kinds of issues that often must be addressed when an employee alleges that she has suffered discriminatory treatment in employment.

Did the Court reach the correct result? Perhaps, but it misrepresented the past jurisprudence in its analysis and seemed to recommend an approach that will yield inconsistent results and may tempt courts to decide issues beyond their competence.

The *Hosanna-Tabor* Court neither specified who counts as a minister for constitutional purposes nor the breadth of immunity conferred on religious institutions when their employees repeatedly violate laws. The implications for institutional autonomy and immunity will only be clear when the case law develops. But the Court's suggestive language and misleading representation of the past jurisprudence does not bode well for a reasoned, nuanced approach to a particularly thorny area of constitutional law.

Notes

1 Watson v. Jones, 80 U.S. 679 (1872).
2 *Id.* at 727.
3 *Id.* at 722.
4 *Id.*
5 *Id.*
6 *Id.* at 723.
7 *Id.*
8 *Id.* at 724.
9 *Id.*
10 *Id.* at 723.
11 *Id.* at 723–24 ("Nor is the principle varied when the organization to which the trust is confided is of the second or associated form of church government. The protection which the law throws around the trust is the same.").
12 *Id.* at 725.
13 *Id.*
14 Lawrence C. Marshall, "The Religion Clauses and Compelled Religious Divorces: A Study in Marital and Constitutional Separations," *Northwestern University Law Review* 80:204–58 (1985), p. 251 (stating that "it is interesting to note that even *Watson v. Jones* required that the Court apply express terms without deferring to the church hierarchy").
15 *Bouldin v. Alexander*, 82 U.S. 131 (1872).
16 *Id.* at 140.
17 *Id.*
18 *Id.*
19 *Gonzalez v. Roman Catholic Archbishop of Manila*, 280 U.S. 1 (1929).
20 *Id.* at 16
21 *Id.*
22 *Id.* at 17.
23 *Kedroff v. St. Nicholas Cathedral of Russian Orthodox Church in North America*, 344 U.S. 94 (1952).
24 *Id.* at 105.
25 *Id.* at 105–06.
26 *Id.* at 107.
27 *Id.* at 108–09.
28 *Id.* at 109.
29 *Id.*
30 *Id.* at 120 (noting that nothing in the record indicated a "relinquishment of this power by the Russian Orthodox Church").
31 *Id.* at 116.
32 *Id.* at 120 ("There are occasions when civil courts must draw lines between the responsibilities of church and state for the disposition or use of property.").
33 *Id.*
34 *Id.* at 120–21.
35 *Presbyterian Church in the United States v. Mary Elizabeth Blue Hull Memorial Presbyterian Church*, 393 U.S. 440 (1969).
36 *Id.* at 443–44.
37 *Id.* at 445.
38 Michael William Galligan, "Judicial Resolution of Intrachurch Disputes," *Columbia Law Review* 83:2007–38 (1983), pp. 2015–16 ("According to the Court, allowing the application of neutral principles in intrachurch property disputes would encourage churches to

clarify their intentions about foreseeable conflicts and disputes through appropriate secular terminology.").
39 *Jones v. Wolf*, 443 U.S. 595 (1979).
40 *Id.* at 598.
41 *Id.* at 602.
42 *Id.* at 606.
43 *Id.*
44 *Id.*
45 *Id.*
46 *Kedroff*, 344 U.S. at 116.
47 *Serbian Eastern Orthodox Diocese for United States of America and Canada v. Milivojevich* 426 U.S. 696 (1976).
48 *Id.* at 712; see also *Gonzalez*, 280 U.S. at 16 ("In the absence of fraud, collusion, or arbitrariness, the decisions of the proper church tribunals on matters purely ecclesiastical, although affecting civil rights, are accepted in litigation before the secular courts as conclusive, because the parties in interest made them so by contract or otherwise.").
49 *Milivojevich*, 426 U.S. at 713.
50 *Id.*
51 *Id.*; see also Lisa J. Kelty, "Malicki v. Doe: The Constitutionality of Negligent Hiring and Supervision Claims," *Brooklyn Law Review* 69:1121–57 (2004), p. 1136 (discussing "the fraud/collusion exception to the normal rule that neither secular courts nor states should become involved in the clergy selection process of religious groups").
52 *Hosanna-Tabor Evangelical Lutheran Church & School v. Equal Employment Opportunity Commission*, 565 U.S. 171 (2012).
53 *Id.* at 179 (citing 42 U.S.C. § 12101 (2008)).
54 *Id.* at 180.
55 *Id.* at 185.
56 *Id.* at 188.
57 *Id.*
58 *Gonzalez*, 280 U.S. at 16.
59 *Kedroff*, 344 U.S. at 116.
60 *Hosanna-Tabor*, 565 U.S. at 186 (citing *Kedroff*, 344 U.S. at 116).
61 *Id.* at 192.
62 *Id.* at 195.
63 *Id.* at 196.

3 Fighting wars and claims of conscience

Individuals might claim as a matter of conscience to be unable to perform a variety of activities. Merely because an individual makes such a claim, however, does not mean that the state will permit the individual to exempt herself from performing the activity at issue without suffering some sort of penalty. The state might reject the sincerity of the claimed belief. Or, the state might accept the sincerity of the individual's belief but nonetheless assert that the implicated state interest is sufficiently important to override the individual's interest in non-participation.

An individual who can be shown to be falsely claiming to be barred by conscience from performing an activity will not put the state's commitment to the protection of conscience to the test. But one way to assess the strength of the protections afforded to claims of conscience is to see the degree to which such sincere claims are respected even when they conflict with important state interests. A classic example is to see the degree to which a state accommodates pacifist views.

Historically, the state's commitment to the protection of the pacifist conscience arose in two different contexts: (1) when individuals seeking to become citizens were asked to affirm that they would defend the country if called upon to do so, and (2) when individuals seeking to avoid active military duty challenged the denial of their conscientious objector status. Individuals challenging state actions allegedly failing to respect their pacifist convictions sometimes argued that their statutorily conferred rights had been abridged and sometimes argued that their constitutional rights had been abridged. The United State Supreme Court heard and decided several cases pitting individual claims of conscience against the state interest in military preparedness. While commentators disagree about how to interpret specific cases, the Court's understanding of the constitutional guarantees has arguably remained relatively consistent over time in these kinds of cases, while the Court's interpretation of the relevant statutes has not.

Pacifists, benefits, and burdens

Several cases explore the conditions under which the State can impose burdens or confer benefits on those with pacifist views. Some of the cases involve individuals who sought to become United States citizens, while other cases involve United States citizens who argued that they were being treated unfairly because of their pacifist views. While the best interpretation of the Court's decisions remains controversial, the decisions are much easier to reconcile than many seem to believe.

Immigration and naturalization

Some of the earlier cases involved individuals seeking United States citizenship who were asked whether they would be willing to take up arms to defend the United States. After the would-be citizens explained that they could not do so because of their religious convictions, their citizenship applications were denied. Those denials were appealed. The Supreme Court upheld the denial of their citizenship applications. Eventually, an applicant's refusal to bear arms to defend the country was not viewed as a sufficient condition for barring that person from becoming a citizen, although that development was due to a change in the Court's understanding of the relevant statute rather than an expansion of free exercise guarantees.

United States v. Schwimmer[1] involved a denial of Rosika Schwimmer's application for citizenship. She was a Hungarian national, born in 1877, who came to the United States in 1921. About a year after coming here, she manifested an interest in becoming a United States citizen, and in 1926 filed a petition for naturalization. She testified that she understood and fully believed in the principles upon which the country was based and "could wholeheartedly take the oath of allegiance"[2] with one small exception. As an uncompromising pacifist, she answered "No" to the following question on a required form: "If necessary, are you willing to take up arms in defense of this country?"[3]

Schwimmer noted that she would not be called upon to take up arms to defend the country—men of her age (49) were not called upon to do so and, in addition, women at that time were not serving in the military as a general matter. Point that she would not be asked to serve notwithstanding, she believed it important to be honest about her views, even if that honesty would result in her not becoming a citizen. Her petition for naturalization was denied.[4]

That denial may well have been motivated by factors having nothing to do with whether she was in fact likely to be asked to take up arms for her country. She was questioned about the following comments made in private correspondence:

> Highly as I prize the privilege of American citizenship, I could not compromise my way into it by giving an untrue answer to question 22, though for all practical purposes I might have done so, as even men of my age—I was 49 years old last September—are not called to take up arms. . . . That "I have no nationalistic feeling" is evident from the fact that I wish to give up the nationality of my birth and to adopt a country which is based on principles and institutions more in harmony with my ideals.[5]

It may be that her valuing her pacifism more highly than her becoming an American citizen or, perhaps, her willingness to affirm those values to someone else contributed to the denial of the naturalization application. Indeed, when asked if she would communicate her pacifist views to other women, she responded,

> With reference to spreading propaganda among the women throughout the country about my being an uncompromising pacifist and not willing to fight, I am always ready to tell anyone who wants to hear it that I am an uncompromising pacifist and will not fight."[6]

The Court upheld the denial of her application for citizenship, apparently fearing that she might dissuade others from defending the country. "The influence of conscientious objectors against the use of military force in defense of the principles of our Government is apt to be more detrimental than their mere refusal to bear arms."[7] Further, that influence might be exerted even by someone who was not in fact called upon to serve. "The fact that, by reason of sex, age or other cause, they may be unfit to serve does not lessen their purpose or power to influence others."[8] Notwithstanding that she was "a woman of superior character and intelligence"[9] who apparently "believe[d] more than some of us do in the teachings of the Sermon on the Mount,"[10] she was told that she could not become a United States citizen.

A similar result was reached in a few other cases. *United States v. Macintosh*[11] involved a challenge to the denial of an application for citizenship. Douglas Macintosh, a Canadian citizen, was an ordained Baptist minister who was a faculty member at the Yale Divinity School. Macintosh explained that

> [h]e was ready to give to the United States all the allegiance he ever had given or ever could give to any country, but he could not put allegiance to the government of any country before allegiance to the will of God.[12]

His naturalization application was denied because he "would not promise in advance to bear arms in defense of the United States unless he believed the war to be morally justified."[13] Those reservations were construed by the district court as indicating that "he was not attached to the principles of the Constitution."[14]

As Chief Justice Charles Hughes explained in his dissent, the issue before the *Macintosh* Court was a narrow one, namely, whether Congress intended to preclude someone like Macintosh from becoming a United States citizen. This was a matter of statutory construction rather than constitutional interpretation. As the *Macintosh* Court explained:

> The privilege of the native-born conscientious objector to avoid bearing arms comes not from the Constitution, but from the acts of Congress. That body may grant or withhold the exemption as in its wisdom it sees fit; and if it be withheld, the native-born conscientious objector cannot successfully assert the privilege.[15]

This explanation of the source of the right was important because it helped clarify a possible point of confusion. It might have been thought that American citizens have certain constitutionally protected religious rights including an immunity from punishment for refusing to serve in the military because of their conscientious objections to war. However, the argument would run, individuals who are not United States citizens do not enjoy similar constitutional protections of religion and so are not protected when they assert that they cannot perform certain actions because doing so would contravene their sincere religious convictions. The *Macintosh* Court made clear that the United States Constitution did not immunize an American citizen's refusal to serve as a matter of conscience, although such immunity could be conferred by statute.

Merely because the protections were statutory rather than constitutional did not end the discussion, because a case like *Macintosh* was distinguishable from a case like *Schwimmer* in the following way: While the Court feared that individuals like Schwimmer might impede the war effort by dissuading others from participating, the Court did not share those same reservations about Macintosh. As Chief Justice Hughes noted in dissent,

> After the outbreak of the Great War [World War I], he [Macintosh] voluntarily sought appointment as a chaplain with the Canadian Army and as such saw service at the front. Returning to this country, he made public addresses in 1917 in support of the Allies."[16]

So, too, *United States v. Bland*[17] involved an application for citizenship from an individual who was quite unlikely to inspire others to refuse to participate at all in a war effort. Marie Averil Bland was a Canadian citizen who, when applying for United States citizenship, agreed to defend the United States against her enemies "as far as [Bland's] conscience as a Christian will allow."[18] As had been true in Macintosh's case, Bland had willingly taken on noncombatant duties during wartime, "spen[ding] nine months in the service of our government in France, nursing United States soldiers and aiding in psychiatric work."[19] Nonetheless, Bland's citizenship application was denied. In dissent, Chief Justice Hughes argued that Congress had not meant to preclude someone like Bland from becoming a citizen merely because she "ha[d] religious scruples against bearing arms."[20]

Chief Justice Hughes's point that individuals should not be refused citizenship because of their conscientious objections to killing was vindicated in *Girouard v. United States*.[21] James Girouard was a Seventh-Day Adventist who made clear that "he was willing to serve in the army but would not bear arms."[22] The Court noted, "Refusal to bear arms is not necessarily a sign of disloyalty or a lack of attachment to our institutions."[23] Indeed, Congress had manifested its agreement with such an approach, because individuals precluded by conscience from engaging in combat who had performed non-combatant duties were allowed to become citizens. The difficulty for Girouard was that he had not yet performed non-combatant duties, although he had been willing to do so. The Court rejected that Congress intended to distinguish for naturalization purposes between a conscientious objector who had performed non-combatant service from one who had been willing to do so but had not yet served in that capacity.

The *Girouard* Count understood that its holding was incompatible with the analyses offered in *Schwimmer*, *Macintosh*, and *Bland*, and expressly repudiated those decisions. Yet, the *Girouard* Court made clear that it was engaging in statutory construction rather than constitutional analysis, so it was not as if the Court was modifying its understanding of the protections afforded by free exercise guarantees.

University military instruction

One of the early conscientious objection cases involved a requirement that the University of California imposed upon its students. *Hamilton v. Regents of the University of California*[24] involved the constitutionality of "the regents' order, requiring able-bodied male students under the age of twenty-four as a condition of their enrollment to take the prescribed instruction in military science and tactics."[25] Several students challenged the requirement because it conflicted with their sincerely held religious beliefs.

The California Regents were required by federal law to make military training available, but were not required to make it compulsory. The question before the Court was whether California's decision to make military training compulsory deprived the students of the liberty protected by the Fourteenth Amendment.

> [A]ppellants' contentions amount to no more than an assertion that the due process clause of the Fourteenth Amendment as a safeguard of 'liberty' confers the right to be students in the state university free from obligation to take military training as one of the conditions of attendance.[26]

The Court rejected that the Fourteenth Amendment precludes the state from imposing such a requirement, citing *Schwimmer* and *Macintosh* in support.

It is fair to suggest that *Hamilton* was issued after *Schwimmer* and *Macintosh* but before *Girouard*, and that the *Hamilton* Court cited *Schwimmer* and *Macintosh* with approval. Thus, it might be argued that the Court had not yet modified its understanding of applicable law to prevent the imposition of burdens on conscientious objectors. While the chronology is correct, such a point masks an important difference among the cases. *Schwimmer*, *Macintosh*, and *Girouard* were all about how to interpret a particular federal statute. *Hamilton* was about whether the Fourteenth Amendment precluded a state university from making military training compulsory for males of a certain age who were attending that school.[27] *Hamilton*'s interpretation of Fourteenth Amendment requirements is quite compatible with *Girouard*'s interpretation of a particular federal statute, so it may well be that *Hamilton* would have been decided the same way even had the challenge been made post-*Girouard*.

In his *Hamilton* concurring opinion, Justice Benjamin Cardozo explained that the question of whether to make military training compulsory was a matter of legislative discretion. He noted that students "elect to resort to an institution for higher education maintained with the state's moneys, then and only then they are commanded to follow courses of instruction believed by the state to be vital to its welfare."[28] While the state's policy "may be condemned by some as unwise or illiberal or unfair when there is violence to conscientious scruples, either religious or merely ethical,"[29] that alone would not suffice to establish that the policy was unconstitutional. Rather, at issue in this case were "matters of legislative policy, unrelated to privileges or liberties secured by the organic law [i.e., the United States Constitution]."[30] Justice Cardozo argued that "[i]nstruction in military science, unaccompanied here by any pledge of military service, is not an interference by the state with the free exercise of religion."[31]

Justice Cardozo looked to history to inform his reasoning. He explained:

> From the beginnings of our history Quakers and other conscientious objectors have been exempted as an act of grace from military service, but the exemption, when granted, has been coupled with a condition, at least in many instances, that they supply the army with a substitute or with the money necessary to hire one.[32]

While it is true that this historical example establishes that there had long been a practice of exempting from active military service those with conscientious objections, it also establishes that individuals with sincere conscientious objections to active duty were not able to completely avoid promoting military aims. This more direct assistance in lieu of service (providing either a substitute or monies that would be used to pay a substitute) would seem to be a greater affront to conscience than would the receipt of military instruction, and yet this greater affront had never been thought a violation of constitutional guarantees.

Suppose that those with conscientious objections to supporting war efforts were protected by the Constitution from having to find a replacement or from paying monies that might be used to help induce someone else to serve. The recognition of such constitutional protection would have important implications, because individuals might then have to be exempted from paying taxes to support other actions to which they had sincere religious objections.

> The conscientious objector, if his liberties were to be thus extended, might refuse to contribute taxes in furtherance of a war, whether for attack or for defense, or in furtherance of any other end condemned by his conscience as irreligious or immoral.[33]

The fear that robust protection of conscience would severely undermine federal programs has been a recurrent theme in the case law.

Who qualifies for conscientious objector status?

The Court offered further clarification of the conscientious objector jurisprudence in *Sicurella v. United States*.[34] Anthony Sicurella was a Jehovah's Witness who challenged the denial of his conscientious objector status, notwithstanding his "willingness to use . . . force in defense of Kingdom interests and brethren."[35] Sicurella had made clear that "the weapons of his warfare were spiritual, not carnal,"[36] and the Court explained that his "defense of 'Kingdom Interests' has neither the bark nor the bite of war as we unfortunately know it today."[37]

The question for the Court was whether Congress intended to preclude individuals like Sicurella from being accorded conscientious objector status when it said that only individuals objecting to "war in any form"[38] were entitled to that status. Because "Congress had in mind real shooting wars when it referred to participation in war in any form—actual military conflicts between nations of the earth in our time—wars with bombs and bullets, tanks, planes and rockets,"[39] and because Sicurella was not admitting his willingness to participate in that kind of war, the Court held that "the reasoning of the Government in denying petitioner's claim is so far removed from any possible congressional intent that it is erroneous as a matter of law."[40] For all intents and purposes, Sicurella had a conscientious objection to participating in any war, and thus could not be excluded from those who Congress intended to exempt.

Subsequent decisions about conscientious objector status also involved interpretations of congressional intent. In *United States v. Seeger*,[41] the Court offered an authoritative construction of a federal statute that "exempts from combatant training and service in the armed forces of the United States those persons who by reason of their religious training and belief are conscientiously opposed to participation in war in any form."[42] "Religious training and belief" was defined as "an individual's belief in a relation to a Supreme Being involving duties superior to those arising from any human relation, but (not including) essentially political, sociological, or philosophical views or a merely personal moral code."[43]

At issue was what Congress intended when using "the expression 'Supreme Being' rather than the designation 'God.'"[44] The section was challenged as a violation of First Amendment guarantees, and requiring that those receiving an exemption believe in God or even a Supreme Being might be thought to violate either establishment or free exercise guarantees.

Rather than address the constitutional issues, the Court explained that Congress "was merely clarifying the meaning of religious training and belief so as to embrace all religions and to exclude essentially political, sociological, or philosophical views."[45] The Court noted that the conflict was not "between theistic and atheistic beliefs,"[46] but instead a conflict of interpretations of the term "Supreme Being," pitting "the orthodox God . . . [against] the broader concept of a power or being, or a faith, 'to which all else is subordinate or upon which all else is ultimately dependent.'"[47]

It is important to understand why this was not a conflict between theistic and atheistic beliefs. The Court was offering a construction of a statute, deciding whether Congress had intended to restrict exemptions to those who believed in an orthodox God. If Congress had intended to be less restrictive, then Seeger would be entitled to an exemption and his appeal would be sustained.

A separate question is whether Congress's affording an exemption to those with theistic beliefs but not to those with atheistic beliefs would have violated First Amendment guarantees. The Court did not need to address that question because Seeger's beliefs counted as theistic when that term was construed broadly. It should be noted, however, that the First

Amendment prohibits the government from favoring religion over non-religion,[48] so it is not at all clear that a challenge on establishment grounds would be without merit.

The statute precluded certain people from being awarded conscientious objector status—"those whose opposition to war stems from a 'merely personal moral code,'"[49] or "those persons who, disavowing religious belief, decide on the basis of essentially political, sociological or economic considerations that war is wrong and that they will have no part of it."[50] But more had to be said before the statute's meaning was clear. The Court explained that

> the test of belief "in a relation to a Supreme Being" is whether a given belief that is sincere and meaningful occupies a place in the life of its possessor parallel to that filled by the orthodox belief in God of one who clearly qualifies for the exemption.[51]

By interpreting congressional intent that way, the Court was able to "avoid[ ] imputing to Congress an intent to classify different religious beliefs, exempting some and excluding others,"[52] which not only sidestepped the charge that Congress was favoring certain religions over others but also the charge that Congress was favoring religion over non-religion.

The Court discussed various views that would count as religious, including a view identifying "God not as a projection 'out there' or beyond the skies but as the ground of our very being,"[53] and a view of religion that was "anthropocentric, not theocentric,"[54] which involved "the devotion of man to the highest ideal that he can conceive."[55] *Seeger* cited *United States v. Kauten* with approval,[56] an opinion that Justice Felix Frankfurter also cited with approval in a different case when pointing to ways in which state officials could permissibly distinguish between religion and non-religion.

Justice Frankfurter worried that a determination of "whether a cause is, or is not, 'religious' opens up too wide a field of personal judgment to be left to the mere discretion of an official."[57] Nonetheless, he cited to an opinion of Judge Augustus Hand, which involved an "allowable range of judgment regarding the scope of 'religion.'"[58] Judge Hand explained:

> There is a distinction between a course of reasoning resulting in a conviction that a particular war is inexpedient or disastrous and a conscientious objection to participation in any war under any circumstances. The latter, and not the former, may be the basis of exemption under the Act. The former is usually a political objection, while the latter . . . may justly be regarded as a response of the individual to an inward mentor, call it conscience or God, that is for many persons at the present time the equivalent of what has always been thought a religious impulse.[59]

Judge Hand suggested that the issue was not really religious versus non-religious as the terms are traditionally understood but, instead, whether the internal promptings were equivalent (in strength?[60] in operation?[61]) to a religious impulse. That said, religious impulses vary in strength and efficacy, so it may be difficult to figure out whether particular internal promptings are equivalent to a religious impulse without further specification.

Seeger had "declared that he was conscientiously opposed to participation in war in any form by reason of his 'religious' belief,"[62] although "he preferred to leave the question as to his belief in a Supreme Being open."[63] Seeger's sincerity was not at issue. Because "the beliefs which prompted his objection occupy the same place in his life as the belief in a traditional deity holds in the lives of his friends, the Quakers,"[64] the Court held that he was entitled to conscientious objector status—Daniel Seeger, who had a "belief in and devotion to goodness and virtue for their own sakes, and a religious faith in a purely ethical creed"[65] could nonetheless qualify for the exemption.[66]

Seeger was neither denying nor affirming God's existence. His belief system would not have to be characterized as anti-religious, even if atheistic belief systems would be so characterized.[67] The *Seeger* opinion left open whether someone affirmatively denying God's existence could nonetheless qualify as a conscientious objector.

In *Welsh v. United States*,[68] the Court addressed whether an individual could be classified as a conscientious objector when his objection to all wars was expressly non-religious, although Welsh had clarified that "his beliefs were 'certainly religious in the ethical sense of the word.'"[69] Here, too, sincerity was not at issue. The *Welsh* Court addressed whether Congress intended to afford conscientious objector status to an individual who "deeply and sincerely holds beliefs that are purely ethical or moral in source and content but that nevertheless impose upon him a duty of conscience to refrain from participating in any war at any time."[70] The relevant issue was whether the asserted beliefs ethical in source "occupy in the life of that individual 'a place parallel to that filled by . . . God' in traditionally religious persons."[71] Because the relevant section of the federal statute "exempts from military service all those whose consciences, spurred by deeply held moral, ethical, or religious beliefs, would give them no rest or peace if they allowed themselves to become a part of an instrument of war,"[72] the Court held that Welsh had been wrongly denied conscientious objector status.

In his concurrence in the result, Justice John Harlan explained that the judgment below had to be reversed, "not as a matter of statutory construction, but as the touchstone for salvaging a congressional policy of long standing that would otherwise have to be nullified."[73] He thus implied that conscientious objector status had to be afforded as a constitutional matter. However, no other justice joined that concurrence, so it should not be assumed that Justice Harlan's view was shared by the other members of the Court.

One way to test whether conscientious objector status must be accorded as a constitutional rather than as a statutory matter is to consider whether someone with a sincere religious objection to a *particular* war must be afforded an exemption, even though Congress required the objection to be to all wars rather than to one war in particular. In *Sisson v. United States*,[74] the Court considered a case involving an individual who had sincere objections to the Vietnam War in particular rather than to war in general. The jury, who had been instructed that "the crux of the case was whether Sisson's refusal to submit to induction was 'unlawfully, knowingly and wilfully' done,"[75] found the defendant guilty. The district court granted "what it termed a motion in arrest of judgment"[76] and held "that the indictment did not charge an offense based on defendant's 'never-abandoned' Establishment, Free Exercise, and Due Process Clause arguments relating to conscientious objections to the Vietnam war."[77] The district court also ruled that the Selective Service provision at issue

> offends the Establishment Clause because it 'unconstitutionally discriminated against atheists, agnostics, and men, like Sisson, who, whether they be religious or not, are motivated in their objection to the draft by profound moral beliefs which constitute the central convictions of their beings.[78]

The United States Government appealed directly to the United States Supreme Court based "on the 'arresting judgment' provision of the Criminal Appeals Act."[79] The Court rejected that it had jurisdiction based on the "arresting judgment" provision, however, because "the critical requirement is that a judgment can be arrested only on the basis of error appearing on the 'face of the record,' and not on the basis of proof offered at trial."[80]

The Court decided that "the decision was in fact an acquittal rendered by the trial court after the jury's verdict of guilty."[81] To explain why that was a more accurate characterization of what had happened, the Court first hypothesized a different case in which the jury had been offered the following instruction:

> If you find defendant Sisson to be sincere, and if you find that he was as genuinely and profoundly governed by conscience as a martyr obedient to an orthodox religion, you must acquit him because the government's interest in having him serve in Vietnam is outweighed by his interest in obeying the dictates of his conscience. On the other hand, if you do not so find, you must convict if you find that petitioner did wilfully refuse induction.[82]

If that had been the instruction, the Court explained that "there [could] be no doubt that its verdict of acquittal could not be appealed under § 3731 no matter how erroneous the constitutional theory underlying the instructions."[83]

The *Sisson* Court understood that there were differences between the hypothesized case and the one before the Court. In the instant case, the judge rather than the jury found for the defendant, although "judges, like juries, can acquit defendants."[84] Further, the judge in this case found for the defendant after the jury had issued a guilty verdict, although the Federal Rules of Criminal Procedure "expressly allow[ed] a federal judge to acquit a criminal defendant after the jury 'returns a verdict of guilty.'"[85] Finally, the judge "labeled his post-verdict opinion an arrest of judgment,"[86] although that label was inaccurate.

The Court viewed the trial court decision as "a post-verdict directed acquittal,"[87] which meant that the Court did not have jurisdiction to address the merits. The district court's suggestion that the First and Fourteenth Amendments protected an individual's sincere refusal to participate in a particular war would not be addressed on the merits until *Gillette v. United States*.[88]

At issue in *Gillette* was "whether conscientious objection to a particular war, rather than objection to war as such, relieves the objector from responsibilities of military training and service."[89] The Court combined two cases, each involving an individual with sincere objections to participating in the Vietnam War in particular. Guy Gillette "was convicted of wilful failure to report for induction into the armed forces."[90] He claimed that he was a conscientious objector with respect to the Vietnam conflict, although he did not object to war as a general matter. Louis Negre sought a discharge as a conscientious objector after having completed his basic training. Negre, a devout Catholic, believed that he had a duty "to discriminate between 'just' and 'unjust' wars and to forswear participation in the latter."[91] He concluded that the Vietnam conflict was an unjust war and that participation in that war would be a violation of conscience.

The sincerity of Gillette's and Negre's convictions was not in doubt. Rather, the issues before the Court included both the proper interpretation of the conscientious objector section and whether that section so construed would pass constitutional muster. The *Gillette* Court explained: "For purposes of determining the statutory status of conscientious objection to a particular war, the focal language of § 6(j) is the phrase, 'conscientiously opposed to participation in war in any form.'"[92] The Court believed the proper interpretation of this section beyond dispute. "This language, on a straightforward reading, can bear but one meaning; that conscientious scruples relating to war and military service must amount to conscientious opposition to participating personally in any war and all war."[93]

As an initial matter, the *Gillette* Court had to determine whether the current conscientious objector statute exempted Negre and Gillette. Because the exemption only applied to individuals objecting to war in any form, individuals with conscientious objections to participation in a particular war did not qualify for an exemption. But the question then became whether the refusal to afford the exemption to those with religious objections to participating in the Vietnam War in particular passed constitutional muster. The Court accepted that

> even as to neutral prohibitory or regulatory laws having secular aims, the Free Exercise Clause may condemn certain applications clashing with imperatives of religion and conscience, when the burden on First Amendment values is not justifiable in terms of the Government's valid aims.[94]

Rather than question whether the requirement imposed a cognizable burden, the Court noted instead that the requirement was not designed to burden religion and that those burdens were justified by the importance of the state interests at issue. Thus, the Court did not question whether forcing individuals to participate in a particular war against their religious convictions constituted a substantial burden, but instead held that the state had sufficiently important interests that justified maintaining a draft where only those objecting to all wars were exempted.

In discussing the difference between objecting to a particular war and objecting to war as a general matter, the *Gillette* Court cited *Sicurella*, explaining that it was permissible for purposes of qualifying for the exemption for an individual to differentiate between a "theocratic war"[95] and "real shooting wars"[96] and say that he would only be willing to fight in the former. That distinction was not at issue in *Gillette*, however, because in the latter case the plaintiffs "for a variety of reasons consider[ed] one particular 'real shooting war' to be unjust, and therefore oppose[d] participation in that war."[97]

The *Gillette* Court then addressed whether affording an exemption to those who objected to war as a general matter but not to those who objected to a particular unjust war "works a de facto discrimination among religions."[98] After all, some religious traditions oppose war of any sort, while other traditions

> themselves distinguish between personal participation in "just" and in "unjust" wars, commending the former and forbidding the latter, and therefore adherents of some religious faiths—and individuals whose personal beliefs of a religious nature include the distinction—cannot object to all wars consistently with what is regarded as the true imperative of conscience.[99]

The Court rejected the contention that the Government was intentionally favoring certain religious traditions over others, instead noting that the chosen method of differentiation was supported by "a number of valid purposes having nothing to do with a design to foster or favor any sect, religion, or cluster of religions."[100] Those purposes included "the Government's need for manpower"[101] and "the interest in maintaining a fair system for determining 'who serves when not all serve.'"[102] If a religious exemption to a particular war qualified for an exemption, then there would likely be even greater difficulty in determining who was entitled to a conscientious exemption, because "[a]ll the factors that might go into nonconscientious dissent from policy, also might appear as the concrete basis of an objection that has roots as well in conscience and religion."[103] The Court was thus noting that in cases in which an individual objected to participating in a particular war, the Court would likely have great difficulty in distinguishing between those individuals whose objections were purely

50 *Fighting wars and claims of conscience*

policy-driven from those whose objections had some basis in religion or conscience. The Vietnam War was a very unpopular war, so the courts would be very busy indeed if certain kinds of objections to that particular war would provide the basis for conscientious objector status whereas other kinds of objections would not. Further, the *Gillette* Court feared that its attempting to craft a way to distinguish among the kinds of objections to the Vietnam War that would provide the basis for conscientious objection to that war in particular would either severely diminish the number of individuals available to participate in the war effort or would give those with access to savvy counselors a distinct advantage when framing their objections to the war.

There was no readily apparent workable way to distinguish fairly among those objecting to this particular war for purposes of deciding who should receive conscientious objector status and who should not. But that meant that the Court had to offer a plausible justification for the Constitution's not requiring an exemption for those with religious objections to fighting in the Vietnam War.

In cases where the Court upheld or extended the application of a conscientious objector exemption, one would expect the Court to say that forcing such individuals to participate in war constituted a great burden on free exercise. But in a case holding that no exemption was required for those with conscientious objections to fighting in the war, one might have expected the Court to adopt a different tack, for example, deny that forcing an individual to participate in a particular war to which he objected imposed a substantial burden on free exercise. After all, the refusal to afford an exemption would be upheld only if no substantial burden on free exercise were imposed or if the state interests were sufficiently important to justify the imposition of such a burden. Rather than say that no substantial burden was imposed, the Court instead suggested that the state's interests justified the imposition of a substantial burden.

With respect to the Free Exercise challenge in particular, the Court explained that the draft laws were "not designed to interfere with any religious ritual or practice, and d[id] not work a penalty against any theological position."[104] Because "[t]he incidental burdens felt by persons in petitioners' position are strictly justified by substantial governmental interests that relate directly to the very impacts questioned,"[105] the Court held that affording conscientious objector status only to those objecting to all wars did not violate constitutional guarantees.

Here, the Court was making two distinct points. First, it denied that the Congress was targeting a particular religion for adverse treatment. Second, the Court was suggesting that important interests were at stake, and the burdening of religious beliefs was a regrettable byproduct of the need to promote those interests. The Court noted the concern

> of the National Advisory Commission on Selective Service . . . that exemption of objectors to particular wars would weaken the resolve of those who otherwise would feel themselves bound to serve despite personal cost, uneasiness at the prospect of violence, or even serious moral reservations or policy objections concerning the particular conflict.[106]

Thus, the Court accepted that according conscientious objector status to those with religious objections to particular wars might have too severe an impact on the conduct of the war.

Guy Gillette and Louis Negre were each convicted of refusing to serve their country in war, although each had claimed to have conscientious objections to serving in the Vietnam War. Sincerity of belief was not at issue. Further, recognizing that "these petitioners' beliefs concerning war are 'religious' in nature,"[107] the Court did not base its decision on the exclusion related to "essentially political, sociological, or philosophical views, or a merely personal moral code."[108] Nonetheless, the Court expressly rejected that Congress intended to offer conscientious objector status to those objecting to a particular war rather than to war in general.

Perhaps *Gillette* can be explained by talking about the difficulty in distinguishing between those with sincere religious objections to the war and those with merely political objections to it. Yet, the Court accepted that firmly held political or moral objections to war as a general matter could be the basis of conscientious objector status in *Welsh*, so the Court should presumably be taken at its word that it believed a different decision might seriously impair the war effort. In any event, *Gillette* does not represent a particularly robust protection of religious liberty. Basically, the Court suggested that recognition of conscientious objector status was a matter of legislative discretion rather than constitutional mandate. Further, the view that the conscientious objector cases do not represent as robust an example of free exercise protections as might be thought is further strengthened when one considers an additional case in which the Court *may* have implicitly modified what qualifies as a substantial burden for free exercise purposes.

At issue in *Johnson v. Robison*[109] was whether conscientious objectors could be denied the education benefits to which those who had been active in the military were entitled. Congress created this benefit to ease the transition from military to civilian life. While conscientious objectors who performed alternative service also had their lives disrupted, the term of service was shorter than and different from the term of service of those who served in the military.

The *Robison* Court rejected that affording educational benefits to those in the military and not to those in alternative service was invidiously discriminatory. "When . . . the inclusion of one group promotes a legitimate governmental purpose, and the addition of other groups would not, we cannot say that the statute's classification of beneficiaries and nonbeneficiaries is invidiously discriminatory."[110] The motivation behind the differentiation was not to target conscientious objectors—the Court rejected that there was "any legislative design to interfere with their free exercise of religion."[111] Instead, the "withholding of educational benefits involve[d] only an incidental burden upon appellee's free exercise of religion,"[112] because extending those benefits to conscientious objectors "would not rationally promote the Act's purposes."[113]

The provision of educational benefits was designed to "make military service more attractive,"[114] so an individual might be more willing to serve in the military if accorded those benefits. However, one precluded by conscience from serving would presumably be unwilling to serve even if offered educational benefits. "[B]ecause a conscientious objector bases his refusal to serve in the Armed Forces upon deeply held religious beliefs, we will not assume that educational benefits will make military service more attractive to him."[115] The Court thereby implied that it was reasonable not to offer those benefits to conscientious objectors, because doing so would not have promoted the state's desired end.[116] But the Court's explanation of why conscientious objectors should not receive educational benefits was not persuasive for a few reasons.

First, an individual who had conscientious objections to participating in any war would nonetheless be offered those educational benefits as an inducement to serve and not to seek conscientious objector status. Perhaps the Court was correct that many conscientious objectors would not consider the offer a sufficient inducement to overcome their reservations about participating in a war. But that would merely mean that the educational benefits would make military service more albeit not sufficiently attractive to overcome the dictates of conscience. The goal—making service more attractive—would have been achieved, even if service would not thereby have been made sufficiently attractive to overcome the individuals' conscientious objections.

It is not as if the educational benefits were only awarded to individuals for whom those benefits played a role in convincing that person to become a part of or remain in the military. Individuals anxious to join the military as a matter of patriotic duty (and thus needing no incentive) would still be entitled to those benefits, as would individuals who had no need for an educational benefits inducement because avoidance of prosecution was more than sufficient as an inducement. Further, an individual who had (mild?) conscientious objections to war who served anyway because of the educational benefits would also receive those benefits. Basically the rationale offered by the Court—the benefits were provided to induce individuals to serve—was not plausible, given that individuals needing no inducement were also accorded those benefits.

A more plausible rationale was that the individuals who served were accorded those benefits as a reward for their putting their lives at risk for serving their country. But characterizing the benefits as a reward supported Robison's contention that he in effect was being taxed for his convictions—Congress had effectively "increase[ed] the price he [the conscientious objector] must pay for adherence to his religious beliefs."[117] The Court was unpersuaded because the statute at issue did "not require appellee and his class to make any choice comparable to that required of the petitioners in *Gillette*,"[118] and the imposition of the burden on Gillette had been upheld.

The Court was correct that the price of following one's conscience in *Gillette* was incarceration, whereas the price of following one's conscience in *Robison* was merely the opportunity cost associated with not having the government pay for one's education. But there were other dissimilarities between the cases that made the Court's analysis unconvincing. Regrettably, the *Robison* Court implied that the government's interests at stake in *Robison* and *Gillette* were comparable—"the Government's substantial interest in raising and supporting armies, is of 'a kind and weight' clearly sufficient to sustain the challenged legislation."[119]

Yet, this was a surprising argument to make. In *Gillette*, the Court implied that requiring exemptions for individuals with conscientious objections about a particular war would put the fate of the whole draft at risk. There was great importance in having "fair, evenhanded, and uniform decisionmaking"[120] with respect to who would be drafted, and "the interest in fairness would be jeopardized by expansion [of the exemption] to include conscientious objection to a particular war."[121] The *Gillette* Court had accepted that expanding the exemption to those whose consciences forbade participation in a particular conflict might seriously impair "the Government's interest in procuring the manpower necessary for military purposes."[122]

Similar concerns were not implicated in *Robison*. Those whose educational benefits were at issue were already exempted from active military duty, and the Court expressly rejected that the provision of military benefits would affect the decision-making of those claiming a conscientious objection. But that means that the state's interest was not in whether the draft could survive, especially because the United States had shifted to an all-volunteer army,[123] but merely in whether the United States would have to bear the additional costs implicated in footing the educational costs of conscientious objectors. Yet, it is not at all clear that protection of the federal fisc sufficed to justify the imposition of a substantial burden on religion, so it is difficult to tell whether the Court implicitly changed its analysis with respect to the kind of burden that will trigger free exercise guarantees or whether, instead, the Court somehow thought the integrity of the (former) draft was predicated on conscientious objectors not receiving these education benefits.

Conclusion

The conscientious objector cases are not free from interpretive difficulty. Nonetheless, the interpretation that bests accounts for these cases is that the First Amendment's free exercise guarantees are not particularly robust in this context. Congress is permitted but not required to extend citizenship to those who would qualify but for their conscientious objections to war. Congress is permitted but not required to exempt from military service those who have conscientious objections to war. While some commentators would suggest that the draft cases provide good reason to believe that the Constitution offers robust protection of religious conscience, a closer examination of the relevant cases does not support that conclusion. Indeed, the existing robust protections are statutorily rather than constitutionally required and conscience tends to be understood in a way that does not privilege (traditional) religious conscience.

The conscientious objector cases might have established the robustness of free exercise protections if the Court had held that conscientious objectors must be granted an exemption, notwithstanding the state's compelling interest in being able to prosecute wars. However, precisely because the state has such a compelling interest in waging war, for example, to assure its own survival, the Constitution's permitting conscientious objectors to be refused an exemption from military service does not establish that free exercise guarantees are weak. The next chapter discusses how claims of conscience have fared when asserted in a context other than one involving a refusal to fight a war.

Notes

1 *United States v. Schwimmer*, 279 U.S. 644 (1929) (overruled in part by *Girouard v. United States*, 328 U.S. 61 (1946)).
2 *Id.* at 647.
3 *Id.*
4 See Barry Cushman, "The Secret Lives of the Four Horsemen," *Virginia Law Review* 83:559–84 (1997), p. 582 (discussing "the preposterous denial of citizenship to 49-year-old pacifist Rosika Schwimmer on the ground that she would not swear to take up arms in defense of the United States.").
5 *Schwimmer*, 279 U.S. at 648.
6 *Id.* at 648–49.
7 *Id.* at 651.
8 *Id.*
9 *Id.* at 653 (Holmes, J., dissenting).
10 *Id.* at 655 (Holmes, J., dissenting).
11 *United States v. Macintosh*, 283 U.S. 605 (1931) (overruled in part by *Girouard v. United States*, 328 U.S. 61 (1946)).
12 *Id.* at 618.
13 *Id.* at 627.
14 *Id.*
15 *Id.* at 624.
16 *Id.* at 629 (Hughes, C.J., dissenting).
17 *United States v. Bland*, 283 U.S. 636 (1931) (overruled in part by *Girouard v. United States*, 328 U.S. 61 (1946)).
18 *Id.* at 636.
19 *Id.* at 637 (Hughes, C.J. dissenting).

20 *Id.* (Hughes, C.J., dissenting).
21 *Girouard v. United States*, 328 U.S. 61 (1946).
22 *Id.* at 62.
23 *Id.* at 64.
24 *Hamilton v. Regents of the University of California*, 293 U.S. 245 (1934).
25 *Id.* at 265.
26 *Id.* at 262.
27 See *Coale v. Pearson*, 290 U.S. 597 (1933). The United States Supreme Court dismissed for want of a substantial federal question an appeal of a Maryland Supreme Court decision (*Pearson v. Coale*, 167 A. 54 (Maryland 1933)) upholding the suspension of a student from the University of Maryland who refused as a matter of conscience to take a required military training course at the University.
28 *Hamilton*, 293 U.S. at 266 (Cardozo, J., concurring).
29 *Id.* (Cardozo, J., concurring).
30 *Id.* (Cardozo, J., concurring).
31 *Id.* (Cardozo, J., concurring).
32 *Id.* at 266–67 (Cardozo, J., concurring).
33 *Id.* at 268 (Cardozo, J., concurring); see also Michael J. White, "The First Amendment's Religion Clauses: 'Freedom of Conscience' versus Institutional Accommodation," *San Diego Law Review* 47:1075–105 (2010), p. 1092 ("If the phrase 'conscientious objection' can be properly applied to any individual demurral from government policy that is sufficiently 'serious' and if that demurral has a recognizably moral basis—or, alternatively, a basis in strong and sincere convictions concerning the 'meaning of life'—an interpretation of free exercise could be developed that would be broad enough to excuse the individual person from compliance with the results of even the most 'democratic decisionmaking.' The result would be that the First Amendment's Free Exercise Clause would become, in effect, a constitutional guarantee of a subjective right to civil disobedience.").
34 *Sicurella v. United States*, 348 U.S. 385 (1955).
35 *Id.* at 389.
36 *Id.*
37 *Id.* at 389–90.
38 *Id.* at 389.
39 *Id.* at 391.
40 *Id.*; see also Donald L. Doernberg, "Pass in Review: Due Process and Judicial Scrutiny of Classification Decisions of the Selective Service System," *Hastings Law Journal* 33:871–902 (1982), p. 889 ("The Supreme Court overturned the conviction, holding that the Department of Justice erred when it stated that Sicurella's willingness to participate in a theocratic war disqualified him under the statute.").
41 *United States v. Seeger*, 380 U.S. 163 (1965).
42 *Id.* at 164–65 (interpreting § 6(j) of the *Universal Military Training and Service Act*, 50 *United States Code* app. § 456(j) (1958)).
43 *Id.* at 165.
44 *Id.*
45 *Id.*
46 *Id.* at 173.
47 *Id.* at 174 (citing *Webster's New International Dictionary*).
48 See *McCreary County, Kentucky v. American Civil Liberties Union of Kentucky*, 545 U.S. 844, 860 (2005) ("[T]he 'First Amendment mandates governmental neutrality between religion and religion, and between religion and nonreligion.'") (citing *Epperson v. Arkansas*, 393 U.S. 97, 104 (1968); *Everson v. Board of Education of Ewing*, 330 U.S. 1, 15–16 (1947)).
49 *Seeger*, 380 U.S. at 173.
50 *Id.*
51 *Id.* at 165–66.
52 *Id.* at 176.
53 *Id.* at 180 (citing Paul Tillich, including a quotation from his book II *Systematic Theology* 12 (1957)).

54 *Id.* at 183.
55 *Id.* (citing Dr. David Saville Muzzey, *Ethics as a Religion* (1951)).
56 See *Seeger*, 380 U.S. at 179 (citing *United States v. Kauten*, 133 F.2d 703 (2d Cir. 1943)).
57 *Saia v. New York*, 334 U.S. 558, 564 (1948) (Frankfurter, J., dissenting); but cf. Kent Greenawalt, "Religion as a Concept in Constitutional Law," *California Law Review* 72:753–816 (1984), p. 762 ("[F]or constitutional purposes, religion should be determined by the closeness of analogy in the relevant respects between the disputed instance and what is indisputably religion.").
58 *Saia*, 334 U.S. at 564 (Frankfurter, J., dissenting) (citing *Kauten*, 133 F.2d at 708).
59 *Kauten*, 133 F.2d at 708.
60 Note, "Conscientious Objectors: Recent Developments and a New Appraisal," *Columbia Law Review* 70:1426–41 (1970), p. 1436 (interpreting Judge Hand to be offering an account partly based on the magnitude of the feelings); Lee J. Strang, "The Meaning of 'Religion' in the First Amendment," *Duquesne Law Review* 40:181–240 (2002), p. 201 (noting that Judge Hand's view takes into account the "intensity of belief").
61 See Note, "Toward a Constitutional Definition of Religion," *Harvard Law Review* 91:1056–89 (1978), p. 1061 (suggesting that Judge Hand "focused on the psychological function of the belief in the life of the individual"). See also Max Dehn, "How It Works: Sobriety Sentencing, the Constitution, and Alcoholics Anonymous," *Michigan State University Journal of Medicine & Law* 10:255–98 (2006), p. 281 (characterizing Judge Hand's approach as involving "an inquiry into the individual's inner life and personal moral center").
62 *Seeger*, 380 U.S. at 166.
63 *Id.*
64 *Id.* at 187.
65 *Id.* at 166.
66 *Id.* at 187 ("In light of his beliefs and the unquestioned sincerity with which he held them, we think the Board, had it applied the test we propose today, would have granted him the exemption.").
67 Cf. *County of Allegheny v. American Civil Liberties Union Greater Pittsburgh Chapter*, 492 U.S. 573, 610 (1989) abrogated by *Town of Greece, New York v. Galloway*, 134 S. Ct. 1811 (2014) ("A secular state . . . is not the same as an atheistic or antireligious state.").
68 *Welsh v. United States*, 398 U.S. 333 (1970).
69 *Id.* at 341.
70 *Id.* at 340.
71 *Id.*
72 *Id.* at 344.
73 *Id.* at 345 (Harlan, J., concurring).
74 *Sisson v. United States*, 399 U.S. 267 (1970).
75 *Id.* at 276.
76 *Id.* at 277.
77 *Id.*
78 *Id.* at 278 (quoting *United States v. Sisson*, 297 F. Supp. 902, 911 (D. Massachusetts 1969)).
79 *Id.* at 278–79 (citing 18 *United States Code* § 3731 (1964)).
80 *Id.* at 281. The Court noted that there was another reason that it did not have jurisdiction to hear the government's appeal, namely that "[t]he second statutory requirement, that the decision arresting judgment be 'for insufficiency of the indictment,' is also not met in this case." See *id.* at 287.
81 *Id.* at 288.
82 *Id.* at 289.
83 *Id.*; see also 18 *United States Code* § 3731: "In a criminal case an appeal by the United States shall lie to a court of appeals from a decision, judgment, or order of a district court dismissing an indictment or information or granting a new trial after verdict or judgment, as to any one or more counts, or any part thereof, except that no appeal shall lie where the double jeopardy clause of the United States Constitution prohibits further prosecution."
84 *Sisson*, 399 U.S. at 290.
85 *Id.* (citing *Federal Rules Criminal Procedure* 29(b)–(c)).
86 *Id.*

87 *Id.*
88 *Gillette v. United States*, 401 U.S. 437 (1971).
89 *Id.* at 439.
90 *Id.*
91 *Id.* at 441.
92 *Id.* at 443.
93 *Id.* (citing *Welsh*, 398 U.S. at 340, 342. But cf. *Macintosh*, 283 U.S. at 635 (Hughes, C.J., dissenting) ("Nor is there ground, in my opinion, for the exclusion of Professor Macintosh because his conscientious scruples have particular reference to wars believed to be unjust.").
94 *Id.* at 462.
95 *Id.* at 446.
96 *Id.* at 446–47.
97 *Id.* at 447.
98 *Id.* at 451–52.
99 *Id.* at 452.
100 *Id.* at 452–53.
101 *Id.* at 455.
102 The Court noted, "The Report of the National Advisory Commission on Selective Service (1967) is aptly entitled *In Pursuit of Equity: Who Serves When Not All Serve?*" See *id.* at n. 20.
103 *Id.* at 455.
104 *Id.* at 462.
105 *Id.*
106 *Id.* at 459–60.
107 *Id.* at 447.
108 *Id.*
109 *Johnson v. Robison*, 415 U.S. 361 (1974).
110 *Id.* at 383.
111 *Id.* at 385.
112 *Id.*
113 *Id.*
114 *Id.* at 382.
115 *Id.*at 382–83.
116 Cf. *id.* at 383 ("[T]he inclusion of one group promotes a legitimate governmental purpose, and the addition of other groups would not . . .").
117 *Id.* at 383.
118 *Id.* at 385.
119 *Id.* (citing *United States Constitution* article I, § 8).
120 *Gillette*, 401 U.S. at 455.
121 *Id.* at 455
122 *Id.* at 462.
123 See Christine Hunter Kellett, "Draft Registration and the Conscientious Objector: A Proposal to Accommodate Constitutional Values," *Columbia Human Rights Law Review* 15:167–81 (1984), p. 168 n. 9 ("The Congress went to an all-volunteer army and ended the draft in 1973.").

4 Early modern free exercise

The United States Supreme Court has had multiple opportunities to address the strength of free exercise guarantees in contexts other than those involving individuals with conscientious objections to serving in the armed forces. Religious beliefs and practices may impact various aspects of daily life, so conflicts between religious duties and civil laws will likely occur in a variety of non-military contexts. When such conflicts arise, plaintiffs often argue that the state must accommodate their religious practices to reduce if not eliminate the burdens imposed.

The United States Constitution does not expressly describe when or how religious practices must be accommodated, and it is unsurprising that the Court has not yet found a satisfying test yielding determinate results in the great range of cases in which such conflicts might arise. Nonetheless, the Court's free exercise jurisprudence is justly criticized not because of the failure to discover some elusive, all-encompassing principle, but because the Court has been inconsistent both with respect to which test determines whether free exercise guarantees have been violated and with respect to how the relevant test should be applied. This inconsistency has created a confused and confusing jurisprudence—sometimes free exercise guarantees seem rather robust while at other times quite weak. The Court's free exercise approach has not only made the jurisprudence difficult if not impossible to understand but has also obscured some of the valuable insights about free exercise that the Court has offered in the case law.

Fulfilling religious obligations in society

Individuals may have religious obligations to act or refrain from acting in particular ways, and religious adherents fulfilling their duties may thereby incur a variety of social or financial costs. The Court has decided several cases exploring the conditions under which individuals should be exempted from generally applicable requirements because of their sincerely held religious beliefs and practices. Regrettably, the Court has offered mixed signals with respect to when the state must accommodate religious practices that are at odds with the way that most people live their lives, which has made it difficult if not impossible to construct a principled and coherent jurisprudence specifying the conditions under which free exercise is protected.

Modern free exercise jurisprudence

In *Cantwell v. Connecticut*, a seminal case in modern free exercise jurisprudence,[1] the Court made clear that religious practice is entitled to increased constitutional protection and, further, that the free exercise guarantees found in the First Amendment to the United States

Constitution also constrain the states. The holding that the Free Exercise Clause also constrains the states was somewhat controversial if only because it was not directly supported by the constitutional text.[2]

The First Amendment to the United States Constitution states: "Congress shall make no law ... prohibiting the free exercise [of religion]."[3] Prior to *Cantwell*, the free exercise guarantees contained in the First Amendment were often interpreted as only applying to the federal government, precisely because the First Amendment expressly barred *Congress* from prohibiting free exercise.[4] After *Cantwell*, the First Amendment's free exercise guarantees imposed constraints on both federal and state governments,[5] although the range and depth of those guarantees were not clearly spelled out.

The *Cantwell* Court provided some insights about what free exercise guarantees protected. For example, employing a distinction made during the previous century, the Court explained that free exercise guarantees cover both an individual's right to believe and her right to act in accord with those beliefs. However, the freedom to believe and the freedom to act do not enjoy the same degree of protection. "[T]he Amendment embraces two concepts, freedom to believe and freedom to act. The first is absolute but ... the second cannot be. Conduct remains subject to regulation for the protection of society."[6]

The Court's pointing out that laws may regulate religious conduct in order to protect society does not provide much guidance. Different laws are designed to avert a whole host of threats ranging from grave dangers to minor inconveniences, and more must be said before the protection of society can be a helpful standard. One of the Court's great failures in free exercise jurisprudence as a general matter has been in failing to offer a consistent position with respect to the kinds of individual and societal interests that will trump religious liberty and the kinds that will not. Without such a position, it is rather difficult to formulate a clear picture about when free exercise rights will be protected or even how heavily they should be weighed.

Cantwell involved a challenge to Cantwell's breach-of-the-peace conviction resulting from his playing a phonograph recording extremely critical of the Catholic Church. On a particular occasion, those listening to the recording had become quite angry and had asked Jesse Cantwell to leave, which he did. The Court concluded that Cantwell's phonograph playing did not constitute a breach of the peace, even though the contents of Cantwell's speech had almost induced his listeners to strike him.

Part of the reason that the speech did not qualify as a breach involved its specific subject matter. While "the contents of the record not unnaturally aroused animosity,"[7] the Court distinguished what Cantwell had played from "provocative language which consisted of profane, indecent, or abusive remarks directed to the person of the hearer."[8] The former, but not the latter, is "communication of information or opinion safeguarded by the Constitution."[9]

The *Cantwell* Court could have ended its analysis after noting that the speech was protected because not profane, indecent, or abusive. But the Court did not stop there, instead suggesting that the religious nature of Cantwell's speech required that the speech be given more leeway by the state—"the power to regulate must be so exercised as not, in attaining a permissible end, unduly to infringe the protected freedom."[10] The referent of the protected freedom was the free exercise of religion.

Cantwell left many questions unanswered. While some additional protection was afforded to Cantwell's speech because it was religious in nature, the Court left open how much extra weight was added because the speech was religious. By the same token, the Court was less clear than might have been desired about when some of the other interests in the balance should be weighed. For example, while the state does not need to wait for violence to break out before acting and can instead act to prevent a probable disturbance,[11] the Court did not explain whether there is some threshold probability that violence will occur that will determine whether religious speech can be treated as a breach of the peace. Suppose, for example, that those offended by the speech had not merely asked Cantwell to leave but instead had assaulted him. Who, if anyone, would have been arrested? Those hoping for answers to these questions would have to wait for future decisions.

Distributing religious tracts

Four years later, the Court decided *Prince v. Massachusetts*,[12] which involved whether child labor laws could constitutionally be applied to children who were distributing religious tracts pursuant to a religious calling. A preliminary issue involved whether the child labor law was even intended to apply to children distributing religious literature in the hopes that they would receive a donation. That was a matter of state law, and the Supreme Judicial Court of Massachusetts had concluded that the law did cover the matter at hand. Because state law covered the activity, the United States Supreme Court had to address whether the First Amendment's free exercise guarantees required that an exemption be granted for those whose tract distribution involved a religious calling.

Sarah Prince, the plaintiff, permitted her children and her niece, Betty Simmons, to hand out the religious tracts "Watchtower" and "Consolation" in exchange for donations. Prince argued that she had the constitutional right to permit her niece (who was also her ward) "to preach the gospel,"[13] both because of Sarah's rights as a parent—Prince had legal custody of Betty—and by virtue of the constitutional protections for religious exercise. The *Prince* Court recognized that the Constitution protects the "rights of children to exercise their religion, and of parents to give them religious training and to encourage them in the practice of religious belief."[14] But that did not mean that Sarah Prince could expose her children to the dangers that might be associated with distributing this literature. That an adult could not be precluded from preaching in this way did not establish that children were also free to do so. The Court held that no religious exemption to the child labor law was required for children who sought to distribute literature for religious reasons in exchange for donations.

Prince is itself a study in mixed messages. The Court recognized that "the custody, care and nurture of the child reside first in the parents" and that there is a "private realm of family life which the state cannot enter."[15] However, "neither rights of religion nor rights of parenthood are beyond limitation."[16] Legislation designed to prevent harm to children "is within the state's police power, whether against the parents [sic] claim to control of the child or one that religious scruples dictate contrary action."[17] The *Prince* Court explained that "the state has a wide range of power for limiting parental freedom and authority in things affecting the child's welfare; and . . . this includes, to some extent, matters of conscience and religious conviction."[18] Thus, the Court was emphasizing on the one hand the constitutional protections accorded to parenting and to religious practice but was also emphasizing on the other hand, that deference must be given to states in their attempts to promote child welfare.

Certainly, the state has an interest in protecting children, and it is unsurprising that the Federal Constitution does not require the states to stand idly by while parents sacrifice their children's lives even if doing so out of sincere religious belief. Yet, there was no evidence that the children were being exposed to grave and immediate danger.[19] Sarah Prince was also handing out tracts that day, so it is not as if she had abandoned the children to be at the mercy of strangers.[20] The difficulty posed by this case was not that the state was asserting its power to protect children when their lives were in danger, but that the state was asserting its power to protect children when the kinds of dangers commonly associated with child labor did not seem applicable. By upholding the application of the law in these circumstances, the Court impliedly accorded the implicated free exercise rights little if any weight, especially because the rights asserted included in addition the parent's right to raise her child.

Sunday closing laws

Just as free exercise rights did not seem to be accorded much weight in *Prince*, they also did not seem to be accorded much weight in *Braunfeld v. Brown*.[21] At issue was whether the enforcement of Sunday closing laws "interfere[d] with the free exercise of appellants' religion."[22] The appellants were Orthodox Jews who closed their businesses from Friday evening to Saturday evening for religious reasons. Forcing the appellants to close on Sunday as well hurt their ability to make a living. These business owners had to make a difficult choice—either "give up their Sabbath observance, a basic tenet of the Orthodox Jewish faith, or . . . [be] at a serious economic disadvantage if they continue[d] to adhere to their Sabbath."[23] The Court did not downplay that enforcement of the law imposed an economic burden on the appellants, but nonetheless reasoned that the "legislative power . . . may reach people's actions when they are found to be in *violation of important social duties or subversive of good order*, even when the actions are demanded by one's religion."[24]

Here, the Court implied either that the appellants' closing their businesses on Sunday was somehow important to society or that their closing their businesses on Saturday but remaining open on Sunday was somehow subversive of good order. But it was difficult to understand why closing their businesses on Sunday would be important to society, given that 21 of the 34 states with Sunday closing laws had exemptions for those whose Sabbaths required rest on another day. By the same token, it was difficult to understand why closing on Saturday but being open on Sunday would be subversive of good order if many states permitted such a practice.

When upholding the constitutionality of the regulation, the Court reasoned that the challenged law did not target any particular religions and did "not make unlawful any religious practices of appellants"[25] but, instead, "simply regulate[d] a secular activity,"[26] thereby making appellants' religious practice more expensive. However, characterizing the law as simply regulating a secular activity in a way making it somewhat more expensive undercut the significance of the burden. Many regulations increase the cost of doing business to some extent, and such a characterization does not distinguish between a regulation having a minimal effect on the bottom line and one that forces a business to close its doors. In the case before the Court, there was testimony that "Sunday closing will . . . render appellant Braunfeld unable to continue in his business, thereby losing his capital investment."[27]

The *Braunfeld* Court noted that it was not as if the law burdened all Orthodox Jews, "but only those who believe it necessary to work on Sunday."[28] A separate issue involved the potential burdens that Orthodox Jews might bear if their would-be employers required Saturday work, but that burden could not be (directly) attributed to the Sunday closing laws. Ironically, the Court did take into consideration the difficulties that workers face when asked to work on their Sabbath, but did so in a way that undermined rather than supported the plaintiffs' case. Were the exemption required, "exempted employers would probably have to hire employees who themselves qualified for the exemption because of their own religious beliefs, a practice which a State might feel to be opposed to its general policy prohibiting religious discrimination in hiring."[29] Thus, the Court implied, because permitting the plaintiffs to remain open on Sunday might result in their refusing to hire workers who could not work on Sunday, the State could force the plaintiffs to choose between staying in business or observing their own Sabbaths by closing on Saturday. At the very least, this differentiation had the appearance of favoring the observance of one Sabbath over another, which raises other constitutional concerns.

There was yet another respect in which the *Braunfeld* Court minimized the burden imposed by the law. While noting that the appellants might have to make some financial sacrifice either by closing on Sunday or by finding other work that did not require them to work on Saturday, the Court nonetheless believed that this forced choice "is wholly different than when the legislation attempts to make a religious practice itself unlawful."[30] The latter would be a direct burden on religious practice and would receive far closer scrutiny than would a statue merely imposing an indirect economic burden on such a practice. Where a direct burden was imposed and religious practices "conflicted with the public interest,"[31] the Court explained that "accommodation between the religious action and an exercise of state authority is a particularly delicate task."[32] But because in *Braunfeld* "the statute at bar d[id] not make unlawful any religious practices of appellants . . . [but merely] operate[d] so as to make the practice of their religious beliefs more expensive,"[33] the Court implied that the case before it was not particularly difficult to decide.

After undercutting the degree to which the requirement was burdensome and implying that the number of people burdened was not very great, the *Braunfeld* Court noted its reluctance to invalidate a law that "imposes only an indirect burden on the exercise of religion."[34] This was not to say that all indirect burdens on religious practice are immune from constitutional invalidation:

> If the purpose or effect of a law is to impede the observance of one or all religions or is to discriminate invidiously between religions, that law is constitutionally invalid even though the burden may be characterized as being only indirect.[35]

Yet, the announced exception describing when the Court would strike down indirect burdens seemed implicated in this case if only because an effect of the Sunday closing laws was to impede the appellants in observing their religion. Being closed on Saturday and Sunday was financially burdensome, which imposed an impediment on the ability of the plaintiffs to act in accord with their religious beliefs.

The *Braunfeld* Court examined whether the state could have achieved its goals in a way that would not have imposed such a burden on religious observance. For example, the state could have mandated that individuals have a day of rest without mandating which day that would be or the state could have exempted from Sunday closing laws all those businesses whose owners observed a Sabbath day other than Sunday. The Court conceded that a policy including such a religious exemption might be wiser, but the Court's "concern [wa]s not with the wisdom of legislation but with its constitutional limitation."[36]

The Court's distinguishing between what might be wise versus what might be constitutionally required is unsurprising as a general matter. In *Williamson v. Lee Optical of Oklahoma, Incorporated*,[37] the Court noted that an Oklahoma law requiring a prescription from an ophthalmologist or optometrist before an optician could fit or duplicate lenses might "exact a needless, wasteful requirement,"[38] but that it was the job of "the legislature, not the courts, to balance the advantages and disadvantages of the new requirement."[39] As the Court explained in *Day-Brite Lighting, Incorporated v. Missouri* a few years before *Williamson*, the Court does "not sit as a super-legislature to weigh the wisdom of legislation nor to decide whether the policy which it expresses offends the public welfare."[40]

Yet, the difficulty posed by the *Braunfeld* Court's emulating the *Williamson* approach by distinguishing between wisdom and constitutionality was that free exercise rights were hanging in the balance. The normal deference to legislative wisdom was not appropriate where burdens on free exercise were at stake, and the state should of course adopt an alternate policy not burdening religious exercise unless there were important reasons not to do so.

If the states who had afforded a religious exemption to their Sunday closing laws had thereby encountered significant problems, that might have been a reason not to require that such an exemption be permitted. However, as Justice Brennan pointed out in his concurring and dissenting opinion, many states with Sunday closing laws included an exemption for those who observed a Sabbath on a different day, and no evidence was presented that "those States are significantly noisier, or that their police are significantly more burdened, than Pennsylvania's."[41]

It is not as if the state had no legitimate interests in requiring Sunday closings; for example, the state arguably had a legitimate interest in

> provid[ing] a weekly respite from all labor and, at the same time, to set one day of the week apart from the others as a day of rest, repose, recreation and tranquility—a day when the hectic tempo of everyday existence ceases and a more pleasant atmosphere is created, a day which all members of the family and community have the opportunity to spend and enjoy together, a day on which people may visit friends and relatives who are not available during working days, a day when the weekly laborer may best regenerate himself.[42]

Further, while the state could require businesses to close one day a week without specifying that it be Sunday, this would impose an administrative burden because "there would be two or more days to police rather than one and it would be more difficult to observe whether violations were occurring."[43] In addition, if everyone had to close on Sunday except for those closing on another day for religious reasons, the Court feared that such an arrangement "might well provide these people with an economic advantage over their competitors."[44]

Yet, the Court should not have found these concerns persuasive. For example, there was testimony that being open on Sunday would merely permit the owners to recoup some of the sales that they were unable to make on their Sabbath. While it might have been somewhat inconvenient to have extra days where required closings had to be policed, the other states affording an exemption to those observing a Sabbath on a day other than Sunday had not found this added inconvenience overly burdensome. Further, there was no reason for the Court to hypothesize the kinds of competitive effects that Sunday closing laws with exemptions would have, because various states had enacted such laws. If the Court's suspicions about economic advantage were to have had some basis in fact, then one would have expected that those states providing such exemptions would have had many problems. No evidence of any difficulties was offered.

The Court offered some arguably legitimate interests supporting Sunday closing laws. But if these state interests were very important rather than merely legitimate, then one would not have expected the majority of states with Sunday closing laws to have provided an exemption for those who observed the Sabbath on a different day. Justice Brennan asked rhetorically: "What overbalancing need is so weighty in the constitutional scale that it justifies this substantial, though indirect, limitation of appellants' freedom?"[45] His answer—"the mere convenience of having everyone rest on the same day"[46]—suggests that the state and the Court overstated the importance of the interest served.

In *Gallagher v. Crown Kosher Super Market of Massachusetts, Incorporated*,[47] a supermarket almost exclusively selling kosher foods challenged the constitutionality of the Massachusetts Sunday closing laws on free exercise grounds, among others. While the market could have opened on Saturday evenings for a few hours after sundown or on Sunday mornings for a few hours, doing so would not have been economical, which meant that the Massachusetts law precluded the market from being open more than four and one-half days per week.

Many of the hypothesized worries discussed in *Braunfeld* seemed inapplicable. For example, permitting this store to remain open would not greatly increase commercial traffic and activity, because it would be the *only* store in the area open on Sunday. Further, given that it almost exclusively sold kosher goods, permitting the market to be open on Sunday would not seem to afford the store much, if any, advantage over its non-kosher competitors. Not only would the latter stores be open on Saturday while this store would be closed, but the stores selling non-kosher foods would likely be less expensive anyway, so non-kosher shoppers planning ahead might well choose to buy less expensive non-kosher goods on Saturday rather than kosher goods on Sunday.

The Court gave short shrift to Crown's free exercise claim, dispensing with it in two paragraphs. Crown claimed that it "will be open only four and one-half days a week, thereby suffering extreme economic disadvantage."[48] But "[t]hese allegations [were] similar, although not as grave, as those made by appellants in *Braunfeld v. Brown*."[49] The Court reasoned that if the indirect burden on religion at issue in *Braunfeld* was permissible even though it might have resulted in Braunfeld's losing his business, then Crown's claims about economic disadvantage (not leading to financial ruin) could hardly win the day.

The *Gallagher* analysis was at best incomplete, because it focused exclusively on the costs associated with engaging in a religious practice and failed to consider the state interests promoted by the legislation. While the Court may have been correct that the burden borne by Crown was less onerous than that borne by Braunfeld, the Court simply did not address whether the state interests implicated in *Braunfeld* were also implicated in *Gallagher*. By failing to do so, the Court implicitly suggested that if a state law is constitutional even though it burdens free exercise to such an extent that it causes an individual to go out of business, then any law imposing a lesser burden on free exercise of course also passes muster.

Employees who cannot work on their Sabbath

Two years after *Braunfeld*'s tepid enforcement of free exercise guarantees,[50] the Court decided *Sherbert v. Verner*.[51] The case involved a free exercise challenge by Adell Sherbert, who was denied unemployment compensation when she, a Seventh-Day Adventist, could not find work because working on Saturdays violated her religious convictions.[52]

The South Carolina Employment Security Commission rejected that her faith-based refusal to accept employment requiring Saturday work qualified as "good cause," which meant that her refusals of offers requiring Saturday work were considered unjustified. For that reason, her claim for unemployment compensation was denied. She unsuccessfully challenged that denial in the state courts. The South Carolina Supreme Court held that

> appellant's ineligibility infringed no constitutional liberties because such a construction of the statute "places no restriction upon the appellant's freedom of religion nor does it in any way prevent her in the exercise of her right and freedom to observe her religious beliefs in accordance with the dictates of her conscience."[53]

When evaluating the merits of Sherbert's challenge, the South Carolina Supreme Court had reasoned that the purpose behind the unemployment statute was to provide compensation for those laid off at work and not for those who "chose" not to work, even if those refusing had compelling reasons such as the need to be home at certain times to care for children or to avoid working on the Sabbath. The state's refusal to award benefits to individuals who chose not to work, even for important reasons, was reasonable in light of the state's goal of providing temporary compensation to those who had been laid off involuntarily. Further, there was no claim that the state intended to punish those of a particular religion or those who wished to be home with children during certain hours of the day, which made the burden incidental and indirect rather than targeted.

When reviewing the South Carolina Supreme Court decision, the United States Supreme Court began its analysis by asking whether Sherbert's "disqualification as a beneficiary . . . [infringed upon] her constitutional rights of free exercise."[54] The Court explained that it did, because "the pressure upon her to forego that [religious] practice is unmistakable."[55] Basically, she was put in the position of having "to choose between following the precepts of her religion and forfeiting benefits, on the one hand, and abandoning one of the precepts of her religion in order to accept work, on the other hand."[56] The Court analogized the choice she faced to one involving a government-imposed penalty: "Governmental imposition of such a choice puts the same kind of burden upon the free exercise of religion as would a fine imposed against appellant for her Saturday worship."[57]

The surprising aspect of the Court's analysis was not in its characterizing Sherbert's situation as involving a forced choice, but rather its analysis of the import of her having been forced to choose between her religion and unemployment benefits. Braunfeld had also been afforded a forced choice—he had to choose between observing the Sabbath on the one hand and keeping his business on the other—but nonetheless was not afforded an exemption. The *Braunfeld* Court had noted that the burden on Braunfeld had been indirect—the law had not made observing the Sabbath on a day other than Sunday illegal—and then had reasoned that because the burden was indirect, the Court had to defer to the State.

The *Sherbert* Court understood that its holding was difficult to reconcile with *Braunfeld* but offered the following justification:

> [T]he state interest asserted in the present case is wholly dissimilar to the interests which were found to justify the less direct burden upon religious practices in *Braunfeld v. Brown*. The Court recognized that the Sunday closing law which that decision sustained undoubtedly served "to make the practice of (the Orthodox Jewish merchants') religious beliefs more expensive." But the statute was nevertheless saved by a countervailing factor which finds no equivalent in the instant case—a strong state interest in providing one uniform day of rest for all workers. That secular objective could be achieved, the Court found, only by declaring Sunday to be that day of rest. Requiring exemptions for Sabbatarians, while theoretically possible, appeared to present an administrative problem of such magnitude, or to afford the exempted class so great a competitive advantage, that such a requirement would have rendered the entire statutory scheme unworkable. In the present case no such justifications underlie the determination of the state court that appellant's religion makes her ineligible to receive benefits.[58]

Thus, the *Sherbert* Court suggested that the law at issue in *Braunfeld* was narrowly drawn to promote compelling state interests, whereas the denial of unemployment benefits in *Sherbert* was not. Yet, such a characterization of the state interests implicated in *Braunfeld* is not plausible.⁵⁹ For example, when the *Braunfeld* Court noted that some states required a day of rest without requiring that everyone rest on Sunday, the Court offered an example of such a statute without describing the experiences of those states. No evidence was presented suggesting that those states incurred great difficulty when affording such flexibility, which undercuts the claim that the state's interest in having Braunfeld closed on Sunday was compelling.⁶⁰ But that makes *Sherbert* and *Braunfeld* difficult to reconcile by appealing to the importance of the implicated state interest, as some of the justices pointed out.⁶¹

Sherbert has been described as rather protective of free exercise rights.⁶² Even so, *Sherbert* qualified the protection it was affording. For example, the Court was careful to note that "the recognition of the appellant's right to unemployment benefits under the state statute [does not] serve to abridge any other person's religious liberties."⁶³ *Sherbert* does not stand for the proposition that free exercise rights of one individual or group must be respected even if doing so would adversely impact others' free exercise interests.

Such a point would seem uncontroversial and not particularly telling if one envisions a world in which differing religious beliefs and practices are unlikely to pose conflicts. However, in a country where many different faiths are represented and where there is a wide range of beliefs and practices, such conflicts are likely to result and the *Sherbert* analysis employing allegedly robust free exercise guarantees will be unlikely to offer much guidance about how such conflicts should be handled.

Decisions about schooling

*Wisconsin v. Yoder*⁶⁴ also seems to represent robust protection of free exercise rights, because the parents were exempted from having to send their children not yet aged 16 to high school. The *Yoder* Court made clear that the exemption was granted because "the claims must be rooted in religious belief,"⁶⁵ and suggested that beliefs that were "philosophical and personal rather than religious [do] . . . not rise to the demands of the Religion Clauses."⁶⁶

It was unclear from the opinion whether the *Yoder* Court was thereby expressing disapproval of *United States v. Seeger*, where the Court accepted that the beliefs at issue were religious in the relevant sense when Seeger cited the writings of "such personages as Plato, Aristotle and Spinoza for support of his ethical belief in intellectual and moral integrity without belief in God, except in the remotest sense."⁶⁷ Plato, Aristotle, and Spinoza were all philosophers, so *Seeger* suggests that an individual's basing her opinions on philosophical writings helps make those sincere convictions religious in the relevant sense. Perhaps *Yoder* was rejecting that philosophical beliefs count as religious for constitutional purposes, although *Seeger* and *Yoder* are compatible if *Yoder* was suggesting that merely personal beliefs may well not count as religious.

Once establishing that the law burdened religious exercise, the *Yoder* Court sought to determine whether the state had sufficiently important interests to justify the imposition of that burden. For example, Wisconsin had argued that "some degree of education is necessary to prepare citizens to participate effectively and intelligently in our open political system if we are to preserve freedom and independence"⁶⁸ and that "education prepares individuals to be self-reliant and self-sufficient participants in society."⁶⁹ While these were and are compelling interests, a separate issue was whether the means chosen were sufficiently closely tailored to promote those ends.

Children who remained in the Amish community would likely not benefit much from the extra couple of years of schooling. Even those who would leave the Amish community might not gain that much from the additional year or two of education, and those individuals might well flourish in any event "with their practical agricultural training and habits of industry and self-reliance."[70] The Court's focus on the additional benefit that high school students might receive from the extra year or two meant the Court closely examined whether the attendance requirement was sufficiently narrowly tailored to promote the state's compelling interests to justify the burden being placed on free exercise. The *Yoder* Court acknowledged that

> activities of individuals, even when religiously based, are often subject to regulation by the States in the exercise of their undoubted power to promote the health, safety, and general welfare, or the Federal Government in the exercise of its delegated powers,

citing both *Braunfeld* and *Gillette*,[71] but rejected that "religiously grounded conduct is always outside the protection of the Free Exercise Clause."[72] Noting that "there are areas of conduct protected by the Free Exercise Clause of the First Amendment and thus beyond the power of the State to control, even under regulations of general applicability," citing *Sherbert*,[73] the Court explained that "[w]here fundamental claims of religious freedom are at stake"[74] the Court must "searchingly examine the interests that the State seeks to promote . . . and the impediment to those objectives that would flow from recognizing the claimed . . . exemption."[75]

The Court was unpersuaded that the state had a compelling interest in assuring that Amish children attend high school, in part because expert testimony suggested that Amish children became "productive members of the Amish community."[76] In addition, other evidence helped establish that the Amish had "an excellent record as law-abiding and generally self-sufficient members of society."[77] Indeed, the Court noted that the Amish "reject public welfare in any of its usual modern forms"[78] and, further, that "Congress itself recognized their self-sufficiency by authorizing exemption of such groups as the Amish from the obligation to pay social security taxes."[79]

Some of the *Yoder* opinion suggests that the Amish challenge would have been successful even if the evidence regarding the outcomes for their children had been more equivocal, if only because the state had to pass such a daunting test to justify its free exercise infringement. "[O]nly those interests of the highest order and those not otherwise served can overbalance legitimate claims to the free exercise of religion."[80] Yet, a different part of the opinion undercuts the strength of the constitutional protections for free exercise. The Court explained that

> when the interests of parenthood are combined with a free exercise claim of the nature revealed by this record, more than merely a "reasonable relation to some purpose within the competency of the State" is required to sustain the validity of the State's requirement under the First Amendment.[81]

This passage provides the basis for interpreting *Yoder* in two very different ways. On one interpretation, the Court simply provided even more support for its holding, because it noted that parents have a fundamental interest in directing the education of their children as found in *Meyer v. Nebraska*[82] and *Pierce v. Society of Sisters*.[83] Not only must an exemption be granted because of free exercise guarantees,[84] but the parental rights recognized in *Meyer* and *Pierce* provide an independent and adequate ground to support the Amish parent's right to keep his child home from a public school that will undermine important values.[85]

A different interpretation is that free exercise guarantees were respected only because parenting rights were also implicated.[86] According to that interpretation, free exercise guarantees would not alone have sufficed to justify requiring an exemption for the Amish.[87]

The *Yoder* Court seemed to strike a blow for tolerance and diversity when suggesting that "[a] way of life that is odd or even erratic but interferes with no rights or interests of others is not to be condemned because it is different."[88] This passage might also be read in a different way, because it might be taken to mean that the free exercise rights of the Amish were respected only because doing so would not have interfered in any way with others' rights or interests.

Refusing to make war weapons

Yoder raises a number of questions including the degree to which beliefs must be shared by others before they will trigger free exercise guarantees. The Court in *Thomas v. Review Board of Indiana Employment Security Division*[89] made clear that an individual might have sincere religious compunctions about making war materials even if others of his faith did not share those compunctions.

Once it was established that Thomas's refusal to work implicated free exercise guarantees, the state had to establish that its interests were sufficiently compelling and the means chosen sufficiently closely tailored to justify its infringement of Thomas's religious liberty. The Court rejected the state's suggestion that "the number of people who find themselves in the predicament of choosing between benefits and religious beliefs is large enough to create 'widespread unemployment,' or even to seriously affect unemployment."[90] Basically, the Court believed *Sherbert* was controlling and struck down Indiana's refusal to award the benefits. Ironically, in this case the fact that relatively few individuals would be affected spoke in favor of protecting free exercise, whereas in *Braunfeld* the Court implied that because relatively few would be affected the Sunday closing law should be upheld.

Indiana was burdening the free exercise of religion by attaching significant costs to Thomas's acting in light of his beliefs, just as South Carolina had burdened the free exercise of Sherbert's religious beliefs. The *Thomas* Court explained:

> Where the state conditions receipt of an important benefit upon conduct proscribed by a religious faith, or where it denies such a benefit because of conduct mandated by religious belief, thereby putting substantial pressure on an adherent to modify his behavior and to violate his beliefs, a burden upon religion exists. While the compulsion may be indirect, the infringement upon free exercise is nonetheless substantial. Thus, free exercise guarantees may be implicated where benefits, rather than rights, are at issue. Even indirect pressure to forego religious practice is enough to trigger constitutional protections of religion.[91]

Using language that might well have led to a different result in *Robison* and *Braunfeld*, the *Thomas* Court reasoned that "a burden upon religion exists"[92] if "the state conditions receipt of an important benefit upon conduct proscribed by a religious faith"[93] or if the state "denies such a benefit because of conduct mandated by religious belief."[94] The test is not whether the individual changes his conduct or even whether he is likely to do so; instead, the question is whether the state puts "substantial pressure on an adherent to modify his behavior and to violate his beliefs."[95] But if denying unemployment compensation imposed pressure on religious beliefs, then denying educational benefits might also be thought to impose pressure on those asserting conscientious objections. So, too preventing stores from being open on Sunday would impose pressure on those wishing to observe their Sabbaths on a different day of the week.

Conclusion

The Court's free exercise jurisprudence from *Cantwell* through *Thomas* is subject to very different interpretations. The jurisprudence might seem ambiguous or self-contradictory, especially because the alleged differences between *Braunfeld* and *Sherbert* were not persuasive. So, too, *Prince* and *Yoder* might seem difficult to reconcile because both involved a combination of parental rights and free exercise.

A different interpretation would be that *Braunfeld*, *Gallagher*, and *Prince* were simply outliers and that *Sherbert*, *Yoder*, and *Thomas* establish that free exercise guarantees are rather robust. Such an interpretation might suggest that the Court was working out its position in *Prince*, *Braunfeld*, and *Gallagher*, and ultimately settled on a more protective approach in *Sherbert*, *Thomas*, and *Yoder*. The next chapter discusses several cases in which the Court's free exercise jurisprudence becomes increasingly difficult to understand and characterize.

Notes

1 Mark E. Chopko, "Continuing the Lord's Work and Healing His People: A Reply to Professors Lupu and Tuttle," 2004 *Brigham Young University Law Review* 2004:1897–920 (2004), p. 1914 (discussing "the seminal case *Cantwell v. Connecticut*"); William Drabble, "Righteous Torts: *Pleasant Glade Assembly of God v. Schubert* and the Free Exercise Defense in Texas," *Baylor Law Review* 62:267–89 (2010), p. 269 (discussing "the seminal case of *Cantwell v. Connecticut*"); William P. Marshall, "In Defense of the Search for Truth as a First Amendment Justification," *Georgia Law Review* 30:1–39 (1995), p. 11 ("*Cantwell v. Connecticut* . . . is . . . a seminal free exercise case.").
2 Bruce B. Jackson, "Secularization by Incorporation: Religious Organizations and Corporate Identity," *First Amendment Law Review* 11:90–147 (2012), p. 110 ("In 1940, a significant change occurred when the Supreme Court applied the Free Exercise Clause to a state for the first time. It did this in a creative, unusual, and controversial way: by incorporating the First Amendment into the Fourteenth Amendment, and then asserting the state had abridged the claimant's Fourteenth Amendment right to 'liberty' without due process.").
3 See *United States Constitution*, amendment I.
4 See, for example, *People ex rel. Ring v. Board of Education of District 24*, 92 N.E. 251, 252 (Illinois 1910) ("The first amendment to the federal Constitution prohibits Congress from making any law respecting an establishment of religion or prohibiting the free exercise thereof. That instrument contains no restriction in this respect upon the Legislatures of the states, which are thus left free to enact such laws in respect to religion as they may deem proper, restrained only by the limitations of the respective state Constitutions."); *Gerhardt v. Heid*, 267 N.W. 127, 129 (North Dakota 1936) ("The First Amendment to the Federal Constitution provides: 'Congress shall make no law respecting an establishment of religion, or prohibiting the free exercise thereof; or abridging the freedom of speech, or of the press; or the right of the people peaceably to assemble, and to petition the Government for a redress of grievances.' This amendment merely restricts the power of Congress, and is not restrictive of the states.")
5 *Cantwell v. Connecticut*, 310 U.S. 296, 303 (1940) ("The First Amendment declares that Congress shall make no law respecting an establishment of religion or prohibiting the free exercise thereof. The Fourteenth Amendment has rendered the legislatures of the states as incompetent as Congress to enact such laws.").
6 *Id*. at 303–04.
7 *Id*. at 311.

8 *Id.* at 309.
9 *Id.* at 310.
10 *Id.* at 304.
11 *Id.* at 309 ("One may, however, be guilty of the offense if he commit acts or make statements *likely* to provoke violence and disturbance of good order.") (emphasis added).
12 *Prince v. Massachusetts*, 321 U.S. 158 (1944).
13 *Id.* at 164.
14 *Id.* at 165 (citing *West Virginia Board of Education v. Barnette*, 319 U.S. 624 (1943)).
15 *Id.* at 166.
16 *Id.*
17 *Id.* at 168–69.
18 *Id.* at 167.
19 *Id.* at 175 (Murphy, J., dissenting) ("[T]here is not the slightest indication in this record, or in sources subject to judicial notice, that children engaged in distributing literature pursuant to their religious beliefs have been or are likely to be subject to any of the harmful 'diverse influences of the street.'").
20 See *id.* at 175 (Murphy, J., dissenting) ("Jehovah's Witness children invariably make their distributions in groups subject at all times to adult or parental control, as was done in this case.").
21 *Braunfeld v. Brown*, 366 U.S. 599 (1961).
22 *Id.* at 601.
23 *Id.* at 602.
24 *Id.* at 603–04 (emphasis added).
25 *Id.* at 605.
26 *Id.*
27 *Id.* at 601.
28 *Id.* at 605.
29 *Id.* at 609.
30 *Id.* at 606.
31 *Id.* at 605.
32 *Id.* (citing *Prince*, 321 U.S. at 165). That said, however, laws are sometimes upheld even when imposing a direct burden on religion. See *id.* (discussing two instances in which the Court had upheld laws criminalizing religious practice—*Reynolds v. United States*, 98 U.S. 145 (1878) (upholding polygamy ban) and *Prince*, 321 U.S. 158 (upholding child labor law which in effect precluded children from proselytizing)).
33 *Id.*
34 *Id.* at 606.
35 *Id.* at 607.
36 *Id.* at 608.
37 *Williamson v. Lee Optical of Oklahoma, Incorporated*, 348 U.S. 483 (1955).
38 *Id.* at 487.
39 *Id.*
40 *Day-Brite Lighting, Incorporated v. Missouri*, 342 U.S. 421, 423 (1952); cf. Comment, "Zoning Ordinances Affecting Churches: A Proposal for Expanded Free Exercise Protection," *University of Pennsylvania Law Review* 132:1131–62 (1984), p. 1144 ("Measured against [a] lenient standard, the Sunday closing law was upheld.").
41 *Braunfeld*, 366 U.S. at 614–15.
42 *Id.* at 607
43 *Id.* at 608.
44 *Id.*
45 *Id.* at 614.
46 *Id.*
47 *Gallagher v. Crown Kosher Super Market of Massachusetts, Incorporated*, 366 U.S. 617 (1961).
48 *Id.* at 630.
49 *Id.* at 631 (citing *Braunfeld v. Brown*, 366 U.S. 599 (1961)).
50 Donald Falk, "*Lyng v. Northwest Indian Cemetery Protective Association*: Bulldozing First Amendment Protection of Indian Sacred Lands," *Ecology Law Quarterly* 16:515–70 (1989), p. 564 (describing *Braunfeld*'s free exercise protection as "weak").

70 *Early modern free exercise*

51 *Sherbert v. Verner*, 374 U.S. 398 (1963).
52 *Id.* at 399 ("Appellant, a member of the Seventh-day Adventist Church was discharged by her South Carolina employer because she would not work on Saturday, the Sabbath Day of her faith."); *id.* at 399–400 ("[S]he was unable to obtain other employment because from conscientious scruples she would not take Saturday work.").
53 *Id.* at 401 (citing *Union Naval Stores Company v. United States*, 240 U.S. 286, 303–04 (1916) and *Sherbert v. Verner*, 125 S.E.2d 737, 746 (South Carolina 1962)).
54 *Id.* at 403.
55 *Id.* at 404.
56 *Id.*
57 *Id.*
58 *Id.* at 408–09 (citing *Braunfeld*, 366 U.S. at 605).
59 See Steven M. Rosato, "Saving Oklahoma's 'Save Our State' Amendment: Sharia Law in the West and Suggestions to Protect Similar State Legislation from Constitutional Attack," *Seton Hall Law Review* 44:659–93 (2014), p. 672 ("*Sherbert v. Verner* . . . seems in direct conflict with the holding in *Braunfeld*.").
60 See *Braunfeld*, 366 U.S. at 613–14 (Brennan, J., concurring and dissenting) ("What, then, is the compelling state interest which impels the Commonwealth of Pennsylvania to impede appellants' freedom of worship? What overbalancing need is so weighty in the constitutional scale that it justifies this substantial, though indirect, limitation of appellants' freedom? . . . It is the mere convenience of having everyone rest on the same day. It is to defend this interest that the Court holds that a State need not follow the alternative route of granting an exemption for those who in good faith observe a day of rest other than Sunday."); *McGowan v. Maryland*, 366 U.S. 420, 561 (1961) (Douglas, J., dissenting) ("If the 'free exercise' of religion were subject to reasonable regulations, as it is under some constitutions, or if all laws 'respecting the establishment of religion' were not proscribed, I could understand how rational men, representing a predominantly Christian civilization, might think these Sunday laws did not unreasonably interfere with anyone's free exercise of religion and took no step toward a burdensome establishment of any religion. But that is not the premise from which we start."); Sidney A. Rosenzweig, "Restoring Religious Freedom to the Workplace: Title VII, RFRA and Religious Accommodation," *University of Pennsylvania Law Review* 144:2513–35 (1996), p. 2530 (describing the *Braunfeld* Court as "applying rational basis review").
61 See *Sherbert v. Verner*, 374 U.S. 417 (1963) (Stewart, J., concurring in the result) ("I cannot agree that today's decision can stand consistently with *Braunfeld v. Brown*."); *id.* at 421 (Harlan, J., dissenting) ("[D]espite the Court's protestations to the contrary, the decision necessarily overrules *Braunfeld v. Brown*, 366 U.S. 599, which held that it did not offend the 'Free Exercise' Clause of the Constitution for a State to forbid a Sabbatarian to do business on Sunday."). See also Nicholas Nugent, "Toward a RFRA That Works," *Vanderbilt Law Review* 61:1027–66 (2008), p. 1034 ("[T]he burden on free exercise in *Sherbert* seemed similar to that in *Braunfeld* . . ."); Douglas W. Kmiec, The Original Understanding of the Free Exercise Clause and Religious Diversity, *University of Missouri Kansas City Law Review* 59:591–609 (1991), p. 607 ("[N]either *Sherbert* nor *Braunfeld* merit exemption because the government actions in their cases were simply not prohibitory.").
62 Charles Cowan, "Creationism's Public and Private Fronts: The Protection and Restriction of Religious Freedom," *Mississippi Law Journal* 82:223–56 (2013), p. 244 ("The Supreme Court decision in *Sherbet v. Verner* best demonstrates a strong Free Exercise Clause—one that is protective of religious practice in the United States.").
63 *Sherbert*, 374 U.S. at 409.
64 *Wisconsin v. Yoder*, 406 U.S. 205 (1972).
65 *Id.* at 215.
66 *Id.* at 216.
67 *United States v. Seeger*, 380 U.S. 163, 166 (1965) (internal quotation marks omitted).
68 *Yoder*, 406 U.S. at 221.
69 *Id.*
70 *Id.* at 224.
71 *Id.* at 220 (citing *Gillette v. United States*, 401 U.S. 437 (1971) and *Braunfeld v. Brown*, 366 U.S. 599 (1961)).

72 *Id.* at 219–20.
73 *Id.* at 219–20 (citing *Sherbert v. Verner*, 374 U.S. 398 (1963)).
74 *Id.* at 221.
75 *Id.* (citing *Sherbert v. Verner*, 374 U.S. 398 (1963)).
76 *Id.* at 212.
77 *Id.* at 212–13.
78 *Id.* at 222.
79 *Id.*
80 *Id.* at 215.
81 *Id.* at 233.
82 *Meyer v. Nebraska*, 262 U.S. 390, 400 (1923).
83 *Pierce v. Society of Sisters*, 268 U.S. 510, 534–35 (1925).
84 Cf. John W. Whitehead, "The Conservative Supreme Court and the Demise of the Free Exercise of Religion," *Temple Political & Civil Rights Law Review* 7:1–139 (1997), pp. 2–3 ("*Yoder* has been interpreted as decisively establishing the supremacy of free exercise.").
85 Cf. Jeffrey Shulman, "The Parent As (Mere) Educational Trustee: Whose Education Is It, Anyway?" *Nebraska Law Review* 89:290–357 (2010), p. 338 (noting that "*Meyer* and *Pierce* have been read to state broad claims about the fundamental nature of parental rights").
86 Cf. *Employment Division v. Smith*, 494 U.S. 872, 881 (1990) ("The only decisions in which we have held that the First Amendment bars application of a neutral, generally applicable law to religiously motivated action have involved not the Free Exercise Clause alone, but the Free Exercise Clause in conjunction with other constitutional protections, such as freedom of speech and of the press.").
87 Cf. James R. Mason, III, "*Smith*'s Free-Exercise 'Hybrids' Rooted in Non-Free-Exercise Soil," *Regent University Law Review* 6:201–59 (1995), p. 243 ("In other words, the outcome for the parents in *Yoder* was correct, but the free-exercise exemption analysis was not.").
88 *Yoder*, 406 U.S. at 224.
89 *Thomas v. Review Board of the Indiana Employment Security Division*, 450 U.S. 707 (1981).
90 *Id.* at 719.
91 *Id.* at 717–18.
92 *Id.* at 718.
93 *Id.* at 717.
94 *Id.* at 717–18.
95 *Id.* at 718.

5 Free exercise becomes (more) chaotic

After issuing *Prince*, *Braunfeld*, and *Gallagher*, the Court seemed to adopt a fairly consistent position in the *Sherbert–Thomas* line of cases. But even if that is so, some explanation of the apparent disconnect between the earlier cases and those following them must be offered. One possibility is that the Court overruled the earlier cases *sub silentio* and embraced robust free exercise guarantees. According to this interpretation, *Braunfeld* and *Gallagher* would have been decided differently had the Court heard them after having issued *Sherbert*.

Several cases decided after *Thomas* laid to rest any hope that the Court had adopted a consistent jurisprudence, much less one in which free exercise guarantees were treated as offering robust protection. Rather, the Court issued several decisions, some supporting and others undermining any contention that the Constitution's free exercise guarantees provide substantial protection. These decisions were inconsistent both with respect to the appropriate test and with respect to how particular tests should be applied. The cases during this period present an incoherent jurisprudence that is as incomprehensible as it is indefensible.

On government rules and religious exemptions

Government rules and regulations affect a variety of areas of life whether involving taxes, labor practices, or the conditions under which particular benefits will be accorded. Religious beliefs and practices may affect whether individuals can in good conscience do what the government requires them to do, and several cases involved the conditions under which government requirements must accommodate religious practices. Regrettably, the Court decisions in this next set of cases made the free exercise jurisprudence utterly unprincipled, thwarting all attempts to offer a plausible and coherent approach to the difficult issues posed by conflicts between religious and civil requirements.

Social Security

One year after *Thomas*, the Court in *United States v. Lee*[1] seemed to renege on its commitment to the existence of robust free exercise guarantees. Edwin Lee, a member of the Old Order Amish, employed several Amish employees to work on his farm and in his carpentry shop. Lee did not pay the employer's share of Social Security taxes and failed to withhold Social Security taxes from his employees' paychecks. He refused to do so as a matter of conscience—the Amish have religious objections to the Social Security system, because they believe that they themselves must provide for the elderly and those in need.[2] The Amish are not only barred from accepting Social Security benefits but they are also barred from making contributions to that system.[3] Basically, requiring Lee to pay into the system would be a *direct* infringement of free exercise, because such contributions were expressly prohibited by his religion.

The Court understood the significance of those beliefs: "Because the payment of the taxes or receipt of benefits violates Amish religious beliefs, compulsory participation in the social security system interferes with their free exercise rights."[4] However, the Court rejected that the mere fact of direct infringement established that an exemption was required. That there is "a conflict between the Amish faith and the obligations imposed by the social security system is only the beginning . . . and not the end of the inquiry."[5]

Like the *Yoder* Court, the *Lee* Court noted that Congress had exempted self-employed Amish from participating in the Social Security system. However, that exemption was "available only to self-employed individuals and does not apply to employers or employees."[6] While not explaining why Congress had imposed that limitation on the exemption, the Court did cite to the statute, which provided in part:

> In order to qualify for the exemption, the applicant must waive his right to all social security benefits and the Secretary of Health and Human Services must find that the particular religious group makes sufficient provision for its dependent members.[7]

It would be unsurprising if Congress had limited the provision to those self-employed because it did not want to be in the position of exempting an employer from paying into the Social Security system for an employee who wished to remain eligible for Social Security payments.[8] While the need to protect employees might explain Congress's unwillingness to afford an employer a religious exemption at the expense of his employees, such an analysis would have been more applicable in a different case. In *Lee*, the challenge to the law was that "imposition of the social security taxes violated . . . [Lee's] First Amendment free exercise rights and *those of his Amish employees*."[9] Here, there was no divergence of interests between employee and employer—all of the parties had religious objections to participating in the Social Security system.

The Court offered a possible reason that Congress chose to exclude only the self-employed. That way, Congress would have limited the exception to "a narrow category which was readily identifiable."[10] Yet the Court did not cite any evidence establishing that a broader accommodation could not be granted,[11] and it was not clear what compelling interest prevented extending that exemption to employers and employees objecting to Social Security because of their religious beliefs.[12] Further, while the state might prefer to have a narrow category of readily identifiable individuals if only because that would make the policy easier to administer, administrative convenience is not the kind of compelling interest that normally justifies burdening free exercise.

The question before the Court was whether the Constitution required that Lee be granted an exemption. The Court explained that "[n]ot all burdens on religion are unconstitutional"[13] and that the "state may justify a limitation on religious liberty by showing that it is essential to accomplish an overriding governmental interest."[14]

The Social Security system is predicated upon employer and employee contributions, and "mandatory participation is indispensable" to its "fiscal vitality."[15] A system based on voluntary contribution simply would not work.[16] However, Lee was not proposing a purely voluntary system but, instead, was seeking an exemption, and the question at hand was whether a religious accommodation would too severely undermine the implicated state interests. The Court explained that "it would be difficult to accommodate the comprehensive social security system with myriad exceptions flowing from a wide variety of religious beliefs."[17] In addition, the Court worried that there was "no principled way . . . to distinguish between general taxes and those imposed under the Social Security Act,"[18] which might mean that if

> a religious adherent believes war is a sin, and if a certain percentage of the federal budget can be identified as devoted to war-related activities, such individuals would have a similarly valid claim to be exempt from paying that percentage of the income tax.[19]

Yet, it was not at all clear that granting Lee an exemption would have opened up the floodgates. Congress recognized that some Amish (the self-employed) should be exempted from participating in the Social Security system, presumably because where a self-employed person requests an exemption there is no worry that the employer and employee might disagree about whether to participate in the system. But if the telling consideration is that the employer and employee are of one mind with respect to non-participation rather than that the employer and the employee share the same body, then other exemptions would also be appropriate to recognize.

The Court rejected that the most important consideration was whether the employer and employee were of one mind, instead reasoning that Congress had already made a religious accommodation "to the extent compatible with a comprehensive national program."[20] Because the self-employed "are distinguishable from the generality of wage earners employed by others,"[21] expanding the exemption would allegedly be too destructive to the federal system.[22]

In his concurrence, Justice John Paul Stevens explained that the refusal to award the exemption in this case could not simply be explained as an attempt to save money. "As a matter of fiscal policy, an enlarged exemption probably would benefit the social security system because the nonpayment of these taxes by the Amish would be more than offset by the elimination of their right to collect benefits."[23] This exemption request had to be rejected because of the other requests that would be made. The Court explained that it "rejects the particular claim of this appellee, not because it presents any special problems, but rather because of the risk that a myriad of other claims would be too difficult to process."[24]

What was Lee to do? He could violate his conscientious beliefs and pay the tax. Or, he could abide by his religious beliefs and then pay the penalty for his failure to pay into the Social Security system. Or, he might reduce the size of his business. Were he to fire all of his employees and simply be self-employed, then he would be able to opt out of paying into Social Security.

Requiring him to drastically reduce the size of his business as a price of staying true to his religious beliefs would be a rather harsh penalty. But, the Court might have pointed out, the Sunday closing law was constitutional even if its enforcement would cost Braunfeld his business, and forcing Lee to reduce the size of his business was less severe than putting him out of business entirely. If drastically reducing the size of Lee's business was not an option and he would have to close his business to avoid breaking the law, *Braunfeld* established that free exercise guarantees do not always require the law to exempt businesses from generally applicable laws, even if those businesses might otherwise be forced to close.

While the Court did not focus on its having upheld the constitutionality of a statute possibly forcing Braunfeld out of business (and thus why the burden on Lee was not too onerous), the Court did cite *Braunfeld* with approval,[25] which itself had certain implications. For example, after *Lee*, it was clear that *Braunfeld* had not been impliedly overruled and also clear that free exercise guarantees will not always be treated as rather robust. But this meant that the interpretation of the post-*Braunfeld* cases must take account of the relative strength of the free exercise guarantees as reflected in *Braunfeld* and *Gallagher*. After *Lee*, it could not plausibly be argued that the view represented in *Braunfeld* and *Gallagher* had subsequently been superseded.

Lee undercut the existing jurisprudence in yet another way. *Braunfeld* suggested that there is an important constitutional difference between direct and indirect infringement of free exercise rights. Following the *Braunfeld* analysis, one might have expected the Court to note that Braunfeld could have closed his business on Sunday without violating his religious duty, whereas Lee could not have participated in the Social Security system in any way without compromising his religious beliefs.[26] Thus, one might have expected that the *Braunfeld* Court would have upheld the Sunday closing law but would have required an exemption to participating in the Social Security system. By holding instead that no exemption was required under the Free Exercise Clause even though Lee had religious objections to participating in the program, the *Lee* Court seemed to give even less weight to free exercise guarantees than the *Braunfeld* Court had.

When citing *Braunfeld*,[27] the *Lee* Court did not emphasize the difference between direct and indirect infringement, instead noting that in a religiously diverse nation like the United States "some religious practices [must] yield to the common good."[28] While it is not particularly controversial to suggest that some religious practices must yield, the Court failed to articulate any differentiating principle to make clear which free exercise practices would be protected and which not.

Consider the unemployment compensation cases. Both South Carolina and Indiana had wished to protect public resources when denying unemployment compensation to those who had refused to work for religious reasons. In both *Sherbert* and *Thomas*, the Court rejected that those indirect burdens on free exercise passed muster. But those states might have made good use of the argument apparently accepted in *Lee*, namely, that the great diversity of religious viewpoints might allow many individuals to claim that they could not work for religious reasons and were thus entitled to unemployment compensation.

The Court was unpersuaded that Indiana and South Carolina would face crushing unemployment compensation burdens if the state had to respect Sherbert and Thomas's free exercise claims.[29] Yet, it is not at all obvious that terrible results would have occurred if Lee had been exempted from paying into the Social Security system for employees who also objected to receiving such benefits. Indeed, Congress eventually exempted individuals in Lee's position from paying into the system,[30] which at least suggests that the Court overstated the difficulties that would have resulted from according such an exemption.

The *Lee* Court explained,

> When followers of a particular sect enter into commercial activity as a matter of choice, the limits they accept on their own conduct as a matter of conscience and faith are not to be superimposed on the statutory schemes which are binding on others in that activity.[31]

This characterization of the limits of free exercise guarantees in the commercial context would need further clarification in the subsequent case law. That said, however, such a characterization did not helpfully describe the existing case law, because that very rationale might have been offered to explain why Thomas and Sherbert were not entitled to employment compensation, especially where the statutory schemes merely imposed indirect costs on free exercise. After all, workers are also in the marketplace as a matter of choice and, arguably, the limitations individuals set on their own conduct should not be superimposed on the applicable statutory scheme. In short, the *Lee* Court offered no persuasive justification for its holding in light of *Sherbert* and *Thomas*, which themselves could not be persuasively distinguished from *Braunfeld* and *Gallagher*.

Other labor limitations

State regulation of commercial activity was also at issue in *Tony and Susan Alamo Foundation v. Secretary of Labor*,[32] where the Court addressed whether the Fair Labor Standards Act (FLSA) was applicable to employees of a religious foundation engaged in commercial activities.[33] The Tony and Susan Alamo Foundation was a nonprofit religious organization that derived its income from a variety of commercial activities. The businesses were staffed by associates who did not receive salaries but were provided food, clothing, and shelter, among other benefits.[34]

The *Alamo* Court explained that two conditions must be met for the Foundation's commercial activities to be subject to FLSA: "First, the Foundation's businesses must constitute an '[e]nterprise engaged in commerce or in the production of goods for commerce.' Second, the associates must be 'employees' within the meaning of the Act."[35] The Court held that both prongs were met in this case, and that application of the Act to the Foundation's commercial activities did not violate First Amendment guarantees.[36]

Lest it be thought that the Foundation was simply exploiting its staff, the Court noted that most of the associates were "drug addicts, derelicts, or criminals before their conversion and rehabilitation by the Foundation."[37] Thus, the Foundation was doing important work by helping these individuals become responsible and productive members of society. Further, the "associates who had testified at trial had vigorously protested the payment of wages, asserting that they considered themselves volunteers who were working only for religious and evangelical reasons."[38] As had been true in *Lee*, however, the fact that both the employer and the employees supported the employer's failure to abide by the law did not justify a free exercise exemption.

The Court recognized that those challenging the law were those who the law was designed to protect and thus it might seem that there would be no harm in granting that exemption. However, affording an exemption to businesses whose employees were willing to work without being paid wages would give employers an unfair advantage.

> If an exception to the Act were carved out for employees willing to testify that they performed work "voluntarily," employers might be able to use superior bargaining power to coerce employees to make such assertions, or to waive their protections under the Act.[39]

Thus, one explanation for the Court's reluctance to grant an exemption was that employees might thereby be put at risk. The Court might have made a similar argument in *Lee*, namely, that if employers like Lee were exempted from paying into Social Security as long as their employees waived their eligibility for such payments, there might be at least two foreseeable, undesirable consequences: (1) would-be employees might be pressured into waiving their right to Social Security benefits, and (2) the employer would have been incentivized to hire individuals with conscientious objections to participating in the Social Security system rather than individuals with no such compunctions, just as the *Braunfeld* Court had worried that granting an exemption would have incentivized hiring workers who did not observe a Sunday Sabbath.

The *Alamo* district court had noted that although the Foundation was a nonprofit religious corporation, "its businesses were 'engaged in ordinary commercial activities in competition with other commercial businesses.'"[40] This was important, because such a finding was necessary for the Fair Standards Labor Act to be applicable. It was also important because "the payment of substandard wages would undoubtedly give petitioners and similar organizations an advantage over their competitors."[41] Thus, "the admixture of religious motivations does not alter a business' effect on commerce."[42] Here, the district court was offering the rationale that had been offered in *Braunfeld*, namely, that free exercise guarantees may have to yield to "protect[ ] competitors against unfair competition."[43]

The *Alamo* Court recognized that the Foundation was a nonprofit religious organization, but rejected that subjecting the Foundation to the requirements of the Fair Labor Standards Act would violate the associates' free exercise rights.[44] That was at least in part because "the Free Exercise Clause does not require an exemption from a governmental program unless, at a minimum, inclusion in the program actually burdens the claimant's freedom to exercise religious rights."[45] Because wages need not be in the form of cash, the Court could not see how the requirement imposed a burden on free exercise—"the associates [could] simply continue to be paid in the form of benefits."[46] Even "if the associates' beliefs precluded them from accepting the statutory amount, there is nothing in the Act to prevent the associates from returning the amounts to the Foundation, provided that they do so voluntarily."[47] But if that was so, then it was unclear how "the Act would interfere with the associates' right to freely exercise their religious beliefs."[48]

While the Court's point that associates could always voluntarily donate to the Foundation was eminently reasonable, it was nonetheless surprising in a number of respects. The relevant question was not whether the Court believed that application of the statute imposed a burden on the employees' religious beliefs, but whether the *employees* believed that. The *Thomas* Court suggested that "religious beliefs need not be acceptable, logical, consistent, or comprehensible to others in order to merit First Amendment protection."[49] Not only was it important to focus on the claimants' rather than the justices' beliefs, but it might also have been important to focus on the contents of the particular beliefs at issue. Thus, if part of the belief was that the individuals should not *receive* "excess" wages rather than merely that they should not *keep* excess wages, then one would have expected the Court to discuss why the state had a compelling interest at stake and why allowing an exemption would have severely undermined that interest.

One might have expected the *Alamo* Court to have discussed *Braunfeld* or, at least, to have cited it. The Court did not do so, even though both decisions took seriously the anti-competitive effects that might result from requiring an exemption and, further, the possible negative implications for some employees that might result from requiring that the requested exemption be granted.

That potential anti-competitive effects on business and negative implications for workers are considered does not establish how heavily these factors are weighed in the calculus determining whether the implicated state interests are sufficiently weighty to override free exercise guarantees. So, too, precisely because the *Alamo* Court did not focus on the specific contents of the employees' beliefs, for example, with respect to not receiving versus not keeping "excess" wages, one does not know how heavily the Court weighs the protection of specific religious beliefs and practices in the calculus determining the conditions under which exemptions must be granted. Thus, one explanation of *Alamo* is that free exercise guarantees did not require a different result because the employees' religious beliefs and practices were not adversely impacted by enforcement of FLSA requirements. Such an interpretation leaves open what would have happened had those religious beliefs and practices been adversely affected.

In the same year that *Alamo* was decided, the Court addressed another workplace regulation. *Estate of Thornton v. Caldor, Incorporated*[50] involved a Connecticut statute granting individuals a right not to work on their Sabbath day.[51] While Connecticut was presumably trying to accommodate differing religious traditions, the Court noted that "the statute takes no account of the convenience or interests of the employer or those of other employees who do not observe a Sabbath."[52] Further, as Justice Sandra Day O'Connor noted in her concurrence, "[a]ll employees, regardless of their religious orientation, would value the benefit which the statute bestows on Sabbath observers—the right to select the day of the week in which to refrain from labor."[53] She then elaborated on the difficulty involved in solely focusing on those who might object to working on the Sabbath: "Connecticut requires private employers to confer this valued and desirable benefit only on those employees who adhere to a particular religious belief."[54] A reasonable observer would have a predictable reaction to the statute: "The message conveyed is one of endorsement of a particular religious belief, to the detriment of those who do not share it."[55] The Court held that "the Connecticut statute, which provides Sabbath observers with an absolute and unqualified right not to work on their Sabbath, violates the Establishment Clause of the First Amendment."[56]

The Court's considering the interests of employers and of non-religious employees is commendable. Yet, the *Thornton* establishment analysis suggests a possible difficulty raised by the *Sherbert* free exercise analysis. Individuals who had very good, non-religious reasons that they were no longer available for work, e.g., the loss of reliable childcare, might also have appreciated being eligible for unemployment compensation, and the *Sherbert* Court rejected that any worrisome constitutional issues were raised when it distinguished between an individual like Sherbert who was unavailable for work on her Sabbath and an individual who was not available for work on a certain day because of the loss of a reliable babysitter. While there are ways to distinguish between *Thornton* and *Sherbert*, the *Thorton* analysis did not do enough to show why analogous reasoning would have required a different result in *Sherbert*, which undercuts the persuasiveness of *Sherbert* and gives support to Justice Harlan's *Sherbert* dissent.[57]

AFDC benefits

Bowen v. Roy[58] suggests that free exercise guarantees may not do much work even when religious beliefs and practices are greatly undermined by state requirements. At issue was whether the provision of welfare benefits could be conditioned on acceptance of a Social Security number when use of that number would impose a burden on free exercise. Stephen Roy and Karen Miller had applied for and received benefits under the Aid to Families with Dependent Children (AFDC) and Food Stamp programs. However, they refused to comply with a condition of the programs, namely, that they provide the Social Security number of any dependents living in their household. The refusal was based on Roy's sincere religious belief that he must keep his daughter's person and spirit unique. The uniqueness of the Social Security number as an identifier, coupled with the uses of the number, would serve to "rob the spirit" of his daughter and prevent her from attaining greater spiritual power.[59]

The district court concluded that "the public interest in maintaining an efficient and fraud resistant system can be met without requiring use of a social security number for Little Bird of the Snow."[60] This was so, at least in part, because so few people have religious objections to the use of that number that the amount of fraud that might occur as a result of ruling in

Roy's favor would be minimal. Just as the Court in *Sherbert* and *Thomas* expressed doubt that affording compensation to the plaintiffs would put the respective unemployment compensation systems at risk by those pretending to have the relevant beliefs or because there would many others claiming to have religious beliefs that prevented them from working, the district court did not believe that many would express similar reservations about using Social Security numbers.

The Supreme Court was utterly unsympathetic to Roy's claim, noting that the Court had never "interpreted the First Amendment to require the Government *itself* to behave in ways that the individual believes will further his or her spiritual development or that of his or her family."[61] Yet, more had to be said to distinguish this case from the other free exercise cases, since those did not stand for the proposition that individuals' religious beliefs cannot dictate the Government's particular "internal procedures."[62] For example, South Carolina had refused unemployment compensation to those who refused jobs offers because unavailable for work on a required day. But one way of understanding this policy was that South Carolina had an internal procedure whereby individuals would not be found eligible for unemployment compensation if refusing a job offer for scheduling reasons. So, too, Indiana might be understood to have had an internal policy of refusing to award unemployment compensation to those whose refusal to work was not for good cause. While the Court distinguished *Sherbert* and *Thomas*, that explanation was neither based on whether the Government itself was being asked to behave in certain ways nor on whether the individual was seeking government benefits.

The *Bowen* Court distinguished *Sherbert* and *Thomas* from what was before it by noting that in the unemployment compensation cases the state had "created a mechanism for individualized exemptions."[63] Where the state already has in place a system for evaluating whether individual exemptions should be made, the state's "refusal to extend an exemption to an instance of religious hardship suggests a discriminatory intent."[64] Because the state was already willing to make judgments on a case-by-case basis, "it was appropriate to require the State to demonstrate a compelling reason for denying the requested exemption."[65] But this rationale is unpersuasive. South Carolina had rejected making case-by-case determinations with respect to unavailability—the state did not want to distinguish between the person unavailable for work for religious reasons and the person who was unavailable for work because that person's children could not be left alone.[66] Further, there was no evidence that South Carolina was attempting to discriminate on the basis of religion,[67] just as there was no evidence that Indiana was attempting to discriminate against Thomas because of his religion.[68] While it may well be that neither Indiana nor South Carolina had adequate reasons to deny unemployment compensation to the plaintiffs, neither *Sherbert* nor *Thomas* suggested that the respective states were targeting religion for adverse treatment.

The *Bowen* Court having appealed to whether there was already a system in place for making exemptions was ironic in light of *Lee*. The *Lee* Court had recognized that Congress had exempted some Amish from paying into Social Security but had been unwilling to expand that exemption. Thus, even if the difference between a policy with exceptions versus a policy without exceptions could somehow ground the differing results in *Bowen* on the one hand and *Thomas* and *Sherbert* on the other, that difference could not explain the difference between *Lee* on the one hand and *Thomas* and *Sherbert* on the other.

The *Bowen* Court noted that the challenged requirement "may indeed confront some applicants for benefits with choices,"[69] although it did not "affirmatively compel appellees, by threat of sanctions, to refrain from religiously motivated conduct or to engage in conduct that they find objectionable for religious reasons."[70] While the Court was correct that Roy had not been subject to sanction for failing to engage in religiously motivated conduct, it was also true that neither Sherbert nor Thomas had been subject to such sanctions. Roy was being compelled (or at least incentivized) to engage in religiously objectionable conduct because he would otherwise not be awarded certain benefits. So, too, Sherbert and Thomas were also incentivized to engage in religiously objectionable conduct because they would otherwise not be awarded certain benefits.

The Court understood that Roy was being asked to do something to which he had religious objections. However, it was not as if Roy was simply minding his own business when the Government spontaneously imposed this new requirement on him. Rather

> it is appellees who seek benefits from the Government and who assert that, because of certain religious beliefs, they should be excused from compliance with a condition that is binding on all other persons who seek the same benefits from the Government.[71]

The Court seemed to be making two related points. The government's imposition of a burden was only in response to Roy having sought something, and the burden itself was the denial of a benefit rather than, for example, the imposition of a criminal penalty. While benefits are important, the kind of burden imposed here was qualitatively different from the kind of burden imposed where the government criminalizes religious practice.

> [W]e cannot ignore the reality that denial of such benefits by a uniformly applicable statute neutral on its face is of a wholly different, less intrusive nature than affirmative compulsion or prohibition, by threat of penal sanctions, for conduct that has religious implications.[72]

That did not make the burden imposed in this kind of case immunized from review. "A governmental burden on religious liberty is not insulated from review simply because it is indirect."[73] That said, however, "the nature of the burden is relevant to the standard the government must meet to justify the burden."[74]

Where the burden is indirect and there is no evidence of any intent to discriminate, neutral and generally applicable laws will be upheld as long as they are reasonably related to the promotion of legitimate government interests.[75] What about the state's decision with respect to whether it would create a process for case-by-case decision-making? The Court explained that

> a policy decision by a government that it wishes to treat all applicants alike and that it does not wish to become involved in case-by-case inquiries into the genuineness of each religious objection to such condition or restrictions is entitled to substantial deference.[76]

Yet, South Carolina's desire not to have to address the genuineness of each religious objection to work received little or no deference rather than great deference.

The difficulty posed by South Carolina's system was not in its refusing to award unemployment compensation benefits to those who as a general matter had very good reasons that they were unavailable for work, for example, because very young children were at home in need of supervision. Instead, the difficulty was in the state's failure to create an exception for those whose work unavailability was due to their religious beliefs. But the *Sherbert* analysis casts doubt on the *Bowen* Court's pronouncement that a government's refusal to adopt a case-by-case analysis is entitled to great deference.

Arguably, it is reasonable not to force a government to adopt a system in which individualized assessments must be made. A government might be reluctant to institute such a system where the state could not determine prospectively whether such a system would create more problems than it would solve. Yet, such an explanation is much less persuasive if other governments have already established that setting up such an individualized system would yield great benefits.

Suppose that other governments have adopted a case-by-case system to protect free exercise interests without encountering feared difficulties. That might make a state's refusal to adopt such an approach suspicious. Just as the Court was willing to impute discriminatory intent when a state was willing to employ individualized assessment for non-religious considerations but not for religious ones, the Court might impute discriminatory intent if the state was unwilling to set up an individualized system to protect free exercise when other states had done so rather successfully. But the *Braunfeld* Court deferred to Pennsylvania's refusal to afford an exemption to those observing Sabbath on a day other than Sunday, even though many states affording such an exemption had not encountered difficulties when doing so.

The *Bowen* Court concluded that the "Appellees may not use the Free Exercise Clause to demand Government benefits, but only on their own terms, particularly where that insistence works a demonstrable disadvantage to the Government in the administration of the programs."[77] Yet, the unemployment compensation cases essentially required the government to afford compensation on the appellants' own terms, and one reason that the states might not have wanted to afford such benefits to those refusing to work for religious reasons could have involved a reluctance to inquire "into the genuineness of each religious objection to such condition or restrictions."[78]

There was yet another respect in which the *Bowen* analysis did not seem to account for prior jurisprudence. Consider *Gillette*, where the government was already doing a case-by-case analysis so that individuals with conscientious objections to all wars could escape active service. The Court suggested that the federal government had a compelling interest in not also affording an exemption to individuals with conscientious objections to a particular war, citing both fairness and manpower concerns. Yet, it may well be that the Court was too willing to accept the Government's asserted justifications without subjecting them to close examination. Many individuals would not have been able to establish their sincere *religious* objections to participating in that war in particular when the individualized review was performed, which would mean that many would not qualify for the exemption in any event. Further, service members may well not have thought it any more unfair to exempt those with sincere conscientious objections to a particular war than to exempt those with sincere conscientious objections to all wars.[79] Prior case law did not privilege the case-by-case analysis offered by the *Bowen* Court, both in that neutral and general laws were not always given deference (as *Yoder* illustrates) and in that laws with such exceptions did not trigger the demanding scrutiny that the Court implied would thereby be triggered (as *Lee* illustrates).

Often, free exercise analysis involves weighing an individual's free exercise interests against state interests. Here, however, the state interests were on both sides of the balance. The state has an interest in making sure that only the proper individuals receive benefits, which is facilitated by requiring the use of Social Security numbers for identification purposes. But the state also has an interest in assuring that children receive adequate support, and that interest might also be weighed in the balance. The failure to exempt those who have religious objections to submitting Social Security numbers might simply result in the children not receiving the support that they otherwise would receive, which neither promotes the interests of society as a whole nor of the particular individuals involved.

Subsequent change of religion

The validity of the *Bowen* analysis was questioned the very next year in *Hobbie v. Unemployment Appeals Commission of Florida*.[80] At issue was whether an individual who converted to the Seventh-Day Adventist faith could be denied unemployment compensation when she refused to work on Saturdays.[81]

When Paula Hobbie was initially hired, she did not have any reservations about working on Saturday. However, when she converted to the Seventh-Day Adventist faith, she could no longer work on Friday evenings or Saturdays.[82] At first the company was able to accommodate her religious requirements,[83] but she was later informed that she would either have to work during her scheduled shifts or resign from the company.[84] Hobbie refused to resign and was fired.[85] She filed for unemployment benefits but her application was rejected.[86]

Florida law permitted individuals to receive unemployment compensation if they were not at fault for the loss of their jobs.[87] In effect, the issue before the Court was whether the refusal to work at certain times for religious reasons constituted "misconduct"[88] that would justify the denial of unemployment benefits.

The Florida Unemployment Appeals Commission argued that its decision should be evaluated "under the less rigorous standard articulated in Chief Justice Warren Burger's opinion in *Bowen v. Roy.*"[89] That weaker standard provided that

> [a]bsent proof of an intent to discriminate against particular religious beliefs or against religion in general, the Government meets its burden when it demonstrates that a challenged requirement for governmental benefits, neutral and uniform in its application, is a reasonable means of promoting a legitimate public interest.[90]

Needless to say, Florida's defense of its statute would have been much easier if the standard announced in *Roy* had been applicable. The *Hobbie* Court simply rejected the *Roy* analysis rather than hold that this case fell within the exception recognized under *Roy* or, perhaps, that the facts of *Hobbie* made the case distinguishable.

Presumably, the *Hobbie* Court was trying to correct what it perceived to be an error in the *Bowen* analysis, which was why the latter opinion was rejected "in toto."[91] *Bowen* seemed to be telling states that their neutral and exceptionless policies would be much less vulnerable to invalidation than would more nuanced policies. But such an approach disincentivized attempting to tailor policies to meet individual needs, because creating one exception might put a whole program at risk. In any event, the *Hobbie* Court's attempt to neutralize the *Bowen* analysis had a rocky start, if only because Justice Powell in his concurrence suggested that "the Court's rejection of *Roy*'s reasoning is dictum."[92]

Sacred ground

If the *Hobbie* Court had been committed to rejecting the *Bowen* analysis, then Justice Powell's having called the rejection mere dictum would not have carried much weight. In subsequent cases, the Court could simply have reaffirmed that the *Bowen* analysis had no place in free exercise jurisprudence. But the very next year the Court offered an analysis that was reminiscent of *Bowen* in *Lyng v. Northwest Indian Cemetery Protective Association*.[93]

At issue was

> whether the First Amendment's Free Exercise Clause prohibits the Government from permitting timber harvesting in, or constructing a road through, a portion of a National

Forest that has traditionally been used for religious purposes by members of three American Indian tribes in northwestern California.[94]

The Forest Service was trying to connect two towns by creating a 75-mile paved road. In order to complete the project, it was necessary to "build a 6-mile paved segment through the Chimney Rock section of the Six Rivers National Forest."[95]

The Forest Service had commissioned a study of "American Indian cultural and religious sites in the area."[96] That study concluded that "constructing a road along any of the available routes 'would cause serious and irreparable damage to the sacred areas which are an integral and necessary part of the belief systems and lifeway of Northwest California Indian peoples.'"[97] Because the road would be so destructive, the report recommended that the road not be built. The Forest Service disagreed with that conclusion, however, instead choosing to build the road in a way that would minimize the cultural harm thereby caused.

The tribes argued that

> the burden on their religious practices is heavy enough to violate the Free Exercise Clause unless the Government can demonstrate a compelling need to complete the . . . road or to engage in timber harvesting in the Chimney Rock area.[98]

When analyzing the challenge, the Court noted that "[t]he building of a road or the harvesting of timber on publicly owned land cannot meaningfully be distinguished from the use of a Social Security number in *Roy*."[99] While "the challenged Government action would interfere significantly with private persons' ability to pursue spiritual fulfillment according to their own religious beliefs,"[100] the Court reasoned that it could not be said that "the affected individuals [would] be coerced by the Government's action into violating their religious beliefs."[101] Further, it also could not be maintained that the "governmental action penalize[s] religious activity by denying any person an equal share of the rights, benefits, and privileges enjoyed by other citizens."[102]

When denying that the challenged action would deny anyone an equal share of rights, benefits, or privileges, the Court was not denying "that the logging and road-building projects at issue in this case could have devastating effects on traditional Indian religious practices."[103] Nonetheless, the Court explained that "the Constitution simply does not provide a principle that could justify upholding respondents' legal claims."[104] The difficulty was that the "government simply could not operate if it were required to satisfy every citizen's religious needs and desires."[105] Indeed, because the same government activities might promote the spiritual requirements of some groups while undermining the spiritual requirements of others,[106] the Court concluded, "Whatever rights the Indians may have to the use of the area, however, those rights do not divest the Government of its right to use what is, after all, *its* land."[107]

Regrettably, much of the Court's analysis was unpersuasive. For example, the Court's point that particular government policies might promote the spiritual interests of some and undermine the spiritual interests of others might be important were the question at hand which exceptionless policy should be adopted—there, the government could not help but offend someone's religious beliefs. But individuals who request a free exercise exemption are not seeking implementation of an exceptionless policy; instead, they are seeking to have a policy not applied to them in particular because of their religious beliefs. Thus, the response to the point that a particular government policy might be compatible with the religious beliefs of some but not others is that the latter group might be exempted from the policy (unless doing so would itself be too costly).

In *Lyng*, respecting the religious wishes of the tribes would have meant stopping the logging and road-building altogether. If refraining from engaging in those activities would have undermined a compelling state interest, then the Forest Service could have proceeded with its plans in any event. The Court seemed reluctant, however, to apply the compelling interest test when the Government's use of its own property was at issue. Yet, the unemployment compensation cases involved the Government's use of its own resources, although the resources in those cases did not involve land.

The *Lyng* analysis raised another concern. When religious practices are substantially burdened, the Court will sometimes judge the constitutionality of the challenged action in light of the compelling interest test and at other times will not. But without some principle to determine when the state must meet that standard, there is a great danger that the Court would appear to respect the free exercise rights of some groups but not of others.[108] Indeed, some read the Court's free exercise jurisprudence as favoring majority over minority religion free exercise rights.[109]

Idiosyncratic beliefs

Frazee v. Illinois Department of Employment Security[110] involved an individual's sincere refusal to work based on his "personal professed religious belief."[111] While William Frazee did not belong to a particular sect and was not a member of a particular church, he nonetheless was asserting sincere religious convictions. The Court nonetheless expressly "reject[ed] the notion that to claim the protection of the Free Exercise Clause, one must be responding to the commands of a particular religious organization."[112]

There are numerous ways to read *Frazee*. In some ways, the opinion suggests that free exercise guarantees also protect minority viewpoints in that Frazee did not belong to a particular church and his religious views were somewhat idiosyncratic. Yet, it is also true that he self-identified as belonging to a majority faith.

In some ways, *Frazee* fits into a fairly narrow understanding of free exercise guarantees. He, like Sherbert, Thomas, and Hobbie, was merely seeking unemployment compensation benefits. Recognition of his claim would not seem to open up the floodgates to requiring the receipt of other kinds of benefits, just as *Sherbert* was not understood to provide the basis in free exercise to require the receipt of other kinds of benefits.

Sales and use taxes

At issue in *Jimmy Swaggart Ministries v. Board of Equalization of California*[113] was whether California's generally applicable sales and use tax could be applied to the "distribution of religious materials by a religious organization"[114] without offending constitutional guarantees. The Court upheld the application of the tax, because there was no evidence that the state was targeting religion and no reason to think that the tax would in some way compromise sincerely held religious beliefs. Indeed, there was no claim that the payment of taxes violated religious beliefs, although such a belief would likely have proven unavailing in any event.

The Court reasoned that because

> the sales and use tax is not a tax on the right to disseminate religious information, ideas, or beliefs *per se*; rather, it is a tax on the privilege of making retail sales of tangible

personal property and on the storage, use, or other consumption of tangible personal property in California,[115]

it could not be claimed that California was somehow targeting religious organizations or products for disadvantageous treatment. Requiring the payment of taxes on the sales of religious retail items did not impose a "constitutionally significant burden on appellant's religious practices or beliefs."[116] Because that was so, the Free Exercise Clause "does not *require* the State to grant appellant an exemption from its generally applicable sales and use tax."[117]

Here, there was perhaps an implicit worry that the failure to impose the tax would have anti-competitive effects, because "[t]he use tax, as a complement to the sales tax, reaches out-of-state purchases by residents of the State."[118] That said, the concern was not only with items bought interstate. In addition, "appellant held 23 crusades in California—each lasting 1 to 3 days, with one crusade lasting 6 days."[119] At the event, the appellant "sold religious books, tapes, records, and other religious and nonreligious merchandise."[120]

When explaining that the appellant was not being singled out for disadvantageous treatment, the Court noted that

> California treats the sale of a Bible by a religious organization just as it would treat the sale of a Bible by a bookstore; as long as both are in-state retail sales of tangible personal property, they are both subject to the tax regardless of the motivation for the sale or the purchase.[121]

Any other approach would give the religious entity a competitive advantage.

Conclusion

The Court's free exercise jurisprudence from *Lee* to *Swaggart* was chaotic. The standard announced for determining whether free exercise guarantees had been violated would be applied one way in one case, a different way in a different case, and ignored or expressly rejected in other cases. The Court would sometimes claim to be protecting employer or employee interests, although those interests were not dispositive. The Court would sometimes claim that free exercise guarantees did not require the state to modify the way that it disposed of its own property, but that interpretation was undercut by the unemployment compensation cases. The Court issued a series of decisions, sometimes protecting free exercise and sometimes not, without offering persuasive rationales for those decisions. This chaotic jurisprudence led to what was perceived to be a groundbreaking decision, which is discussed in the next chapter.

Notes

1 *United States v. Lee*, 455 U.S. 252 (1982).
2 *Id.* at 255.
3 *Id.*
4 *Id.* at 257.
5 *Id.*
6 *Id.* at 256.
7 *Id.* at 255 n. 4 (citing 26 U.S.C. § 1402(g)).
8 See *id.* at 261 ("Granting an exemption from social security taxes to an employer operates to impose the employer's religious faith on the employees.").

9 *Id.* at 255 (emphasis added).
10 *Id.* at 261.
11 Michelle O'Connor, "The Religious Freedom Restoration Act: Exactly What Rights Does It "Restore" in the Federal Tax Context?," *Arizona State Law Journal* 36:321–402 (2004), p. 337 (footnote omitted) ("The Court's holding was not based on any evidence concerning the feasibility of the taxpayer's requested accommodation. Consequently, the Court did not find that the sought-after accommodation was not viable. Rather, the Court reached that conclusion by relying on its own 'common sense' and the government's bare contention that exempting Amish employees from Social Security taxes would impose a significant burden on the system.").
12 Michael S. Paulsen, "A RFRA Runs Through It: Religious Freedom and the U.S. Code," *Montana Law Review* 56:249–94 (1995), p. 267 ("Congress had exempted self-employed Amish but not Amish employers. But how could the federal government's interest in mandatory participation be thought so compelling as to override conflicting Amish beliefs, where the government did not always pursue that interest, and where its decision not to pursue that interest was premised on the fact that doing so would conflict with Amish beliefs?").
13 *Lee*, 455 U.S. at 257 (citing *Prince v. Massachusetts*, 321 U.S. 158 (1944); *Reynolds v. United States*, 98 U.S. 145 (1879)).
14 *Id.* (citing *Thomas v. Review Board*, 450 U.S. 707 (1981); *Wisconsin v. Yoder*, 406 U.S. 205 (1972); *Gillette v. United States*, 401 U.S. 437 (1971); *Sherbert v. Verner*, 374 U.S. 398 (1963)).
15 *Id.* at 258.
16 *Id.* ("[A] comprehensive national social security system providing for voluntary participation would be almost a contradiction in terms and difficult, if not impossible, to administer.").
17 *Id.* at 259–60.
18 *Id.* at 260.
19 *Id.*
20 *Id.*
21 *Id.* at 261
22 *Id.* ("Congress drew a line in § 1402(g), exempting the self-employed Amish but not all persons working for an Amish employer. The tax imposed on employers to support the social security system must be uniformly applicable to all, except as Congress provides explicitly otherwise.").
23 *Id.* at 262 (Stevens, J., concurring).
24 *Id.*
25 *Id.* at 259.
26 *Id.* at 255.
27 *Id.* at 259.
28 *Id.*
29 See *Sherbert*, 374 U.S. at 406–08; *Thomas*, 450 U.S. at 711.
30 26 *United States Code* § 3127 ("Exemption for employers and their employees where both are members of religious faiths opposed to participation in Social Security Act programs.").
31 *Lee*, 455 U.S. at 261.
32 *Tony and Susan Alamo Foundation v. Secretary of Labor*, 471 U.S. 290 (1985).
33 See *id.* at 291–92.
34 *Id.* at 292.
35 *Id.* at 295 (citing 29 *United States Code* § 203(s) (2006)).
36 *Id.* at 306.
37 *Id.* at 292.
38 *Id.* at 293.
39 *Id.* at 302 (citing *Barrentine v. Arkansas-Best Freight System, Incorporated*, 450 U.S. 728 (1981)).
40 *Id.* at 293. (quoting *Donovan v. Tony & Susan Alamo Foundation*, 567 F. Supp. 556, 573 (W.D. Arkansas 1982)).
41 *Id.* at 299.
42 *Id.*

43 See *Tony & Susan Alamo Foundation*, 567 F. Supp. at 574 (citing *Braunfeld*)
44 *Tony and Susan Alamo Foundation*, 471 U.S. at 303.
45 *Id.* (citing *United States v. Lee*, 455 U.S. 252, 256–57 (1982); *Thomas v. Review Board. Indiana Employment Security Division*, 450 U.S. 707, 717–18 (1981)).
46 *Id.* at 304.
47 *Id.*
48 *Id.* at 304–05.
49 *Thomas*, 450 U.S. at 714.
50 *Estate of Thornton v. Caldor, Incorporated*, 472 U.S. 703 (1985).
51 *Id.* at 708 ("The Connecticut statute challenged here guarantees every employee, who 'states that a particular day of the week is observed as his Sabbath,' the right not to work on his chosen day.") (citing Connecticut General Statutes § 53–303e(b) (1985)).
52 *Id.* at 709.
53 *Id.* at 711 (O'Connor, J., concurring).
54 *Id.* (O'Connor, J., concurring).
55 *Id.* at 711 (O'Connor, J., concurring). Justice O'Connor was willing to announce what the reasonable observer would think on other occasions as well. See, e.g., *Corporation of Presiding Bishop of Church of Jesus Christ of Latter-Day Saints v. Amos*, 483 U.S. 327, 349 (1987) (O'Connor, J., concurring) ("[I]n my view the objective observer should perceive the Government action as an accommodation of the exercise of religion rather than as a Government endorsement of religion.").
56 *Thornton*, 472 U.S. at 710–11; see also *Trans World Airlines, Incorporated v. Hardison*, 432 U.S. 63, 84–85 (1977) ("By suggesting that TWA should incur certain costs in order to give Hardison Saturdays off the Court of Appeals would in effect require TWA to finance an additional Saturday off and then to choose the employee who will enjoy it on the basis of his religious beliefs. While incurring extra costs to secure a replacement for Hardison might remove the necessity of compelling another employee to work involuntarily in Hardison's place, it would not change the fact that the privilege of having Saturdays off would be allocated according to religious beliefs.").
57 See *Sherbert*, 374 U.S. at 422 (Harlan, J., dissenting) ("The State, in other words, must single out for financial assistance those whose behavior is religiously motivated, even though it denies such assistance to others whose identical behavior (in this case, inability to work no Saturdays) is not religiously motivated.").
58 *Bowen v. Roy*, 476 U.S. 693 (1986).
59 *Id.* at 696.
60 *Id.* at 698 (quoting *Roy v. Cohen*, 590 F. Supp. 600, 607 (M.D. Pennsylvania 1984)).
61 *Id.* at 699.
62 *Id.* at 700.
63 *Id.* at 708.
64 *Id.*
65 *Id.*
66 See *Sherbert*, 374 U.S. at 416 (Stewart, J., concurring in the result) ("South Carolina would deny unemployment benefits to a mother unavailable for work on Saturdays because she was unable to get a babysitter.").
67 See *id.* (Stewart, J., concurring in the result) ("Thus, we do not have before us a situation where a State provides unemployment compensation generally, and singles out for disqualification only those persons who are unavailable for work on religious grounds. This is not, in short, a scheme which operates so as to discriminate against religion as such.").
68 *Thomas*, 450 U.S. at 723 (Rehnquist, J., dissenting) ("[I]t cannot be said that the State discriminated against Thomas on the basis of his religious beliefs or that he was denied benefits *because* he was a Jehovah's Witness.").
69 *Bowen*, 476 U.S. at 703.
70 *Id.*
71 *Id.*
72 *Id.* at 704.
73 *Id.* at 706 (citing *Thomas*, 450 U.S. at 717–18).
74 *Id.* at 707.

75 *Id.* at 707–08 ("Absent proof of an intent to discriminate against particular religious beliefs or against religion in general, the Government meets its burden when it demonstrates that a challenged requirement for governmental benefits, neutral and uniform in its application, is a reasonable means of promoting a legitimate public interest.").
76 *Id.* at 707.
77 *Id.* at 711–12.
78 *Id.* at 707.
79 *See* Michael J. Davidson, "War and the Doubtful Soldier," *Notre Dame Journal of Law, Ethics & Public Policy* 19:91–161 (2005), p. 139 ("An expansion of the conscientious objector exemption would comport with our deep-rooted tradition of accommodating those members of our citizenry with sincere moral or religious objections to participating in a war.").
80 *Hobbie v. Unemployment Appeals Commission of Florida*, 480 U.S. 136 (1987).
81 *Id.* at 138 ("[A]fter a meeting with Hobbie and her minister, the general manager informed appellant that she could either work her scheduled shifts or submit her resignation to the company. When Hobbie refused to do either, Lawton discharged her.").
82 *Id.* ("In April 1984, Hobbie informed her immediate supervisor that she was to be baptized into the Seventh-Day Adventist Church and that, for religious reasons, she would no longer be able to work on her Sabbath, from sundown on Friday to sundown on Saturday.").
83 *Id.* ("The supervisor devised an arrangement with Hobbie: she agreed to work evenings and Sundays, and he agreed to substitute for her whenever she was scheduled to work on a Friday evening or a Saturday.").
84 *Id.* ("[T]he general manager informed appellant that she could either work her scheduled shifts or submit her resignation to the company.").
85 *Id.*
86 See *id.* at 139.
87 *Id.* at 138. ("Under Florida law, unemployment compensation benefits are available to persons who become 'unemployed through no fault of their own.'") (citing *Florida Statutes* § 443.021 (1985)).
88 See *id.* at 139.
89 *Id.* at 141 (citing *Bowen*, 476 U.S. at 707–08).
90 *Bowen*, 476 U.S. at 707–08.
91 See *Hobbie*, 480 U.S. at 147 (Powell, J., concurring in the judgment) ("[T]he Court reaches out to reject the reasoning of *Roy in toto*.").
92 *Id.* (Powell, J., concurring in the judgment).
93 *Lyng v. Northwest Indian Cemetery Protective Association*, 485 U.S. 439 (1988).
94 *Id.* at 441–42.
95 *Id.* at 442.
96 *Id.*
97 *Id.*
98 *Id.* at 447.
99 *Id.* at 449.
100 *Id.*
101 *Id.*
102 *Id.*
103 *Id.* at 451.
104 *Id.* at 452.
105 *Id.*
106 *Id.* ("A broad range of government activities . . . will always be considered essential to the spiritual well-being of some citizens. . . . Others will find the very same activities deeply offensive, and perhaps incompatible with . . . the tenets of their religion.").
107 *Id.* at 453 (citing *Bowen*, 476 U.S. at 724–27 (O'Connor, J., concurring in part and dissenting in part)).
108 See Rebekah J. French, "Free Exercise of Religion on the Public Lands," *Public Land Law Review* 11:197–209 (1990), p. 209 ("The Supreme Court's refusal to apply the traditional balancing test to free exercise claims brought by Native Americans demonstrates the extent of their hostility to the religious beliefs of that minority.").

109 John M.A. DiPippa, "God and Guns: The Free Exercise of Religion Problems of Regulating Guns in Churches and Other Houses of Worship," *Marquette Law Review* 98:1103–46 (2015), p. 1128 ("[O]f the successful claimants, majority religions win more often than non-majority religions.")
110 *Frazee v. Illinois Department of Employment Security*, 489 U.S. 829 (1989).
111 *Id.* at 831. (citing *Frazee*, 512 N.E.2d at 790).
112 *Id.* at 834.
113 *Jimmy Swaggart Ministries v. Board of Equalization of California*, 493 U.S. 378 (1990).
114 *Id.* at 380.
115 *Id.* at 389.
116 *Id.* at 392.
117 *Id.*
118 *Id.* at 381.
119 *Id.* at 382.
120 *Id.*
121 *Id.* at 390.

6 The *Smith* revolution

The case law from *Lee* to *Swaggart* is somewhat difficult to characterize jurisprudentially—the Court seems ambivalent about the appropriate test for free exercise cases. Even when there was agreement about which test was appropriate, members of the Court were not of one mind about how to apply it. To make matters even more complicated, rationales that did a lot of work in one case did little or no work in others. This confused and confusing jurisprudence set the stage for the issuance of *Employment Division, Department of Human Resources of Oregon v. Smith*,[1] a controversial decision supported by some commentators and roundly criticized by others.[2]

The *Smith* Court claimed to be offering a consistent account of the past jurisprudence but proposed an account of free exercise that seemed ad hoc and, further, involved fairly weak protections. In reaction to that decision, Congress attempted to offer more protection for religious exercise via federal statute, although the statutes passed in reaction to *Smith* were not themselves free from difficulty.

Smith and its aftermath

Smith was a controversial decision in part because of how it characterized past cases and in part because it seemed to treat free exercise protections as rather weak. Many of the criticisms of the decision are deserved. Nonetheless, *Smith* may have taken on an impossible task—making sense of an internally inconsistent set of cases previously decided by the Court. If that is so, then criticisms of the decision should be tempered in light of the Court's having taken on an impossible task, and congressional attempts to reinstate the former protections in a clear and principled way via statute will fail because the past cases were irreconcilable.

The free exercise revolution

At issue in *Smith* was a claim for unemployment compensation by two drug counselors, Alfred Smith and Galen Black, who had been fired from their jobs for using peyote sacramentally in accordance with their religious tradition. Their applications for unemployment compensation were denied, because they had been fired for work-related misconduct. Yet, a clear lesson of the *Sherbert–Frazee* line of cases is that alleged work misconduct such as failing to come to work for religious reasons may not provide a sufficient justification for the denial of unemployment compensation benefits.

Smith and Black challenged the denial of benefits in the state courts. The Oregon Supreme Court held that the denial of unemployment compensation violated federal but not state constitutional guarantees. That interpretation of federal guarantees was appealed to the United States Supreme Court.

In *Smith I*, the United States Supreme Court addressed the Oregon Supreme Court's holding that Smith and Black could not be denied unemployment benefits for the sacramental use of peyote, notwithstanding that individuals convicted of peyote possession could receive up to ten years in prison for that offense. The Court rejected that "the illegality of an employee's misconduct is irrelevant to the analysis of the federal constitutional [free exercise] claim."[3] Using a greater includes the lesser approach, the *Smith I* Court reasoned that

> if a State has prohibited through its criminal laws certain kinds of religiously motivated conduct without violating the First Amendment, it certainly follows that it may impose the lesser burden of denying unemployment compensation benefits to persons who engage in that conduct.[4]

The Court noted in addition that "if Oregon does prohibit the religious use of peyote, and if that prohibition is consistent with the Federal Constitution, there is no federal right to engage in that conduct in Oregon."[5] But that would mean that if there was no exception for the sacramental use of peyote in Oregon, then "the State [would be] free to withhold unemployment compensation from respondents for engaging in work-related misconduct, despite its religious motivation."[6]

Yet, it is not at all clear that the *Smith I* Court's approach was consistent with the prevailing jurisprudence. The Court seemed to be making the following argument: Suppose that Statute 1 criminalizes certain religious behavior. Suppose further that Statute 2 imposes a lesser burden, for example, a less severe fine or fewer years in prison, on individuals engaging in that same religious behavior. One would expect that if Statute 1 is constitutional because narrowly tailored to promote certain compelling interests, then Statute 2 would also be constitutional.

While the greater includes the lesser analysis might seem applicable at first, further reflection makes that approach less attractive. This is not a straightforward difference in degree scenario for a variety of reasons including that the difference between direct and indirect burdens complicates the analysis. In one sense, the penalties at issue here represent greater and lesser penalties in that direct burdens such as criminal sanctions for the performance of religiously mandated conduct are thought a greater infringement of religious liberty than are indirect burdens such as the denial of benefits for an individual who chose to engage in a practice (itself not criminalized). Yet, direct burdens are not always thought more burdensome than indirect burdens. Suppose, for example, that the direct penalty for observing one's Sabbath is a $1 fine, whereas the indirect penalty is losing one's job. If given the choice, many would choose to have the (allegedly greater) direct burden imposed rather than the (allegedly lesser) indirect one.

The greater includes the lesser approach is especially inapt in the free exercise context. Consider the factual scenarios of *Sherbert* and *Braunfeld*. A court accepting the greater includes the lesser approach might be expected to say either: (1) if Sherbert cannot be forced to forego unemployment compensation for having exercised her right to observe her Sabbath then Braunfeld cannot be forced to lose his business for exercising his right to observe his Sabbath, or (2) if Braunfeld can be forced to close his business as a cost of observing his Sabbath then Sherbert can also be forced to forego unemployment benefits as a cost of observing her Sabbath. In these scenarios (1) uses greater/lesser by suggesting that if free exercise rights are so robust that the state is constitutionally precluded from forcing an individual to incur a financial penalty for observing the Sabbath, then the state is constitutionally precluded from forcing an individual to incur an even greater financial penalty for observing the Sabbath; and (2) uses greater/lesser by suggesting that if the State can constitutionally impose a great financial penalty as a cost of observing the Sabbath, then it can also constitutionally impose a less severe financial penalty as a cost of observing the Sabbath. But the Court did not opt for either (1) or (2), instead upholding the constitutionality of the law imposing the greater financial burden but rejecting the constitutionality of the law imposing the lesser financial burden.

The analysis is even trickier when comparing direct and indirect burdens. Merely because a law directly imposing a criminal penalty on a religious practice is narrowly tailored to promote a compelling state interest does not also establish that a law indirectly imposing a burden on a religious practice is also narrowly or even closely tailored to promote a compelling state interest Both the ends and the means might well differ in the two kinds of statutes. The direct burden imposed by the criminal law might be justified if the purpose was to prevent certain activity thought very dangerous to others, whereas the indirect burden might not be thought justified if the purpose was simply to protect the public fisc.

At least one more complicating factor should be considered. This was not a case about someone convicted of a crime whose punishment was loss of unemployment benefits rather than ten years in jail. Instead, the greater/lesser analysis was used to justify denying unemployment compensation to someone who had not only not been sentenced to ten years imprisonment but who also had not even be tried or convicted.

The *Smith I* Court remanded the case to the Oregon Supreme Court for a determination of whether Oregon law exempted religious use of peyote from the criminal law, commenting that "a necessary predicate to a correct evaluation of respondents' federal claim is an understanding of the legality of their conduct as a matter of state law."[7] Basically, the Court suggested that if Oregon exempted the sacramental use of peyote from the criminal law, then the respondents' conduct might well be constitutionally protected. If Oregon did not offer that exemption, then the Court might well have to decide "whether the ingestion of peyote for sincerely held religious reasons is a form of conduct that is protected by the Federal Constitution from the reach of a State's criminal laws."[8]

On remand, the Oregon Supreme Court held that Oregon law did not exempt sacramental peyote use from criminal prosecution but that the First Amendment to the United States Constitution required that unemployment compensation be awarded. That decision was appealed to the United States Supreme Court.

When considering whether the Oregon Supreme Court was correct that Smith and Black could not be denied unemployment compensation benefits, the *Smith II* Court had a number of issues to consider. They included whether a criminal prohibition of sacramental peyote use violated constitutional guarantees and, if not, whether constitutional guarantees were violated by the denial of unemployment compensation benefits to those who had engaged in sacramental peyote use, criminal prohibition notwithstanding. An additional issue of importance involved clarification of the jurisprudence as a general matter—prior case law was inconsistent with respect to the appropriate standard to determine whether free exercise guarantees required an exemption, and the *Smith II* Court offered its own interpretation of the prevailing jurisprudence.

Smith and Black argued that "their religious motivation for using peyote places them beyond the reach of a criminal law that is not specifically directed at their religious practice."[9] They suggested that the *Sherbert* balancing test should be used, and that "governmental actions that substantially burden a religious practice must be justified by a compelling governmental interest."[10] The Court rejected this approach, announcing instead that "the First Amendment bars application of a neutral, generally applicable law to religiously motivated action . . . [only when] the Free Exercise Clause in conjunction with other constitutional protections" have been implicated.[11] Thus, *Smith* suggests that the Free Exercise Clause will not invalidate a neutral, generally applicable law limiting religious action unless that law also implicates other constitutional guarantees. As examples, the Court cited *Cantwell v. Connecticut*,[12] described as also including "freedom of speech and of the press,"[13] and *Wisconsin v. Yoder*,[14] described as "invalidating compulsory school-attendance laws as applied to Amish parents who refused on religious grounds to send their children to school."[15] The Court explained that the case at bar did not involve "a hybrid situation."[16]

The *Smith II* analysis does not capture the past jurisprudence in a few different respects. First, hybrids need not trigger strict scrutiny. In *Prince*, free exercise rights plus the right of a parent (guardian) to direct the upbringing of her child were not enough to require a free exercise exemption, even though there was no showing that the children involved in that case faced the kinds of potential harms commonly associated with child labor. Thus, the existence of a hybrid involving free exercise and the right to parent did not suffice to trigger strict scrutiny. Further, past case law did not require a hybrid right to be at issue in order for strict scrutiny to be triggered.[17] In *Sherbert*, the Court held that unemployment compensation had to be accorded to an individual who could not work on Saturdays for religious reasons.[18]

It was not as if the *Smith II* Court overlooked *Sherbert*; on the contrary, the Court expressly acknowledged that "[u]nder the *Sherbert* test, governmental actions that substantially burden a religious practice must be justified by a compelling governmental interest."[19] Further, the Court admitted that application of that test in three different cases resulted in the "invalidat[ion] [of] state unemployment compensation rules that conditioned the availability of benefits upon an applicant's willingness to work under conditions forbidden by his religion."[20] But the Court did not view the *Sherbert–Frazee* line as providing the appropriate framework for analyzing free exercise cases as a general matter.[21] Instead, the Court implied that this set of cases represented a limited, anomalous exception to the announced rule; after all, the Court had "never invalidated any governmental action on the basis of the *Sherbert* test except the denial of unemployment compensation."[22]

The Court's point that the only successful non-hybrid free exercise challenges had involved unemployment compensation was surprising for at least two distinct reasons. First, Smith was merely arguing that the *Sherbert* test was applicable.[23] Even if many of the cases in which the test was triggered had not resulted in a victory for those claiming the exemption, that would not have somehow established the inapplicability of the test.[24] As Justice O'Connor noted in her concurrence in the judgment, "it is surely unusual to judge the vitality of a constitutional doctrine by looking to the win–loss record of the plaintiffs who happen to come before [the Court]."[25]

The Court's focus on the unemployment compensation exception was surprising for yet another reason—the claim at issue also involved unemployment compensation. Thus, it might seem that the facts of this case would trigger strict scrutiny, even assuming that the Court was correct that most cases implicating free exercise should not trigger that protective test.[26] However, the Court distinguished the cases in the *Sherbert–Frazee* line by suggesting that those protections should not be applied "to require exemptions from a generally applicable criminal law."[27]

The *Smith II* Court might have argued, as did Justice O'Connor in her concurring opinion, that the War Against Drugs involved such a compelling interest that the Oregon law should be upheld under strict scrutiny.[28] Yet, there was reason to believe that the

Oregon statute's failure to provide a religious exemption would not have passed muster under strict scrutiny.[29] First, the state did not even enforce the prohibition against religious users, undercutting the importance of the claimed state interest.[30] Second, the state did not provide any evidence that the religious use of peyote had ever harmed anyone,[31] which may have been due to the "carefully circumscribed ritual context in which respondents used peyote . . . [unlike] the irresponsible and unrestricted recreational use of unlawful drugs."[32] Not only did the church limit the context in which peyote would be used religiously, but it also prohibited peyote use for non-religious purposes. In addition, other states had afforded an exemption for religious use of peyote without being subject to some of the difficulties Oregon hypothesized, for example, that granting an exemption would open the floodgates to a whole host of claims.[33]

After noting that "[t]he *Sherbert* test . . . was developed in a context that lent itself to individualized governmental assessment of the reasons for the relevant conduct,"[34] the *Smith II* Court reasoned that the individualized assessment rule was inapplicable because the Oregon criminal law was exceptionless. But that was false—there was an exception under the Oregon criminal law if the controlled substance at issue was prescribed.[35] However, Oregon argued, the exception did not include prescriptions for Schedule 1 drugs.[36] Thus, the state claimed, while the statute did include an exception, it was not the right kind of exception to help the *Smith II* plaintiffs.

Yet, such an explanation should not have been thought persuasive if only because of how the analogous claim would have been treated in *Sherbert*. South Carolina had been unwilling to award unemployment compensation benefits to those who claimed to be unavailable for work, even though the state was willing to award unemployment compensation for those unable to work for other reasons.

The claim here is not that a physician had prescribed peyote for Smith or Black. Nor is the claim that the state would have honored such a prescription had one been obtained. The point is merely that the past jurisprudence did not permit the state to permit some exceptions and nonetheless to refuse to include a religious exception because the latter exception was not in the correct exception category. Else, South Carolina's refusal to award Sherbert unemployment compensation would have been upheld as long the exceptions South Carolina did recognize did not include an unavailable-to-work-on-that-particular-day exception.

Not only did the Oregon criminal law include an exception, but the Oregon unemployment compensation system involved individualized assessment, which was yet another reason that the *Sherbert* rule should have been triggered. Basically, not only was the *Smith II* Court's exposition of the past jurisprudence inaccurate but the very rule announced was misapplied.

The *Smith II* Court modified the prevailing jurisprudence in two ways: First, the Court announced that the "narrowly tailored to promote compelling interests" test was not triggered when neutral and generally applicable laws burdening free exercise were at issue.[37] The Court thereby weakened free exercise protections in that courts were no longer to apply the tougher test in many situations.[38] Second, the Court weakened the very test that it announced, because the challenge in *Smith II* was to the refusal to use the narrowly tailored to promote compelling state interests test in a context (unemployment compensation benefits denial) in which a case-by-case approach was utilized.[39]

Smith II has the potential to change the jurisprudence even more than is commonly appreciated. Basically, the existence of an unenforced law was enough to justify the denial of unemployment benefits. Suppose, however, that Oregon did not have such a law, even though such a law would not have violated constitutional guarantees. One would expect that Justice Scalia would use the greater includes the lesser argument to suggest that the fact that the state *could have* passed such a criminal law and then imposed a penalty would have justified the state denial of benefits, which after all would have been a lesser penalty.

Justice Scalia took something akin to this approach in his dissent in *Romer v. Evans*,[40] which involved a referendum that precluded the state of Colorado and its localities from affording anti-discrimination protection on the basis of sexual orientation.[41] At the time, the Supreme Court had not yet held that adult consensual relations are constitutionally protected.[42] Although Colorado had been one of the first states to repeal its sodomy law,[43] Justice Scalia nonetheless suggested that because the state *could have* passed such a law, the state was constitutionally permitted to pick out a group who would or might engage in sodomitical relations and preclude that group from receiving anti-discrimination protections.[44]

Justice Scalia's view did not win the day in *Romer*.[45] Nonetheless, his approach could be imported into the free exercise context. The constitutionality of criminalizing particular conduct (even if the state had not in fact criminalized it) would entail that the state did not violate constitutional guarantees by imposing civil burdens on individuals performing that conduct, even if they were doing so for religious reasons. Such a view would make free exercise protections even weaker than they already are.

As the *Smith II* Court pointed out, a salient difference between *Smith II* and those other cases was that *Smith II* involved a criminal statute whereas the other cases did not. Yet, the Court did not make clear why this difference was dispositive. Nor did the Court make clear why neutral and generally applicable laws were virtually immune from free exercise challenges. As Justice O'Connor noted in her concurrence,

> [t]here is nothing talismanic about neutral laws of general applicability or general criminal prohibitions, for laws neutral toward religion can coerce a person to violate his religious conscience or intrude upon his religious duties just as effectively as laws aimed at religion.[46]

The *Smith II* Court announced a test that did not capture the past jurisprudence. But that was unsurprising, because the pre-*Smith* jurisprudence was itself inconsistent with respect to what was required to justify the state imposition of a substantial burden on religious practice. While the *Sherbert* Court discussed the need for "some compelling state interest . . . [to] justif[y] the substantial infringement of appellant's First Amendment right,"[47] the *Bowen* Court suggested that even substantial burdens, if indirect, would be subjected to a lesser standard of review.

The *Smith II* Court misapplied the very test that it announced, both because the allegedly exceptionless criminal law had an exception built into it and because the unemployment compensation system whose judgment was being upheld was designed to make the individualized assessments that could easily have taken into account particular religious practices. It was as if the Court had a standard and result that it had in mind, and the Court was not going to permit the actual law or the facts of the case to get in the way of the Court's adopting and applying (or, perhaps, misapplying) that standard. That said, the Court did capture the spirit of the past jurisprudence when suggesting that courts are not competent to judge the centrality of religious beliefs.[48] Further, the Court was correct that applying a version of strict scrutiny that has not been watered down would mean that many laws will have to include religious exemptions in order to pass constitutional muster.[49]

Basically, the Court recognized that it had often upheld state practices burdening free exercise while allegedly employing strict scrutiny, and that in many of those cases the state had not been able to meet the burden that the strict scrutiny standard usually required. If the Court was going to have integrity when applying strict scrutiny and nonetheless be no less deferential to state practices burdening free exercise, then something would have to change. Instead of questioning which practices were religious or magnifying the alleged harms of the practice at issue, the Court instead modified the conditions under which state practices burdening but not targeting religious practices would trigger strict scrutiny. *Smith* was a clumsy attempt to force "a square peg into a round hole"[50] by pretending to offer a consistent account of an inconsistent jurisprudence and by ignoring that neither the law nor the facts before the Court provided a good opportunity for doing what the Court seemed so desperately to want to do.

Targeting religion

The focus of *Smith II* was on neutral and generally applicable laws. A separate question involved the appropriate standard of review for a statute *designed* to burden particular religious practices. The Court made clear in *Church of the Lukumi Babalu Aye, Incorporated v. City of Hialeah*[51] that the deferential *Smith* standard should not be applied when the state targets religious practices for unfavorable treatment.

At issue before the *Hialeah* Court were three ordinances adopted by the Hialeah City Council regulating "religious animal sacrifice."[52] The ordinances targeted the killing of animals for religious purposes for unfavorable treatment, although those ordinances included an express exemption for "kosher slaughter."[53] The Court noted that "few if any killings of animals are prohibited other than Santeria sacrifice"[54] under the Hialeah laws, suggesting that the ordinances were adopted specifically to burden Santeria rituals. Further, if consideration of the wording of the ordinances themselves was insufficient to justify an inference of targeting a particular religion, various city officials had stated that Santeria religious practice violated Biblical teachings[55] and that the religion was "a sin, 'foolishness,' 'an abomination to the Lord,' and the worship of 'demons.'"[56] Because of the animus manifested towards the Santeria religion and because the ordinances picked out Santeria practices for unfavorable treatment, the Court found the ordinances at issue in violation of free exercise guarantees.

The *Hialeah* Court affirmed "the general proposition that a law that is neutral and of general applicability need not be justified by a compelling governmental interest even if the law has the incidental effect of burdening a particular religious practice."[57] That said, "the protections of the Free Exercise Clause pertain if the law at issue discriminates against some or all religious beliefs or regulates or prohibits conduct because it is undertaken for religious reasons."[58] If there are religious exemptions for some but not for others, the law will be struck down if that exemption favors one religion over another. For example, "a municipal ordinance was applied in an unconstitutional manner when interpreted to prohibit preaching in a public park by a Jehovah's Witness but to permit preaching during the course of a Catholic mass or Protestant church service."[59]

The *Hialeah* Court cautioned that "laws burdening religious practice must be of general applicability."[60] Yet, the Court was not thereby suggesting that no differentiation is permissible—"[a]ll laws are selective to some extent."[61] Rather, the Court's point was that the "categories of selection are of paramount concern when a law has the incidental effect of burdening religious practice."[62]

Free exercise guarantees are violated "when a legislature decides that the governmental interests it seeks to advance are worthy of being pursued only against conduct with a religious motivation."[63] Targeting religious conduct because of its religious nature is exactly what the Free Exercise Clause precludes. "The principle that government, in pursuit of legitimate interests, cannot in a selective manner impose burdens only on conduct motivated by religious belief is essential to the protection of the rights guaranteed by the Free Exercise Clause."[64]

Hialeah clarifies a few issues. The decision illustrates that states will have great difficulty successfully defending statutes targeting religious practice in particular, but also reaffirms the *Smith II* approach—neutral and generally applicable laws will not trigger strict scrutiny merely because they incidentally impose a burden on religion.

The very year that the Court decided *Hialeah*, Congress reacted to *Smith II*[65] by passing the Religious Freedom Restoration Act (RFRA),[66] which was intended to require both state and federal governments to meet a very difficult test in order to justify their substantially burdening free exercise rights.[67] This difficult test would be triggered even when the government was not targeting religious practice but, instead, was burdening that practice as a result of a "rule of general applicability."[68] Congress specifically referred to the test used in *Sherbert* and *Yoder*, requiring that it be used to evaluate whether government burdening of free exercise was permissible.[69]

RFRA provides:

(a) Government shall not substantially burden a person's exercise of religion even if the burden results from a rule of general applicability, except as provided in subsection (b).
(b) Government may substantially burden a person's exercise of religion only if it demonstrates that application of the burden to the person—

  (1) is in furtherance of a compelling governmental interest; and
  (2) is the least restrictive means of furthering that compelling governmental interest.[70]

RFRA and the states

RFRA's constitutionality was tested in *City of Boerne v. Flores*.[71] Saint Peter Catholic Church, located in an historic district, wished to accommodate the needs of its growing congregation by expanding its facilities. When the request for a building permit was denied, the Archbishop brought suit to challenge that denial, arguing that RFRA precluded the city from denying the permit.

RFRA implicates a number of issues. To some extent, the law might be read as a rebuke of the *Smith II* Court for its (allegedly mistaken) interpretation of free exercise guarantees. The *Boerne* Court in a few different places implied that Congress had violated separation of powers by attempting to perform a judicial function, explaining: "Legislation which alters the meaning of the Free Exercise Clause cannot be said to be enforcing the Clause."[72] The Court also noted that "Congress does not enforce a constitutional right by changing what the right is,"[73] and that the Constitution has not accorded Congress "the power to determine what constitutes a constitutional violation."[74] Finally, the *Boerne* Court expressly reminded Congress that the judiciary has the responsibility of interpreting the Constitution.

> The judicial authority to determine the constitutionality of laws, in cases and controversies, is based on the premise that the "powers of the legislature are defined and limited; and that those limits may not be mistaken, or forgotten, the constitution is written."[75]

After suggesting that Congress had been attempting to usurp the powers of a coordinate branch when passing RFRA, the Court examined whether that law's limitations on the states passed constitutional muster. The Court began its analysis by noting that "the most far-reaching and substantial of RFRA's provisions [are] those which impose its requirements on the States."[76] The constitutionality of those requirements would be assessed by determining whether there was "a congruence and proportionality between the injury to be prevented or remedied and the means adopted to that end."[77]

The Supreme Court described the "[s]weeping coverage" of the Act,[78] which "displac[ed] laws and prohibit[ed] official actions of almost every description and regardless of subject matter."[79] To illustrate that point, the Court noted that "RFRA's restrictions apply to every agency and official of the Federal, State, and local Governments."[80] Further, "RFRA applies to all federal and state law, statutory or otherwise, whether adopted before or after its enactment."[81] Finally, "RFRA has no termination date or termination mechanism."[82]

Such an all-inclusive, open-ended remedy could only be proportional if the harms to be remedied were of great magnitude. But the legislative record supporting RFRA's passage did not include "examples of modern instances of generally applicable laws passed because of religious bigotry,"[83] and none of the incidents mentioned had occurred in the past four decades. This meant that the law lacked the requisite congruence and proportionality: "RFRA is so out of proportion to a supposed remedial or preventive object that it cannot be understood as responsive to, or designed to prevent, unconstitutional behavior."[84]

When explaining why RFRA was disproportionate, the *Boerne* Court wrote that "[i]f an objector can show a substantial burden on his free exercise, the State must demonstrate a compelling governmental interest and show that the law is the least restrictive means of furthering its interest."[85] Yet, that point alone does not establish that RFRA would severely limit the ability to legislate. For example, if it were extremely difficult to establish that a neutral law imposed a substantial burden on free exercise, then RFRA's protections would not often be triggered. However, "[c]laims that a law substantially burdens someone's exercise of religion will often be difficult to contest,"[86] which suggests that there might be many such claims. Further, the Court was not claiming that individuals would be falsely claiming that the laws substantially burdened their free exercise. On the contrary, "[i]t is a reality of the modern regulatory state that numerous state laws . . . impose a substantial burden on a large class of individuals,"[87] even though "the persons affected [may not] have been burdened any more than other citizens, let alone burdened because of their religious beliefs."[88]

Here, the Court was making several points. First, precisely because there is a great deal of regulation, many individuals might find their free exercise substantially burdened by various laws. Second, that burdening would not have been a result of the state having targeted religious practice, although the burdens would exist nonetheless. Third, while it might well be true that some of the individuals affected would have had their free exercise rights substantially burdened, it would also be true that many other individuals would have been burdened by the limitation, although members of this latter group would have chosen to engage in the practice at issue for non-religious reasons.

The *Boerne* Court offered a number of reasons that RFRA could not pass muster. Because "RFRA contradicts vital principles necessary to maintain separation of powers and the federal balance,"[89] the Court struck it down, at least as applied to the states. Perhaps because the issue was not before the Court, the decision does not make clear whether RFRA passes constitutional muster insofar as it imposes limitations on federal law.

If *Boerne* is interpreted as emphasizing the importance of maintaining the federal balance and preventing the federal government from imposing disproportionate limitations on the states, then the decision would seem to have relatively little import for the constitutionality of RFRA's limiting the ability of the federal government to impose substantial burdens on free exercise. If instead the decision is interpreted as striking down RFRA because Congress attempted to perform a judicial function (interpreting the Constitution) and thus violated separation of powers, then *Boerne* would have important implications for the constitutionality of RFRA as applied to federal law.

The *Boerne* Court's point that in our modern world many state laws inadvertently impose a substantial burden on religious practice is equally applicable to federal law, which means that many religious exemptions to federal laws and regulations may have to be accorded unless RFRA's reach is limited in some way. That said, however, there is an important difference between RFRA's limitations on the states and RFRA's limitations on the federal government. Were states to find RFRA unduly burdensome, they could not change the law themselves but, instead, would have to ask Congress to change it. In contrast, if Congress found that RFRA was proving unduly burdensome, Congress could amend the law or, perhaps, expressly exempt certain federal laws from RFRA limitations.

RLUIPA and the Establishment Clause

The *Boerne* Court's description of some of the defects of RFRA led Congress to try again by passing a law that was much narrower in scope.[90] Section Two of the Religious Land Use and Institutionalized Persons Act (RLUIPA) reads:

> No government shall impose or implement a land use regulation in a manner that imposes a substantial burden on the religious exercise of a person, including a religious assembly or institution, unless the government demonstrates that imposition of the burden on that person, assembly, or institution—
>
> (A) is in furtherance of a compelling governmental interest; and
> (B) is the least restrictive means of furthering that compelling governmental interest.[91]

This subsection applies where:

> (A) the substantial burden is imposed in a program or activity that receives Federal financial assistance, even if the burden results from a rule of general applicability;
> (B) the substantial burden affects, or removal of that substantial burden would affect, commerce with foreign nations, among the several States, or with Indian tribes, even if the burden results from a rule of general applicability; or
> (C) the substantial burden is imposed in the implementation of a land use regulation or system of land use regulations, under which a government makes, or has in place formal or informal procedures or practices that permit the government to make, individualized assessments of the proposed uses for the property involved.[92]

This section seemed focused on preventing religious institutions from receiving less favorable treatment than non-religious institutions. The law specifies that "[n]o government shall impose or implement a land use regulation in a manner that treats a religious assembly or institution on less than equal terms with a nonreligious assembly or institution."[93] Further, the law bars the government from "impos[ing] or implement[ing] a land use regulation that discriminates against any assembly or institution on the basis of religion or religious denomination."[94] In addition, the law prevents jurisdictions from entirely fencing out religious institutions—"No government shall impose or implement a land use regulation that—(A) totally excludes religious assemblies from a jurisdiction; or (B) unreasonably limits religious assemblies, institutions, or structures within a jurisdiction."[95]

Section 3 reads:

> No government shall impose a substantial burden on the religious exercise of a person residing in or confined to an institution, as defined in section 1997 of this title, even if the burden results from a rule of general applicability, unless the government demonstrates that imposition of the burden on that person—
>
> (1) is in furtherance of a compelling governmental interest; and
> (2) is the least restrictive means of furthering that compelling governmental interest.[96]

This law applies in cases where

> (1) the substantial burden is imposed in a program or activity that receives Federal financial assistance; or (2) the substantial burden affects, or removal of that substantial burden would affect, commerce with foreign nations, among the several States, or with Indian tribes.[97]

Congress was thus tying the law to its spending power and to its interstate commerce power.

RLUIPA's constitutionality was challenged in *Cutter v. Wilkinson*.[98] The Court explained that RLUIPA "protects institutionalized persons who are unable freely to attend to their religious needs and are therefore dependent on the government's permission and accommodation for exercise of their religion."[99] Rejecting that RLUIPA would "elevate accommodation of religious observances over an institution's need to maintain order and safety,"[100] the Court was confident that "RLUIPA would . . . be applied in an appropriately balanced way, with particular sensitivity to security concerns."[101] The Court rejected a challenge to RLUIPA's constitutionality under the Establishment Clause, and remanded the case for further proceedings.[102]

RFRA and the federal government

A year after *Cutter*, the Court addressed one of the questions left open in *Boerne*—whether RFRA was unconstitutional as a general matter or, instead, was unconstitutional only as applied to the states. The Court explained in *Gonzales v. O Centro Espirita Beneficente Uniao do Vegeta*[103] that the

> Religious Freedom Restoration Act of 1993 . . . prohibits the Federal Government from substantially burdening a person's exercise of religion, unless the Government "demonstrates that application of the burden to the person" represents the least restrictive means of advancing a compelling interest.[104]

At issue were the practices of a Christian Spiritist sect (UDV) whose practices included "receiving communion through hoasca . . . , a sacramental [hallucinogenic] tea made from two plants unique to the Amazon region."[105] United States Customs inspectors intercepted a shipment of hoasca and threatened to prosecute the sect. The UDV filed suit, claiming that the federal government violated RFRA when attempting to apply the Controlled Substances Act to prevent their sacramental use of the tea. The government argued that its actions passed muster under strict scrutiny because it was protecting UDV members, preventing diversion of the drugs to others, and meeting United States treaty obligations. The government further argued that there would be no way to cabin an exception for the UDV. Basically, the government argued that "there is no need to assess the particulars of the UDV's use or weigh the impact of an exemption for that specific use, because the Controlled Substances Act serves a compelling purpose and simply admits of no exceptions."[106]

The Court rejected the Government's position, instead suggesting that RFRA requires a "more focused" inquiry: the government must "demonstrate that the compelling interest test is satisfied through application of the challenged law 'to the person'—the particular claimant whose sincere exercise of religion is being substantially burdened."[107] Under this approach, a mere recitation of generalities will not suffice. The Court reasoned that because there was no indication that Congress had considered the particular use of hoasca at issue here, and because no evidence had been presented that permitting an exemption in this case would cause the same kind of administrative harm as would have occurred in *Lee* and *Braunfeld*, "the Government failed to demonstrate . . . a compelling interest in barring the UDV's sacramental use of hoasca."[108]

There is no small irony in the *O Centro* Court comparing the administrative harms at issue in that case with those presented in *Lee* and *Braunfeld*. In *Braunfeld*, the experience of other states indicated that a religious exemption could be afforded without imposing too great a burden on the state, and no evidence was presented in *Lee* that expanding the exemption to include businesses where all of the parties objected to participation in the Social Security system would be too burdensome. That said, *O Centro* might be understood to stand for the proposition that there must be evidence that Congress considered and ultimately rejected the desired exemption before the Court will accept that a compelling state interest is at stake and that the statute is sufficiently closely tailored to promote that interest.

The *Gonzales* opinion is important both because it applied RFRA to federal law, thereby indicating that RFRA was constitutional at least in that context, and because it required that the Government establish how "application of the burden to the person"[109] would be necessary to promote compelling state interests.[110] Federal law impacts many areas of individuals' lives and, for some, religion governs most or all aspects of life. Challenges to a federal law's failure to include an RFRA-required exemption should be expected to arise in a variety of areas. Further, because the Government must show why the refusal to accord an exemption to this particular individual is narrowly tailored to promote compelling interests,[111] one would expect the Government to have difficulty meeting this requirement in many instances.[112]

Conclusion

Smith II modified free exercise jurisprudence in important ways, modifying the circumstances under which the state burdening free exercise rights would trigger strict scrutiny. The *Smith II* Court did not offer a plausible interpretation of the past jurisprudence and seemed to misapply the very test that it had announced. Yet, the *Smith II* Court was correct to suggest that the strict scrutiny allegedly employed in many of the free exercise cases seemed rather weak, and it is not at all clear that *Smith* would have caused such an uproar if the Court had not announced a new test but instead had merely upheld the refusal to award unemployment compensation benefits using a weak version of strict scrutiny.

Congress reacted to *Smith II* by passing RFRA, seeking to reinstate the *Sherbert* strict scrutiny test in free exercise cases not involving hybrid rights. The Court struck down RFRA as applied to the states, which caused Congress to pass RLUIPA, a less robust statute also designed to reinstate *Sherbert* in certain situations. RLUIPA is still good law, as is RFRA where actions by the federal government allegedly imposing a substantial burden on free exercise rights are at issue.

The controversies surrounding the conditions under which free exercise exemptions must be granted have not abated. However, currently, controversies tend to arise under statutory rather than constitutional guarantees, because *Smith* is still good law with respect to the protections afforded by the Free Exercise Clause. Ironically, many of the difficulties arising under the Court's previous free exercise jurisprudence either have arisen or will likely arise when interpretations of statutory guarantees must be made, as the next chapter will illustrate.

Notes

1 Employment Division, Department of Human Resources of Oregon. v. Smith (*Smith II*), 494 U.S. 872 (1990).
2 See William P. Marshall, "In Defense of *Smith* and Free Exercise Revisionism," *University of Chicago Law Review* 58:308–27 (1991), p. 308 ("I defend *Smith's* rejection of the constitutionally compelled free exercise exemption."); James D. Gordon, III, "Free Exercise on the Mountaintop," *California Law Review* 79:91–116 (1991), p. 114 ("The Court wanted to reach its result in the worst way, and it succeeded."); Michael W. McConnell, "Free Exercise Revisionism and the *Smith* Decision," *University of Chicago Law Review* 57:1109–53 (1990), p. 1120 (suggesting that the Court's "use of precedent is troubling, bordering on the shocking").
3 Employment Division, Department of Human Resources of Oregon. v. Smith (*Smith I*), 485 U.S. 660, 670 (1988).
4 *Id.*
5 *Id.* at 672.
6 *Id.*
7 See *id.*
8 *Id.*
9 *Smith II*, 494 U.S. at 878.
10 *Id.* at 883 (citing *Sherbert*, 374 U.S. at 402–03).
11 *Id.* at 881.
12 *Id.* (citing *Cantwell*, 310 U.S. at 304–07).
13 *Id.*
14 *Id.* (citing *Wisconsin v. Yoder*, 406 U.S. 205 (1972)).
15 *Id.*
16 *Id.* at 882.
17 See *Braunfeld*, 366 U.S. at 599 (suggesting that Sunday closing laws pass muster under strict scrutiny); *United States v. Lee*, 455 U.S. 252 (1982) (suggesting that the refusal to exempt Amish employers from paying into the Social Security system passes muster under strict scrutiny).
18 See *Sherbert*, 374 U.S. at 410 ("Our holding today is only that South Carolina may not constitutionally apply the eligibility provisions so as to constrain a worker to abandon his religious convictions respecting the day of rest.").
19 *Smith II*, 494 U.S. at 883 (citing *Sherbert*, 374 U.S. at 402–03).
20 *Id.* (first citing *Sherbert*, 374 U.S. 398 (1963); then citing *Thomas v. Review Bd. of Indiana Employment Security Div.*, 450 U.S. 707 (1981); and then citing *Hobbie v. Unemployment Appeals Comm'n of Florida*, 480 U.S. 136 (1987)).
21 Christopher C. Lund, "In Defense of the Ministerial Exception," *North Carolina Law Review* 90:1–72 (2011), p. 58 ("Before the Court's decision in *Smith*, free exercise cases had been handled under a strict scrutiny framework. . . . Any burden on religious exercise had to be justified by the government demonstrating a compelling interest pursued by the least restrictive means. *Smith* changed that, saying that burdens on religious exercise required no justification as long as they were neutral and generally applicable.").
22 *Smith II*, 494 U.S. at 883.
23 *Id.* at 882–83 ("Respondents argue that even though exemption from generally applicable criminal laws need not automatically be extended to religiously motivated actors, at least the

claim for a religious exemption must be evaluated under the balancing test set forth in *Sherbert v. Verner*, 374 U.S. 398 (1963).").
24 *Cf. id.* at 896–97 (O'Connor, J., concurring) ("That we rejected the free exercise claims in those cases hardly calls into question the applicability of First Amendment doctrine in the first place.").
25 *Id.* at 897.
26 See Gordon, III (1991), at 114 ("The Court ... distinguished another line of cases as relating to unemployment compensation systems that examine individual reasons for applicants' conduct, when in fact *Smith* itself was such a case.").
27 *Smith II*, 494 U.S. at 884.
28 See *id.* at 907 (O'Connor, J., concurring in the judgment) ("I would therefore adhere to our established free exercise jurisprudence and hold that the State in this case has a compelling interest in regulating peyote use by its citizens and that accommodating respondents' religiously motivated conduct 'will unduly interfere with fulfillment of the governmental interest.'") (citing *Lee*, 455 U.S. at 259).
29 See *id.* at 909–10 (Blackmun, J., dissenting) ("[T]he state interest involved ... is not the State's broad interest in fighting the critical 'war on drugs' that must be weighed against respondents' claim, but the State's narrow interest in refusing to make an exception for the religious, ceremonial use of peyote.").
30 See *id.* at 911 ("[T]he State actually has not evinced any concrete interest in enforcing its drug laws against religious users of peyote. Oregon has never sought to prosecute respondents, and does not claim that it has made significant enforcement efforts against other religious users of peyote.").
31 *Id.* at 911–12 ("The State proclaims an interest in protecting the health and safety of its citizens from the dangers of unlawful drugs. It offers, however, no evidence that the religious use of peyote has ever harmed anyone.").
32 *Id.* at 913.
33 *Id.* at 917 ("Almost half the States, and the Federal Government, have maintained an exemption for religious peyote use for many years, and apparently have not found themselves overwhelmed by claims to other religious exemptions.").
34 *Id.* at 884.
35 See *id.* at 874 ("Oregon law prohibits the knowing or intentional possession of a "controlled substance" unless the substance has been prescribed by a medical practitioner. Ore.Rev.Stat. § 475.992(4) (1987).").
36 Douglas Laycock and Steven T. Collis, "Generally Applicable Law and the Free Exercise of Religion," *Nebraska Law Review* 95:1–27 (2016), p. 22 ("'Controlled substance' covers a wide range of drugs, and Oregon told the Court that the exception did not apply to Schedule I drugs, including peyote.").
37 John D. Inazu, "More Is More: Strengthening Free Exercise, Speech, and Association," *Minnesota Law Review* 99:485–534 (2014), pp. 498–99 ("*Smith* also introduced another significant doctrinal change in free exercise law: the move from strict scrutiny to rational basis scrutiny for claims challenging generally applicable laws.").
38 See Conor B. Dugan, "Religious Liberty in Spain and the United States: A Comparative Study," *Notre Dame Law Review* 78:1675–730 (2003), p. 1718 ("[T]he *Smith* decision ... weakened free exercise protections.").
39 See *Oregon Revised Statutes* § 657.176(2) (2015) (specifying the conditions under which an individual would not be eligible to receive benefits).
40 517 U.S. 620, 636 (1996) (Scalia, J., dissenting).
41 See *id.* at 624.
42 See *Lawrence v. Texas*, 539 U.S. 558 (2003).
43 See *Romer*, 517 U.S. at 645 (Scalia, J., dissenting) ("Colorado not only is one of the 25 States that have repealed their antisodomy laws, but was among the first to do so.") (citing 1971 *Colorado Session Laws* 388).
44 *Id.* at 642 ("If it is rational to criminalize the conduct, surely it is rational to deny special favor and protection to those with a self-avowed tendency or desire to engage in the conduct.").
45 See *id.* at 635 ("Amendment 2 violates the Equal Protection Clause.").

46 *Smith II*, 494 U.S. at 901 (O'Connor, J., concurring in the judgment).
47 *Sherbert*, 374 U.S. at 406.
48 See *Smith II*, 494 U.S. at 887 ("Judging the centrality of different religious practices is akin to the unacceptable 'business of evaluating the relative merits of differing religious claims.'") (citing *Lee*, 455 U.S. at 263 n.2 (Stevens, J., concurring)).
49 *Id*. at 888 ("Moreover, if 'compelling interest' really means what it says (and watering it down here would subvert its rigor in the other fields where it is applied), many laws will not meet the test.").
50 *Rowland v. California Men's Colony, Unit II Men's Advisory Council*, 506 U.S. 194, 200 (1993).
51 *Church of the Lukumi Babalu Aye v. City of Hialeah*, 508 U.S. 520 (1993).
52 *Id*. at 527 (noting that the council had "adopted three substantive ordinances addressing the issue of religious animal sacrifice").
53 *Id*. at 536.
54 *Id*.
55 See *id*. at 541. "Councilman Mejides indicated that he was 'totally against the sacrificing of animals' and distinguished kosher slaughter because it had a 'real purpose.' The 'Bible says we are allowed to sacrifice an animal for consumption,' he continued, 'but for any other purposes, I don't believe that the Bible allows that.'" *Id*.
56 *Id*.
57 *Id*. at 531 (citing *Employment Division. v. Smith*, 494 U.S. 872 (1990)).
58 *Id*. at 532 (citing *Braunfeld v. Brown*, 366 U.S. at 607).
59 *Id*. at 533 (citing *Fowler v. Rhode Island*, 345 U.S. 67 (1953)).
60 *Id*. at 542 (citing *Smith II*, 494 U.S. at 879–81).
61 *Id*.
62 *Id*.
63 *Id*. at 542–43.
64 *Id*. at 543.
65 *City of Boerne v. Flores*, 521 U.S. 507, 512–13 (1997) ("Congress enacted RFRA in direct response to the Court's decision in *Employment Division, Department of Human Resources of Oregon v. Smith*, 494 U.S. 872 (1990).").
66 42 *United States Code* § 2000bb *et seq.* (2012).
67 See *Boerne*, 521 U.S. at 507 ("RFRA prohibits '[g]overnment' from 'substantially burden[ing]' a person's exercise of religion even if the burden results from a rule of general applicability unless the government can demonstrate the burden '(1) is in furtherance of a compelling governmental interest; and (2) is the least restrictive means of furthering that . . . interest.' 42 *United States Code* § 2000bb-1. RFRA's mandate applies to any branch of Federal or State Government.").
68 See *id*. at 507.
69 See *Burwell v. Hobby Lobby Stores, Incorporated*, 134 U.S. 2751, 2784–85 (2014).
70 Religious Freedom Restoration Act, 107 Stat 1488, 42 *United States Code* § 2000bb-3 (1993).
71 *City of Boerne v. Flores*, 521 U.S. 507 (1997)
72 *Id*. at 519.
73 *Id*.
74 *Id*.
75 *Id*. at 516 (citing *Marbury v. Madison*, 5 U.S. 137 (1803)).
76 *Id*.
77 *Id*. at 520.
78 *Id*. at 508.
79 *Id*. at 509.
80 *Id*. at 532 (citing 42 *United States Code* § 2000bb-2(1)).
81 *Id*. (citing 42 *United States Code* § 2000bb-3(a)).
82 *Id*.
83 *Id*. at 530.
84 *Id*. at 532.
85 *Id*. at 534.

86 *Id.* (citing *Smith II*, 494 U.S. at 887).
87 *Id.* at 535.
88 *Id.*
89 *Id.* at 536.
90 *Sossamon v. Texas*, 563 U.S. 277, 281 (2011) ("RLUIPA is less sweeping in scope.").
91 42 *United States Code* § 2000cc(a)(1)
92 42 *United States Code* § 2000cc (a)(2)
93 42 *United States Code* § 2000cc(b)(1)
94 42 *United States Code* § 2000cc(b)(2)
95 42 *United States Code* § 2000cc(b)(3)
96 42 *United States Code* § 2000cc-1(a)
97 42 *United States Code* § 2000cc-1(b)
98 *Cutter v. Wilkinson*, 544 U.S. 709 (2005).
99 *Id.* at 721.
100 *Id.* at 722.
101 *Id.*
102 *Id.* at 726.
103 *Gonzales v. O Centro Espirita Beneficente Uniao do Vegeta*, 546 U.S. 418 (2006).
104 *Id.* at 423 (citing 42 *United States Code* § 2000bb-1(b)).
105 *Id.* at 425.
106 *Id.* at 430.
107 *Id.* at 430–31 (citing 42 *United States Code* § 2000bb-1(b) (2012)).
108 *Id.* at 439.
109 Religious Freedom Restoration Act, 107 Stat 1488, 42 *United States Code* § 2000bb-3b (2000).
110 Amit Shah, "The Impact of *Gonzales v. O Centro Espirita Beneficente Uniao Do Vegetal*, 546 U.S. 418 (2006)," *Rutgers Journal of Law & Religion* 10:4–29 (2008), p. 12 ("The Court specifically indicated that the Government must show with specific particularity how even strong governmental interests would be harmed by allowing an exemption.").
111 Aaron D. Bieber, "Constitutional Law—the Supreme Court Can't Have It Both Ways Under RFRA: The Tale of Two Compelling Interest Tests," *Wyoming Law Review* 7:225–57 (2007), pp. 244–45 ("RFRA and its strict scrutiny test required the government to demonstrate that the compelling interest test is satisfied by applying the challenged law 'to the person,' the particular claimant, whose sincere exercise of religion is being substantially burdened."); Jonathan T. Tan, "Nonprofit Organizations, For-Profit Corporations, and the HHS Mandate: Why the Mandate Does Not Satisfy RFRA's Requirements," *University of Richmond Law Review* 47:1301–70 (2013), p. 1333 ("Under RFRA, a law is invalid if it imposes a substantial burden on a person's exercise of religion and the government fails to prove that it is the least restrictive means of furthering a compelling government interest."); Edward J.W. Blatnik, "No RFRAF Allowed: The Status of the Religious Freedom Restoration Act's Federal Application in the Wake of *City of Boerne v. Flores*," *Columbia Law Review* 98:1410–60 (1998), p. 1449 ("RFRA, in particular, assigns courts the duty of determining whether the claimant's religious exercise has been substantially burdened, and, if so, whether the government has a compelling interest for applying the law in question to this person, and, even if so, whether it has chosen the least restrictive means of doing so.").
112 Noah Butsch Baron, "'There Can Be No Assumption . . .': Taking Seriously Challenges to Polygamy Bans in Light of Developments in Religious Freedom Jurisprudence," *Georgetown Journal of Gender & Law* 16:323–46 (2015), p. 341 ("[T]he application of the challenged law 'to the person'—the particular claimant whose sincere exercise of religion is being substantially burdened . . . is significantly more difficult to meet, and would require an individualized analysis for each claim brought under RFRA.") (quoting *O Centro*, 546 U.S. at 420).

7 Corporate conscience

Worried that *Smith II* might permit state burdens on free exercise to be imposed too easily, Congress passed both RFRA and RLUIPA to restore some of the safeguards that had (allegedly) existed prior to that decision. These laws differ in certain respects. Nonetheless, some of the key terms of the laws are defined in the same way, which means that the construction of one of the laws may have important implications for the other's construction.

The Court has not revisited whether *Smith II* was rightly decided. Instead, the Court has offered interpretations of RFRA and RLUIPA to establish when federal statutory protections for free exercise have been violated. But the interpretations of federal statute have been based in part on the Court's previous free exercise jurisprudence, which means that some of those flawed interpretations have been imported into the statutory interpretations. Regrettably, the Court has offered implausible constructions of congressional intent and has turned a blind eye to some of the implications of the statutes so construed. The foreseeable result is that these decisions will have unintended and undesirable consequences and, in addition, may well lead to the kind of chaotic and disingenuous jurisprudence that *Smith II* was attempting to avoid.

On corporate consciences and substantial burdens

Congress announced that it was trying to reinstate some of the religious protections that had existed prior to *Smith*. Yet, one of noteworthy aspect of the pre-*Smith* jurisprudence was that many religious organizations were not afforded exemptions if doing so might give them a competitive advantage, and the Court would not solely focus on the costs to the state of granting an exemption to a *particular* individual when trying to gauge the protections afforded by the Free Exercise Clause. The Court's recent interpretations of federal law have made free exercise protections in some instances more robust that they were prior to *Smith II*, and the Court has not yet shown an appreciation of the implications of that more robust interpretation.

Corporate conscience exemptions

At issue in *Burwell v. Hobby Lobby Stores, Incorporated*[1] was whether the Affordable Care Act substantially burdened the free exercise rights of certain for-profit corporations. These for-profit companies objected to providing health insurance that might result in the destruction of an embryo, and argued that "the HHS [Health and Human Services] mandate demands that they engage in conduct that seriously violates their religious beliefs."[2]

Conesta Wood Specialties is a for-profit corporation with hundreds of employees. The members of the Hahns family are devout Mennonites, and they "exercise sole ownership of the closely held business; they control its board of directors and hold all of its voting shares."[3] They believe that they have to run their business in light of their religious beliefs and principles. One of those principles is that it is immoral to terminate human life after conception, and they are thus unwilling to include certain sorts of contraception that they consider abortifacients within the health insurance coverage for their employees.

The Greens operated Hobby Lobby Stores, a national chain with over 10,000 employees. The Greens retain exclusive control of the company. They also believe that it is immoral to end human life after conception, and they too object to covering certain sorts of contraception under the insurance plan provided for their employees.

The *Hobby Lobby* Court addressed whether RFRA prohibits the United States Department of Health and Human Services ("HHS") from requiring the companies to "provide health-insurance coverage for methods of contraception that violate the sincerely held religious beliefs of the companies' owners."[4] The Court focused on whether RFRA covered closely held for-profit corporations and whether the law's protections were triggered by the HHS requirement.

The issue arose because RFRA limits the conditions under which the federal government may "substantially burden a person's exercise of religion."[5] But the Affordable Care Act imposes requirements on corporations that arguably burdens free exercise, so it was necessary for the Court to determine whether RFRA protections are also extended to for-profit corporations.

RFRA does not specifically address who qualifies as a "person." To help determine whether RFRA protections are triggered when the (possible) free exercise rights of corporations are implicated, the Court looked to the Dictionary Act and found that it includes a variety of types of entities as persons: "corporations, companies, associations, firms, partnerships, societies, and joint stock companies, as well as individuals."[6] The Court noted that statutes are sometimes limited in focus to natural persons (human beings), although the Court was incredulous that the term might be thought to include natural persons and non-profit corporations, but not for-profit corporations.

Two issues might be distinguished: (1) whether Congress had religious non-profits or, perhaps, natural persons in mind when passing RFRA, and (2) whether it is reasonable to accord RFRA protections to non-profit but not for-profit corporations. The former might be determined at least in part by considering the Congressional Record. For example, various members of Congress suggested that they supported RFRA to protect the free exercise rights of natural rather than artificial persons.[7] Yet, merely because some members of Congress wanted to protect only natural persons does not mean that they all had that intent. Nor does it mean that the best interpretation of the law is that it should only be construed to protect natural persons.

Whether or not Congress intended to limit RFRA's protections to natural persons, a separate question is whether HHS might reasonably distinguish between non-profit and for-profit corporations. HHS accorded RFRA protections to religious non-profits, and it might be argued that religious, closely held, for-profit corporations deserved similar treatment.[8] That issue might be analyzed by examining whether there are any relevant differences between the two kinds of entities.[9]

The Court held that RFRA applied to closely held, for-profit corporations. In dissent, Justice Ginsburg argued that the same reasoning would establish that publicly traded corporations are also persons for RFRA purposes. The Court did not deny that RFRA applied to publicly traded corporations, instead offering the consolation that corporate giants like International Business Machines Incorporated (IBM) or the General Electric Company would not often assert RFRA claims. After all, "the idea that unrelated shareholders—including institutional investors with their own set of stakeholders—would agree to run a corporation under the same religious beliefs seems improbable."[10]

Yet, the Court's assurance that publicly traded corporations will not often seek RFRA exemptions is not particularly comforting for at least two distinct reasons. Basically, the Court has suggested that because it is too difficult to distinguish plausibly between non-profits and closely held for-profits and too difficult to distinguish between closely held, for-profits and publicly traded corporations, Congress must have meant to protect them all. Yet, it seems incredible to believe that Congress had intended to protect companies like General Motors when passing RFRA. Precisely because that is so, Congress presumably intended to draw the line between natural and artificial persons or, perhaps, between natural persons and religious non-profits on the one hand and for-profits on the other.

There is an additional reason that there is cold comfort in the Court's assurance that publicly traded companies will not often seek RFRA exemptions. The Court is implicitly recognizing that RFRA also applies to publicly traded corporations, which means that large corporations affecting the lives of many customers and employees may be able to invoke RFRA protections and adversely impact countless individuals. Further, the consolation offered by the Court that such corporations are unlikely to be run under one particular set of religious beliefs does not provide much of a safeguard. While the shareholders of the respective closely held corporations asking for the exemption in *Hobby Lobby* all shared many of the same values, there is no requirement that everyone share the same values before RFRA protections are triggered.

Consider the *Hobby Lobby* Court's focus, which was not on the whole set of religious values embraced by the shareholders but on one value in particular—whether the challenged requirement might result in the destruction of an embryo. Shareholders might disagree about a variety of issues so that the corporation would not be run in accord with one set of values. Nonetheless, there might be one value that individuals of several faiths share, which would mean that the corporation could seek the RFRA exemption insofar as that value was implicated, even if there was no agreement about other values. For example, historically, people of a variety of faiths opposed interracial marriage. There might be other biases that people of a variety of faiths might currently share. Thus, even if the Court is correct that large corporations would be unlikely to be run according to one religious code, that would not preclude such corporations from seeking RFRA exemptions.

Even if shareholders (of differing religious backgrounds) were to agree that a particular practice would contravene their sincerely held religious beliefs, the Government could still seek to establish that the refusal to accord an exemption was narrowly tailored to promote compelling state interests. Thus, a universal shareholder agreement about one issue would not guarantee that the exemption would have to be accorded. In such a case, however, the Government would still have to pass a very difficult test to justify its refusal to grant the exemption.

Suppose there is no universal shareholder agreement about all religious values or even about one value. Nevertheless, RFRA protections might be triggered. In *Hobby Lobby*, the Court did not even explore what percentage of those objecting to being forced to engage in a practice had to do so for religious reasons. Thus, suppose that some shareholders have a sincere religious objection to paying for certain services, such as birth control, while others (not sharing that view) nonetheless welcome having the costs at issue shifted to another payer. A majority of shareholders might approve of a particular policy, such as shifting the costs of insurance to some third party, even though relatively few shareholders have religious objections to providing that insurance. Given the diversity of religious beliefs in the United States, it would not be difficult to find someone who has a sincere religious objection to any number of practices, and the Court did not discuss the number or percentage of shareholders that must have religious objections to the practice at issue to trigger RFRA protections.

Who can seek an exemption under RFRA? That is unclear, although the Court is well aware that companies' owners have religious differences of opinion with or without RFRA. How should such religious disputes within corporations be resolved? The Court noted in *Hobby Lobby* that "[s]tate corporate law provides a ready means for resolving any conflicts by, for example, dictating how a corporation can establish its governing structure."[11] But the Court's reference to state corporation law helps illustrate why the Court was engaging in misdirection when pointing to the very low probability that all shareholders would subscribe to the same religious tenets. If the practice deemed to contravene religious principles were something that fell with ordinary business operations, that practice would not be subject to shareholder control through a proxy fight but, instead, would be left to those who manage the company.

Suppose that those managing the company do not agree about the morality of a particular practice. As long as some (one?) had moral scruples about providing certain benefits and others believed that not providing that benefit would contribute to the corporation's bottom line, then RFRA might require that an exemption be granted. The *Hobby Lobby* Court noted, "HHS has not pointed to any example of a publicly traded corporation asserting RFRA rights, and numerous practical restraints would likely prevent that from occurring."[12] However, there might be benefits to taking advantage of this cost-shifting as long as at least one individual had sincere religious objections to providing particular benefits. Thus, the point is not that the claim would be insincere,[13] but rather that the great diversity of religious belief would make it more likely that some relevant individual or individuals would have the requisite religious belief so that the company could seek an exemption.

Suppose that the matter at issue was not something mundane that should be left to management but, instead, something viewed as involving a significant policy that should be subject to shareholder direction, for example, whether shareholders should be allowed to include within proxy materials a resolution that a company not discriminate on the basis of sexual orientation. Even when federal law is interpreted to require a proxy vote on certain matters that raise significant social policy issues, a separate question is whether that law itself is subject to a required RFRA exemption, since the failure to afford an exemption might burden management's religious beliefs and practices. Would such a burden be substantial and thus trigger RFRA guarantees? That would have to be worked out in the courts, although the *Hobby Lobby* Court did not set a particularly high bar when discussing what would qualify as a substantial burden.

The Court noted: "Health insurance is a benefit that employees value."[14] If a part of the cost of providing that insurance might be shifted to the government, the company might receive some competitive advantage in its efforts to "retain[ ] and attract[ ] skilled workers."[15] How much of an advantage? That is unclear, although the Court did not quantify the advantage when citing it as a reason to refuse to require the exemption in *Braunfeld*. So, too, the Court did not quantify the competitive advantage that might otherwise have been accrued when holding that the Free Exercise Clause did not require that the Tony and Susan Alamo Foundation be exempted from FLSA requirements.

Can a publicly traded corporation engage in religious exercise?[16] The Court rejected the notion that corporations as such are unable to engage in religious exercise and that non-profits are relevantly dissimilar to for-profits.[17] For example, the Court considered an argument offered by the dissent that "nonprofit corporations are special because furthering their religious 'autonomy . . . often furthers individual religious freedom as well.'"[18] But for-profits can further individual religious freedom as well,[19] and permitting the companies at issue to "assert RFRA claims protects the religious liberty of the Greens and the Hahns."[20]

While non-profit and for-profit corporations are distinguishable in that the latter but not the former seek to make a profit,[21] that difference does not establish that for-profits cannot engage in free exercise. The Court noted that "modern corporate law does not require for-profit corporations to pursue profit at the expense of everything else, and many do not do so."[22] For example, corporations may support "charitable causes" or "may exceed the requirements of local law regarding working conditions and benefits."[23] But if they can do that, then "there is no apparent reason why they may not further religious objectives as well."[24]

This suggests yet another way that a publicly traded corporation might assert free exercise rights—by implementing or modifying policies so that they are in accord with the sincerely held religious beliefs of the CEO. Whether a CEO would be permitted to do this is a different matter—that might depend on how valuable her services were thought to be.[25] But the question at hand is whether Congress intended RFRA to include this kind of case.

That corporations might promote religious objectives might seem wise as a matter of public policy. Many religious objectives seem worthy of pursuit whether or not done for religious reasons, for example, providing food and clothing to the poor. Yet, religious objectives might include a wide range of goals. Given the diversity of religious belief and practice, it should not be thought that all religions share the same objectives. Thus, religions might promote clothing and feeding the poor but might also promote leaving the needy alone because they allegedly deserve their fate. While some religious views promote the common good, others do not, and it should not be assumed that religiously motivated conduct cannot be harmful.

Once holding that RFRA applied to closely held for-profit corporations, the Court had to determine whether requiring those corporations to "provide health-insurance coverage for methods of contraception that violate the sincerely held religious beliefs of the companies' owners"[26] sufficed to meet the threshold requirement that their free exercise rights were "substantially burden[ed]."[27] HHS had argued

> that the connection between what the objecting parties must do (provide health-insurance coverage for four methods of contraception that may operate after the fertilization of an egg) and the end that they find to be morally wrong (destruction of an embryo) [was] simply too attenuated [to constitute a substantial burden].[28]

The Court rejected HHS's contention, instead deferring to the corporations' claim that the burden imposed was substantial. These "companies sincerely believe that providing the insurance coverage demanded by the HHS regulations lies on the forbidden side of the line, and it is not for us to say that their religious beliefs are mistaken or insubstantial."[29] Thus, the Court suggested that the corporation's sincere beliefs that a particular practice imposed a substantial burden may itself have been enough to establish that the burden had been met.

That said, the Court did not simply announce that deference was required and then say nothing else. Instead, the Court offered some reasons to believe that the burdens imposed were indeed substantial. The Court noted that the corporate owners "have a sincere religious belief that life begins at conception."[30] Because of those beliefs, the owners objected "on religious grounds to providing health insurance that covers methods of birth control that . . . *may* result in the destruction of an embryo."[31] The Court then explained that by requiring these "companies to arrange for such coverage, the HHS mandate demands that they engage in conduct that seriously violates their religious beliefs."[32]

While the Court's analysis might initially seem appealing, further reflection makes it much less so. The implicit test is very forgiving—if an employer is required to do something that *might* enable an employee to do something that contravenes the employer's faith, then the religious beliefs of the employer have been substantially burdened as long as she believes the burden substantial. The Court does not now treat what *might* happen as having such constitutional significance in other contexts implicating religion. For example, in *Mitchell v. Helms*,[33] the Court considered whether Establishment Clause guarantees had been violated when federal funds were distributed to religious schools to make purchases including "computers, and computer software, and also slide and movie projectors, overhead projectors, television sets, tape recorders, VCR's, projection screens, laboratory equipment, maps, globes, filmstrips, slides, and cassette recordings."[34] One of the difficulties was that the items purchased with federal monies were being used for religious indoctrination. While Justice O'Connor rejected in her concurrence in the judgment that "actual diversion of government aid to religious indoctrination is consistent with the Establishment Clause,"[35] she reasoned that the actual diversion in the case at issue had been *de minimis* and thus was not constitutionally significant.

The *Mitchell* plurality offered a different approach.

> So long as the governmental aid is not itself "unsuitable for use in the public schools because of religious content," and eligibility for aid is determined in a constitutionally permissible manner, any use of that aid to indoctrinate cannot be attributed to the government and is thus not of constitutional concern.[36]

Instead, the indoctrination would be attributed to the private party. Thus, because the government was not distributing sectarian materials to schools, but instead something with no particular religious significance (money), the government did not violate Establishment Clause guarantees.

How would the *Mitchell* plurality's approach work in the *Hobby Lobby* context? Because the insurance might not in fact have been used to cause death post-conception, it is not even clear that the relevant guarantees would be triggered—the mere possibility that monies would be used in a non-approved way would not suffice to trigger the relevant protections. Suppose that the insurance had *once* been used to acquire contraception that caused death post-conception. Even so, that single usage might be viewed as *de minimis* and also as not triggering the relevant protections.

Suppose that the insurance purchased by the corporation had been used by many employees to acquire contraception that caused post-conception death. The decision (and the moral burden) would not be attributed to Hobby Lobby, but instead to the individual employee who chose to use the contraception in question. Just as the alleged fault in *Mitchell* (promoting religion) was not attributed to the government and thus did not trigger the relevant protections, the alleged fault at issue in *Hobby Lobby* (causing the post-conception death of innocents) would be attributable to the employee rather than the employer, and thus would not trigger the relevant guarantees.

Hobby Lobby might claim that it would be religiously offensive to provide monies that would be used even indirectly to cause a death post-conception. But that argument, if credited, would justify a great deal, for example, the corporation's imposing limitations on how the employees used their salaries if the corporation had religious objections to employees using their wages to purchase spirits or items preventing conception or birth.

What could be said to a corporation to establish that there was no substantial burden on its free exercise if the corporation were precluded from limiting employee use of earnings in objectionable ways?[37] After *Hobby Lobby*, it is no answer to say that it was the employee rather than the corporation who was purchasing the forbidden items.

HHS argued that the link between Hobby Lobby and the use of the forbidden contraceptives was too attenuated, but the Court disagreed. The Court's deference to the corporation's beliefs suggests that as long as a corporation sincerely believes that its religious principles are contravened by an employee's use of her salary in a particular way, then any federal law that precludes the corporation from putting restrictions on how salaries are used might itself trigger RFRA protections. A separate issue would be whether there is a compelling interest in assuring that individuals can use their wages as they wish, so that they can purchase alcohol, movie tickets, books, or other items that might run afoul of religious restrictions, but the Court's rationale suggests that RFRA might have to take account of sincere religious beliefs that preclude being indirectly involved in what is viewed as sinful behavior.

The Court's implicit approach to determining whether something constitutes a substantial burden on religion—does the believer (sincerely) claim that it constitutes such a burden?—is quite forgiving. In addition, the Court suggested yet another method by which to establish that a substantial burden had been imposed, namely, focusing on the penalty for non-compliance.[38]

The *Hobby Lobby* Court remarked that if the corporations "do not comply, they will pay a very heavy price—as much as $1.3 million per day, or about $475 million per year, in the case of one of the companies."[39] After noting the substantial financial penalty that would be imposed, the Court commented, "If these consequences do not amount to a substantial burden, it is hard to see what would."[40]

Yet, it is not at all clear that these consequences amount to a substantial burden on free exercise. Consider a religious organization that is required to pay wages to its employees.[41] The money that is being spent on employees might be used in other ways that would promote the organization's religious values. Assume for purposes here that the Court (or perhaps the corporation itself) would reject that requiring a corporation to pay wages to its employees constitutes a substantial burden on free exercise, even though the money saved from not paying wages would otherwise be used to promote religious objectives. Suppose, in addition, that a hefty fine was associated with the failure to observe the wage laws. The question would be whether this fine (which would be imposed on any similarly sized employer failing to follow the law) would itself make the wage law at issue a substantial burden on religion, thereby triggering RFRA guarantees by transforming what would not have been a substantial burden on religion into one.

If the fine itself would be enough to trigger the relevant guarantees, then the only fines that could be imposed without triggering RFRA would be those that would not be particularly onerous and thus not burdensome to pay. But such an approach would almost guarantee the inefficacy of federal law, at least as far as religious organizations were concerned.

Suppose that the State knew that its imposition of non-onerous fines on corporations as a general matter would induce those corporations to violate the law. Rather than promote law-breaking, the state might try to impose more onerous penalties for violations of wage laws on those corporations that could not invoke RFRA protections (those that could not claim that the onerous penalties for breaking the law constituted a substantial burden on religion). This would at the very least create an appearance of favoritism of religion (because religious corporations would be subject to lesser penalties for the same crimes); whether such favoritism violated constitutional guarantees would be a separate matter.[42]

Suppose that Hobby Lobby sincerely opposes being part of a process that might result in what it views as an immoral act. But that might mean that Hobby Lobby not only does not want to pay for the insurance providing contraception coverage, but also does not want to be complicit in a system that results in someone else paying for that service. In that event, imposing a minimal duty on an organization to notify the government of its moral compunctions so that other arrangements might be made is itself problematic.[43] Such a duty might significantly burden an organization's religious beliefs that it should not participate in any way in an immoral process. Because the *Hobby Lobby* Court implied that undermining religious beliefs in any way might constitute substantially burdening them, the Court seems to be interpreting RFRA's substantial burden requirement as having been met as long as the organization sincerely says that its beliefs have been substantially burdened by a federal requirement. If that is so and if the triggered test is not watered down, then it seems likely that many laws will now require exemptions. While a federal requirement imposing a substantial burden on free exercise would still be permissible if narrowly tailored to promote a compelling interest, it would be surprising that Congress intended RFRA's *substantial* burden requirement to be satisfied as long as the organization with religious objections said that it was.

Suppose that a law substantially burdens free exercise. What must the government establish in order for the law to be upheld? The *Hobby Lobby* Court suggested that the government must show why the refusal to grant this particular exemption would undermine important interests, and was confident that the government's requiring the companies to provide the insurance was not the "least restrictive means of furthering th[e] compelling governmental interest."[44] Why not? Because the

> most straightforward way of doing this would be for the Government to assume the cost of providing the four contraceptives at issue to any women who are unable to obtain them under their health-insurance policies due to their employers' religious objections.[45]

Yet, it is difficult to see why that would not be the most "straightforward way" in many instances. For example, suppose that a company objected to providing insurance for immunizations. Would an exemption be required? The *Hobby Lobby* Court explained:

> Our decision should not be understood to hold that an insurance-coverage mandate must necessarily fall if it conflicts with an employer's religious beliefs. Other coverage requirements, such as immunizations, may be supported by different interests (for example, the need to combat the spread of infectious diseases) and may involve different arguments about the least restrictive means of providing them.[46]

But this is a surprising response. Presumably, the company would not be objecting to its employees getting vaccinated but, instead, to its being forced to pay for the vaccinations. The need to combat the spread of disease simply does not speak to who should foot the bill for promoting the public health, so the Court's response is at best a non sequitur. The company could easily say that the most straightforward way of providing vaccinations would be for the government to assume the cost.

The Court's approach when evaluating what constitutes a substantial burden on religion is extremely deferential. An entity need only sincerely claim that a law or regulation imposes a substantial religious burden to meet the relevant standard. Even if an individual cannot claim that the religious burden is substantial, RFRA protections may nonetheless be triggered if the burden imposed for the failure to comply is itself viewed as too onerous. But this very deferential standard almost invites corporations to seek RFRA exemptions to a variety of federal statutes.

Corporations are subject to numerous federal laws, and *Hobby Lobby* creates a great deal of uncertainty with respect to the exemptions that must be accorded under RFRA. Consider the Family and Medical Leave Act (FMLA),[47] whose purposes include "entitl[ing] employees to take reasonable leave for medical reasons, for the birth or adoption of a child, and for the care of a child, spouse, or parent who has a serious health condition."[48]

Suppose that a corporation has religious objections to aiding particular family members, for example, children who were produced through assisted reproductive technologies (ART), because the corporation believes that the use of such technologies is immoral. Or, perhaps, the corporation has religious objections to divorce and believes that permitting an employee to take off time to care for his or her current, previously divorced spouse would be contrary to religious teachings. Because FMLA requirements would in these cases contravene sincerely held religious beliefs, federal law would be imposing a substantial burden on the corporation's religious exercise.

Courts would have to address whether refusing to exempt such a corporation would be the least restrictive means to promote a compelling interest. Perhaps the burden of caring for a sick family member could easily be shifted to a third party. Perhaps not. In any event, it would be unsurprising were the lower federal courts to disagree sharply about whether an exemption to the FMLA could be denied in cases in which recognition of the relationship might be thought to undermine sincerely held beliefs.[49]

Other federal statutes create similar uncertainties. Consider the Employee Retirement Income Security Act of 1974 (ERISA).[50] While the Act covers pension funds, it also covers other areas including health insurance.[51] Now that same-sex marriage is recognized in all 50 states,[52] a same-sex spouse would be recognized as a spouse under ERISA and would be entitled to all of the benefits due to different-sex spouses under that Act.[53] But assuming that recognition of a same-sex spouse would contravene a corporation's religious beliefs, that corporation might seek a RFRA exemption to ERISA.

In any of these cases, the corporation would have to establish that the federal requirement substantially burdened its religious beliefs. But that would not be particularly difficult, either because of the penalty or because fulfillment of the requirement would contravene some religious belief. The Government would then have to show that its refusal to grant an exemption would be the least restrictive means to promoting some compelling interest.[54]

The *Hobby Lobby* Court suggested that the Government could meet that burden in some cases. For example, the Court suggested that the "Government has a compelling interest in providing an equal opportunity to participate in the workforce without regard to race, and prohibitions on racial discrimination are precisely tailored to achieve that critical goal."[55] But it is simply unclear whether the Government has a similarly compelling interest in providing others an equal opportunity and whether prohibitions of others kinds of discrimination are sufficiently closely tailored to meet that critical goal.[56] The Court's discussion of why the tax system is immune to a RFRA challenge only makes matters more confusing, because the Court did not take seriously whether according an exemption to the particular person seeking it was the least restrictive means to promoting a compelling interest.

The *Hobby Lobby* Court indicated that "the Government [should] assume the cost of providing the four contraceptives at issue to any women who are unable to obtain them under their health-insurance policies due to their employers' religious objections."[57] At least one question remaining is whether the Government should foot the bill in other kinds of cases in which a corporation's religious principles would be undermined by paying for family members who did not fit the religiously approved family.[58]

Consider a corporation whose religious principles would be compromised by affording benefits to a particular child, for example, because the child was a product of ART or, perhaps, was born into a non-marital family. Would the Government ever have a less than compelling interest in assuring that a child receives adequate benefits? While such a question might seem rhetorical, the Court might consider the free exercise analysis in *Bowen v. Roy* and then conclude that children receiving adequate benefits may not be so important after all.[59]

Suppose that the courts were to say that the Government has a compelling interest in assuring that every child has adequate support.[60] A separate question would be whether the least restrictive means was being used. The *Hobby Lobby* Court made clear that the "least-restrictive-means standard is exceptionally demanding,"[61] and it would be unsurprising for the lower courts to reach very different conclusions about what would constitute the least restrictive means to assuring that children receive what they need.

The *Hobby Lobby* deferential approach towards what constitutes a substantial burden might have important implications. For example, individuals might seek a RFRA exemption to paying taxes that supported practices contravening their faith.[62] The *Hobby Lobby* Court sought to forestall an onslaught on the tax system, noting that it would be "untenable to allow individuals to seek exemptions from taxes based on religious objections to particular Government expenditures."[63] After all, suppose everyone did that—"[t]he tax system could not function if denominations were allowed to challenge the tax system because tax payments were spent in a manner that violates their religious belief."[64]

The *Hobby Lobby* Court was correct that systemic difficulties would be created if exemptions to the tax code were recognized. But the same point might have been made about recognizing exemptions to providing insurance for health care—if enough entities assert religious objections to providing insurance, then the cost-shifting might become too onerous. The Court's method of distinguishing between taxes and health care insurance was not persuasive, because the rationale endorsed to protect tax collection would also seem to militate in favor of refusing to afford exemptions to for-profit corporations objecting to paying for health care insurance.

The Court's reasoning was disappointing for an additional reason, namely, that it seemed to involve application of the wrong test. On its face, RFRA does not allow for the kind of aggregation employed, where the Court looks at what would happen if everyone sought an analogous exemption. If the Government could justify refusing this person an exemption by appealing to the bad effects that might result by granting the exemption to other people, RFRA's focus on the importance of the Government's denying *this person* an exemption would be undermined.

RFRA on its face requires an individualized assessment because the Government must "demonstrate[ ] that application of the burden *to the person*"[65] passes strict scrutiny. But arguing that dire results would occur if everyone pursued a particular option does not establish that the government has a compelling interest at stake in denying the exemption to the particular person seeking it, much less that the exemption's denial is the least restrictive means of protecting or promoting that interest.

There is no small irony in the *Hobby Lobby* Court's discussion of *Lee*. The *Lee* Court deferred to Congress's judgment about where the relevant line should be drawn—exempting the Amish self-employed from paying into Social Security but refusing to expand the exemption to include Amish employers with Amish employees. In contrast, the *Hobby Lobby* Court rejected the compromise Congress had made when exempting non-profit but not for-profit corporations from the insurance requirement.[66] Instead, the *Hobby Lobby* Court expanded the exemption to include for-profit corporations as well.[67] Thus, because the United States Department of Health and Human Services has already approved a method providing cost-free access to FDA-approved contraception to women employed at religious, non-profit corporations refusing to provide that contraception, the Court suggested that the exemption for non-profits had to be extended to closely held, for-profit corporations.

By expanding the exemption so that the employees of such religious corporations would receive the same benefits as would employees of non-profit religious corporations, the Court did not have to address how to balance the competing interests of employees who might want access to certain forms of contraception on the one hand and employers with religious objections to providing that access on the other. Nor did the Court have to devise an entirely new, less restrictive method whereby the corporation's religious convictions could be respected without putting those employees at risk. Instead, the Court noted that the existing plan could be modified relatively easily.

The Court offered an explanation of how the exemption plan worked for religious non-profits. When a non-profit religiously objects to providing particular coverage, the employer provides notice of that objection to the insurance provider, who will then continue the coverage but not in a way that is attributable to the employer. However, such an insurer will not thereby be forced to incur additional net costs, either because provision of the contraception would provide net savings for the insurer or because other insurer fees would be modified to make up for any increased costs incurred as a result.

Did Congress intend to include protection in RFRA for for-profit corporations? Congress did not say. However, the *Hobby Lobby* Court noted, merchants were permitted to challenge Sunday closing laws in *Braunfeld* as a violation of free exercise guarantees, even if the merchants did not succeed on the merits. The Court then asked rhetorically whether "there [was] any reason to think that the Congress that enacted such sweeping protection put small-business owners to the choice" of accepting RFRA protections but forgoing corporate status or accepting corporate status but losing those protections.[68] Yet, it is somewhat misleading to characterize the issues this way, because Congress had protected small businesses in a different section of ACA,[69] and because there is no necessary connection between a corporation being closely held and its being a "small" business.

The *Hobby Lobby* Court discussed *Braunfeld*, explaining that it involved "five Orthodox Jewish merchants who ran small retail businesses in Philadelphia [and] challenged a Pennsylvania Sunday closing law as a violation of the Free Exercise Clause."[70] The Court then noted:

> According to HHS, however, if these merchants chose to incorporate their businesses—without in any way changing the size or nature of their businesses—they would forfeit all RFRA (and free-exercise) rights. HHS would put these merchants to a difficult choice: either give up the right to seek judicial protection of their religious liberty or forgo the benefits, available to their competitors, of operating as corporations.[71]

Yet, as the Court noted parenthetically, the *Braunfeld* merchants lost on the merits,[72] which makes the HHS-imposed choice regarding incorporation much less difficult than the

Court implies. Losing the right to litigate a challenge that will be unsuccessful on the merits does not seem like such a great sacrifice. If RFRA were interpreted to protect the *Braunfeld* merchants (in an analogous case involving federal rather than state law), then the Court would be correct that incorporation would impose costs that would have to be considered. But the *Hobby Lobby* Court nowhere stated that RFRA would protect the *Braunfeld* merchants were a federal law at issue, and the *O Centro* Court implied that RFRA would not. Interpreting RFRA to provide that protection would not only repudiate *Smith* but would seem to repudiate *Braunfeld* as well, since the Court was allegedly using strict scrutiny there.

One cannot tell whether the Court was suggesting that the federal government substantially burdens free exercise whenever it requires an individual to act in a way that is contrary to any of her religious beliefs.[73] For example, consider the religious prohibition against providing a Social Security number to the federal government. Under RFRA, does the requirement that individuals provide a Social Security number in order to receive government benefits constitute a substantial burden on that religious belief?

So, too, the *Hobby Lobby* Court cited *Gallagher* to support the proposition that for-profit corporations could challenge laws on free exercise grounds:

> It is quite a stretch to argue that RFRA, a law enacted to provide very broad protection for religious liberty, left for-profit corporations unprotected simply because in *Gallagher*—the only pre-*Smith* case in which the issue was raised—a majority of the Justices did not find it necessary to decide whether the kosher market's corporate status barred it from raising a free-exercise claim.[74]

But the kosher market in *Gallagher* did not win on the merits,[75] and the burden placed on *Hobby Lobby* would seem no greater than that which had been placed on the *Braunfeld* merchants or on Crown Kosher Super Market. This suggests that under the pre-*Smith* jurisprudence, Hobby Lobby would not have been successful even assuming that it had standing.[76] By the same token, the *Lee* Court was confident that the exemption went as far as was appropriate. But Congress in ACA offered corporations a variety of options, which suggests that Congress was at least as deliberative with respect to the ACA exemptions as it was with respect to the exemptions in *Lee*. That makes it difficult to understand why use of the *Lee* test in *Hobby Lobby* did not result in deference to Congress with respect to the appropriate breadth of the exemption.[77]

RFRA was designed to restore the pre-*Smith Sherbert* scrutiny to free exercise claims. But for-profits did not fare well under that system, as *Braunfeld*, *Gallagher*, and *Lee* illustrate. Further, non-profits did not do so well either.

Consider *Bob Jones University v. United States*,[78] which involved whether "nonprofit private schools that prescribe and enforce racially discriminatory admissions standards on the basis of religious doctrine, qualify as tax-exempt organizations under § 501(c)(3) of the Internal Revenue Code of 1954."[79] Bob Jones University is a non-profit corporation that is "dedicated to the teaching and propagation of its fundamentalist Christian religious beliefs."[80] Among those beliefs was the sincere conviction that "the Bible forbids interracial dating and marriage."[81] At first, the school's chosen method of assuring that its beliefs would be honored was simply to exclude Black students completely.[82] Then, the university relaxed its policy. "From 1971 to May 1975, the University accepted no applications from unmarried Negroes, but did accept applications from Negroes married within their race."[83]

The University employed other mechanisms to assure that its beliefs were respected. Any student who dated or was married to someone of another race was expelled. Indeed, anyone who advocated interracial dating or belonged to an organization advocating interracial marriage was expelled. The IRS revoked the school's tax-exempt status because of its interracial dating and marriage policies. The University successfully challenged its loss of tax-exempt status on the district court level, although that decision was reversed by the Fourth Circuit on appeal. The Fourth Circuit reasoned, "To be eligible for an exemption under that section, an institution must be 'charitable' in the common law sense, and therefore must not be contrary to public policy."[84] The University appealed and the United States Supreme Court "granted certiorari to decide whether petitioners, nonprofit private schools that prescribe and enforce racially discriminatory admissions standards on the basis of religious doctrine, qualify as tax-exempt organizations under § 501(c)(3) of the Internal Revenue Code of 1954."[85]

Tax exemptions are afforded only when a public benefit would thereby be accrued. Because "racial discrimination in education violates deeply and widely accepted views of elementary justice,"[86] the Court noted that "[i]t would be wholly incompatible with the concepts underlying tax exemption to grant the benefit of tax-exempt status to racially discriminatory educational entities."[87]

The University argued that "even if the Commissioner's policy is valid as to nonreligious private schools, that policy cannot constitutionally be applied to schools that engage in racial discrimination on the basis of sincerely held religious beliefs."[88] Denial of a tax exemption to those schools "violates their free exercise rights under the Religion Clauses of the First Amendment."[89] The Court admitted that "[d]enial of tax benefits will inevitably have a substantial impact on the operation of private religious schools, but will not prevent those schools from observing their religious tenets."[90] Such a denial was nonetheless constitutionally permissible because of the government's compelling interest in eradicating racial discrimination in education and because "no 'less restrictive means' are available to achieve the governmental interest."[91]

Would the current Court find the denial of a tax exemption to a discriminatory religious institution necessary to promote the state's compelling interest in eradicating discrimination? Perhaps, although the justification, "What would happen if many institutions did that?" would not seem responsive to the individualized assessment requirement under RFRA. The Court might wonder whether granting the exemption but making clear that the Government disapproved of racial discrimination would be as effective in combating discrimination as denying the exemption. If so, then denying the exemption to this particular institution might be very difficult to justify. Further, as long as relatively few institutions had such views, the state might be hard-pressed to deny any or all of them the exemption.

Nor is Bob Jones University the only non-profit organization whose religiously motivated practices had to be changed in light of civil law. Tony & Susan Alamo Foundation, "a nonprofit religious organization,"[92] was not accorded an exemption to FLSA requirements.

Hobby Lobby focused on whether corporations could trigger the pre-*Smith* strict scrutiny allegedly required by free exercise guarantees (and reinstated by RFRA). But the Court seemed to ignore that the pre-*Smith* businesses asserting such protections tended to lose on the merits and Hobby Lobby had no stronger claim than many of those businesses. At least one question raised by *Hobby Lobby* is whether RFRA's reinstatement of the pre-*Smith* jurisprudence increases free exercise protection. Regrettably, the Court seemed not to appreciate that its analysis of why Hobby Lobby should prevail would analogously have offered protection in *Braunfeld, Gallagher, Lee,* and *Bowen.* By suggesting that Hobby Lobby was protected but that Braunfeld, Crown Kosher Super Market, Lee, and Roy would not have been protected had their cases been analyzed under a RFRA-like statute, the Court seemed to be going back to the inconsistent and unprincipled use of strict scrutiny that *Smith II* was trying to avoid.

Beard length

The Court has recently had occasion to provide some clarification of RLUIPA. At issue in *Holt v. Hobbs*[93] was an "Arkansas Department of Correction's grooming policy, which prohibits inmates from growing beards unless they have a particular dermatological condition."[94] The petitioner, Gregory Holt,[95] was a devout Muslim who believed that he had a religious duty not to trim his beard at all but was willing as a compromise to have a ½-inch beard. His compromise was rejected.

The Court explained that under RLUIPA, Holt had to show that religious exercise was at issue and that the challenged policy substantially burdened that exercise.[96] Establishing that a substantial burden had been imposed was not difficult because Holt could show that his shaving his beard was a serious violation of his beliefs and that his failure to shave it would have resulted in a serious punishment.[97] That he was allowed to perform other religious practices did not somehow make this burden on religious practice insubstantial.[98] Further, the fact that other Muslims did not share his view about the impermissibility of shaving did not lessen the burden on his free exercise,[99] and the fact that he would not be held blameworthy for having failed to grow a beard as long as he tried to do so also did not mean that the burden was insubstantial.[100]

The *Holt* Court rejected the kind of reasoning that had won the day in *Lee*— "If I make an exception for you, I'll have to make one for everybody, so no exceptions."[101] The Court noted that other prisons had offered an accommodation without suffering ill effects, so the Arkansas Department had to offer some argument as to why a similar accommodation would not be workable.[102] In so doing, the Court refused to adopt the approach that had won the day in *Braunfeld*, where Pennsylvania had not been forced to explain why it could not provide a religious exemption to its Sunday closing law when other states had successfully incorporated a religious exemption to their Sunday closing laws.

The difficulty posed by *Holt* does not lie in the particulars of the case—it does not seem plausible to believe that permitting Holt to have the (compromise length) beard would have been a security risk. Nonetheless, future RLUIPA cases will have to determine what constitutes a substantial burden on religion. Will the religious adherent's say-so plus a penalty for non-compliance suffice?

RLUIPA and RFRA define substantial burden in the same way, which means that post-*Hobby Lobby* courts should be very deferential with respect to what constitutes a substantial burden on free exercise. If in addition the state bears a heavy burden when attempting to show why it is justified in imposing a substantial burden in a particular case, then one would expect that many more exemptions will have to be granted. Or, courts will feel the need to return to the chaotic pre-*Smith* jurisprudence where strict scrutiny is sometimes rather forgiving, relevantly similar burdens will be deemed substantial in some cases but not in others and, perhaps, those with minority beliefs will be told that they cannot require the government to change its own practices.

Conclusion

Was RFRA intended to protect free exercise in a case like *Hobby Lobby*? Probably not. While businesses had been permitted to challenge laws infringing on the free exercise rights of owners, such challenges had not been successful. Those seeking to reinstate the pre-*Smith* jurisprudence did not seem to be worried about cases like *Braunfeld*, *Gallagher*, and *Lee*, and *Hobby Lobby's* reasoning would analogously cast all of these decisions into doubt.

The *Hobby Lobby* approach to RFRA seems to assume that free exercise rights have been substantially burdened whenever a challenger sincerely claims that they have, although it is difficult to believe that Congress intended to make so much federal law susceptible to challenge. In addition, the *Hobby Lobby* approach makes it very difficult to establish when in a particular case the government has a sufficiently important interest to justify overriding free exercise rights. The Court cited examples where the government allegedly met its burden—*Braunfeld*, *Gallagher*, and *Lee*. Those examples were not plausible, however, either because of the experiences of other states (where exemptions were afforded without great difficulty) or because an exception already recognized by Congress could have been slightly expanded easily, just as the *Hobby Lobby* Court expanded an already recognized congressional exception. But this means that the federal government may have great difficulty in meeting the *Hobby Lobby* test, protestations to the contrary notwithstanding.

While RLUIPA has a narrower scope than RFRA, it applies to the states as well as the federal government. In future cases, courts will have to adopt one of two approaches—either many more exceptions will have to be granted, for example, in cases involving zoning or institutionalized settings, or the courts will have to be less deferential with respect to what constitutes a religion or a substantial burden on free exercise or, perhaps, more deferential with respect to when granting an exemption would cause great harm to the state.

Application of the *Hobby Lobby* deferential approach in cases involving RFRA or RLUIPA will likely make the law more chaotic. Either laws will have to include a whole host of exemptions because of the sincerely held beliefs of a religiously diverse population or the courts will have to adopt unprincipled approaches in light of which some exemptions will be granted and others will not.

Smith II is rightly criticized for having misdescribed the existing jurisprudence and for having misapplied the very standard that it was announcing. However, *Smith II* was correct to suggest that the previous jurisprudence had been unprincipled in its application of the prevailing standard. While it is possible that courts will uniformly apply existing doctrine to be more protective of religious liberty, the Court's own description of the previous cases suggests that it (and courts following that example) will return to the unprincipled approach where relevantly similar cases will be handled differently, claims that a uniform standard is being applied notwithstanding

It is possible, perhaps because of some very unpopular exemptions, that the broad interpretation of RFRA and RLUIPA will be narrowed, either by Congress or through the courts. Such a narrowing might have its own difficulties. But the partisan divide in Congress makes it unlikely that a principled legislative fix will be offered any time in the foreseeable future, which means that we can expect relevantly similar cases to be decided in very different ways in the circuits for a long time to come. The plausibility of such a prediction is bolstered when one considers some of the interpretations of the federal statutes or of state RFRAs that have been offered in the lower courts, as the final chapter illustrates.

Notes

1 *Burwell v. Hobby Lobby Stores, Incorporated*, 134 S. Ct. 2751 (2014).
2 *Id.* at 2775.
3 *Id.* at 2764.
4 *Id.* at 2759.
5 Religious Freedom Restoration Act (RFRA) of 1993, 42 *United States Code* § 2000bb-3(b) (2012).
6 *Hobby Lobby.* 134 S. Ct. at 2768. (citing 1 *United States Code* § 1 (2012)).

7 See 160 *Congressional Record* S4211–01, S4212 (Sen. Boxer) ("I voted for the Religious Freedom Restoration Act, and I know why I voted for it. It was a very important piece of legislation which said that individuals can't have their freedom of religion stepped upon. It didn't say corporations."); *id.* S1502–03, S1503–04 (Sen. Murray) (discussing "18 other Senators who were here when Congress enacted the religious protections under the Religious Freedom Restoration Act of 1993 and who . . . know Congress did not intend for a corporation or, furthermore, its shareholders to restrict a woman's access to preventive health care").
8 Cf. *id.* S4473–01, S4475 (Sen. Ayotte) ("The notion that somehow Hobby Lobby as a closely-held corporation would have to give up all their religious beliefs seems to me to be antithetical to what we supported on a bipartisan basis in this Congress.").
9 See, for example, *Hobby Lobby*, 134 S. Ct. at 2771 (noting that for-profits might engage in charitable activities)
10 *Hobby Lobby*, 134 S. Ct. at 2774.
11 *Id.* at 2775.
12 *Id.* at 2774.
13 Cf. *id.* ("Congress was confident of the ability of the federal courts to weed out insincere claims.").
14 *Id.* at 2776.
15 *Id.* at 2777.
16 See *id.* at 2769 ("According to HHS and the dissent, these corporations are not protected by RFRA because they cannot exercise religion.").
17 *Id.* at 2769. ("The corporate form alone cannot provide the explanation because . . . nonprofit corporations can be protected by RFRA.").
18 *Id.* (quoting *id.* at 2794 (Ginsburg, J., dissenting)).
19 *Id.* ("But this principle applies equally to for-profit corporations: Furthering their religious freedom also 'furthers individual religious freedom.'").
20 *Id.*
21 See *id.* ("If the corporate form is not enough, what about the profit-making objective?").
22 *Id.* at 2771.
23 *Id.*
24 *Id.*
25 Cf. *Korte v. Sebelius*, 735 F.3d 654, 704 (7th Cir. 2013). ("Suppose, for example, that a corporation's owners have entirely entrusted the management of the corporation to its longtime CEO, who is the public face of the corporation and who also happens to have strongly held religious beliefs about the way in which the corporation should be run. Are her beliefs attributable to the corporation?").
26 *Hobby Lobby*, 134 S. Ct. at 2759.
27 *See* 42 *United States Code* § 2000bb-1(a) (1993).
28 *Hobby Lobby*, 134 S. Ct. at 2777.
29 *Id.* at 2779.
30 *Id.* at 2775.
31 *Id.* (emphasis added) (citing Brief for HHS in No. 13–354, at 9, n. 4).
32 *Id.*
33 530 U.S. 793 (2000).
34 *Id.* at 803.
35 *Id.* at 840 (O'Connor, J., concurring).
36 *Id.*
37 See Thomas E. Rutledge, "A Corporation Has No Soul—the Business Entity Law Response to Challenges to the PPACA Contraceptive Mandate," *William & Mary Business Law Review* 5:1–53 (2014), p. 49 n. 220 ("If shareholders are permitted to object to the corporate group health insurance plan's coverage of goods and services they consider sinful, there is no clear reason those same shareholders cannot prevent the employees from using other compensation . . . to pay directly for contraceptives, alcoholic beverages . . . or tobacco.").
38 See *Hobby Lobby*, 134 S. Ct. at 2759.
39 *Boerne*, 521 U.S. at 512 ("Congress enacted RFRA in direct response to the Court's decision in *Employment Division, Department of Human Resources of Oregon v. Smith*, 494

U.S. 872 (1990)."); see also *id.* at 529 (stating that the RFRA "invalidate[s] any law which imposes a substantial burden on a religious practice unless it is justified by a compelling interest and is the least restrictive means of accomplishing that interest").

40 See *Hobby Lobby*, 134 S. Ct. at 2759.
41 Cf. *Tony & Susan Alamo Foundation*, 471 U.S. at 306 ("The Foundation's commercial activities, undertaken with a 'common business purpose,' are not beyond the reach of the Fair Labor Standards Act because of the Foundation's religious character, and its associates are 'employees' within the meaning of the Act.").
42 Cf. *Walz v. Tax Commission of City of New York*, 397 U.S. 664, 673 (1970) ("The limits of permissible state accommodation to religion are by no means co-extensive with the noninterference mandated by the Free Exercise Clause.").
43 Cf. *Wheaton College v. Burwell*, 134 S. Ct. 2806, 2807 (2014) ("If the applicant informs the Secretary of Health and Human Services in writing that it is a nonprofit organization that holds itself out as religious and has religious objections to providing coverage for contraceptive services, the respondents are enjoined from enforcing against the applicant the challenged provisions of the Patient Protection and Affordable Care Act and related regulations pending final disposition of appellate review.").
44 *Hobby Lobby*, 134 S. Ct. at 2780 (quoting 42 *United States Code* § 2000bb-1(b)(2)) (internal quotation marks omitted).
45 *Id.* at 2780.
46 *Id.* at 2783.
47 Family and Medical Leave Act of 1993, 29 *United States Code* §§ 2601–654 (2012).
48 Family and Medical Leave Act of 1993, 29 *United States Code* § 2601(b)(2).
49 Compare *Gilardi v. Sebelius*, 926 F. Supp. 2d 273, 275 (D.D.C.) affirmed in part, reversed in part sub nomine *Gilardi v. United States Department of Health & Human Services*, 733 F.3d 1208 (District of Columbia Cir. 2013) certiorari granted, judgment vacated sub nomine *Gilardi v. United States Department of Health & Human Services*, 134 S. Ct. 2902 (2014) and certiorari denied sub nom. *Department of Health & Human Services. v. Gilardi*, 134 S. Ct. 2902 (2014) (holding that ACA did not impose a substantial burden on free exercise of religion), with *Geneva College v. Sebelius*, 988 F. Supp. 2d 511, 514 (W.D. Pennsylvania 2013) reversed sub nomine *Geneva College v. Secretary of United States Department of Health & Human Services*, 778 F.3d 422 (3d Cir. 2015) certiorari granted in part sub nomine *Zubik v. Burwell*, 136 S. Ct. 444 (2015) and certiorari granted sub nomine *Geneva College v. Burwell*, 136 S. Ct. 445 (2015) (holding that ACA imposed substantial burden on free exercise).
50 Employee Retirement Income Security Act of 1974, 29 U.S.C. §§ 1001–461 (2012).
51 Elaine Gareri Kenney, "For the Sake of Your Health: ERISA's Preemption Provisions, HMO Accountability, and Consumer Access to State Law Remedies," *University of San Francisco Law Review* 38:361–89 (2004), p. 362 ("Although most of ERISA's provisions govern the administration of employer-offered pension funds, it also regulates non-pension employee benefits such as disability and health insurance plans.").
52 See *Obergefell v. Hodges*, 135 S. Ct. 2584 (2015).
53 See U.S. Dep't of Justice Report Outlining Obama Administration's Effort to Implement Federal Benefits to Same-Sex Married Couples, *Employment Practice Guide* (CCH) (WL 6698935) ¶ 5417 (2014) (attachment describing Department of Labor "guidance provid[ing] that 'marriage' and 'spouse' include same-sex marriages and individuals in same-sex marriages, respectively, in cases when the marriage is recognized as a marriage under any state law, regardless of where the couple resides").
54 Cf. *Hobby Lobby*, 134 S. Ct. at 2779 ("Since the HHS contraceptive mandate imposes a substantial burden on the exercise of religion, we must move on and decide whether HHS has shown that the mandate both '(1) is in furtherance of a compelling governmental interest; and (2) is the least restrictive means of furthering that compelling governmental interest.'") (citing 42 *United States Code* § 2000bb-1(b)).
55 See *id.* at 2783.
56 Compare Neil S. Siegel and Reva B. Siegel, "Compelling Interests and Contraception," *Connecticut Law Review* 47:1025–43 (2015) (arguing that the state has a compelling interest in preventing sex discrimination), with David E. Bernstein, "Sex Discrimination Laws Versus

Civil Liberties," *University of Chicago Legal Forum* 1999:133–95 (1999) (rejecting that the state has a compelling interest in preventing sex discrimination).
57 *Hobby Lobby*, 134 S. Ct. at 2780.
58 Cf. *id.* at 2804 (Ginsburg, J., dissenting) ("And where is the stopping point to the 'let the government pay' alternative?").
59 See *Bowen*. 476 U.S. at 712 (rejecting that parents who refused to provide a child's Social Security number for religious reasons were still entitled to receive AFDC benefits and concluding that Congress' refusal to grant appellees a special exemption does not violate the Free Exercise Clause).
60 Cf. *Hobby Lobby*, 134 S. Ct. at 2780 ("We will assume that the interest in guaranteeing cost-free access to the four challenged contraceptive methods is compelling within the meaning of RFRA.").
61 *Id.* at 2780 (citing *Boerne*, 521 U.S. at 532).
62 *Id.* at 2784.
63 *Id.*
64 *Id.* (citing *Lee*, 455 U.S. at 260).
65 Religious Freedom Restoration Act (RFRA) of 1993, 42 *United States Code* § 2000bb-3(b) (2012) (emphasis added).
66 See *Hobby Lobby*, 134 S. Ct. at 2782 ("HHS has already established an accommodation for nonprofit organizations with religious objections.").
67 See *id.* at 2785 ("The contraceptive mandate, as applied to closely held corporations, violates RFRA.").
68 *Id.* at 2767.
69 *Id.* at 2764 (citing 26 *United States Code* § 4980H(c)(2) (2012)) ("And employers with fewer than 50 employees are not required to provide health insurance at all.").
70 *Id.* at 2767 (discussing *Braunfeld v. Brown*, 366 U.S. 599 (1961)).
71 *Id.*
72 *Id.*
73 See *id.* at 2787 (Ginsburg, J., dissenting) ("In a decision of startling breadth, the Court holds that commercial enterprises, including corporations, along with partnerships and sole proprietorships, can opt out of any law (saving only tax laws) they judge incompatible with their sincerely held religious beliefs.").
74 *Id.* at 2773.
75 See *id.* at 2772–73.
76 See *id.* at 2806 (Breyer and Kagan, JJ., dissenting) ("We agree with Justice Ginsburg that the plaintiffs' challenge to the contraceptive coverage requirement fails on the merits. We need not and do not decide whether either for-profit corporations or their owners may bring claims under the Religious Freedom Restoration Act of 1993.").
77 The *Hobby Lobby* Court implied that it agreed with the result in *Lee*. See *id.* at 2784 ("*Lee* was a free-exercise, not a RFRA, case, but if the issue in *Lee* were analyzed under the RFRA framework, the fundamental point would be that there simply is no less restrictive alternative to the categorical requirement to pay taxes.").
78 461 U.S. 574 (1983).
79 *Id.* at 577.
80 *Id.* at 580.
81 *Id.*
82 *Id.* ("To effectuate these views, Negroes were completely excluded until 1971.").
83 *Id.* The university had a different policy for its employees. See *id.* at n. 5 ("Beginning in 1973, Bob Jones University instituted an exception to this rule, allowing applications from unmarried Negroes who had been members of the University staff for four years or more.").
84 *Id.* at 582; see also *Bob Jones University v. United States*, 639 F.2d 147, 151 (4th 1980).
85 *Bob Jones*, 461 U.S. at 577.
86 *Id.* at 592.
87 *Id.* at 595.
88 *Id.* at 602–03.
89 *Id.* at 603.
90 *Id.* at 603–04.

91 *Id.* at 604 (quoting *Thomas*, 450 U.S. at 718).
92 *Tony & Susan Alamo Foundation*, 417 U.S. at 292.
93 *Holt v. Hobbs*, 135 S. Ct. 853, 859 (2015).
94 *Id.*
95 *Id.* ("Petitioner Gregory Holt, also known as Abdul Maalik Muhammad . . .").
96 *Id.* at 862 ("In addition to showing that the relevant exercise of religion is grounded in a sincerely held religious belief, petitioner also bore the burden of proving that the Department's grooming policy substantially burdened that exercise of religion.").
97 *Id.*
98 *Id.* ("RLUIPA's 'substantial burden' inquiry asks whether the government has substantially burdened religious exercise (here, the growing of a ½-inch beard), not whether the RLUIPA claimant is able to engage in other forms of religious exercise.").
99 *Id.* at 862–63 ("[T]he protection of RLUIPA, no less than the guarantee of the Free Exercise Clause, is 'not limited to beliefs which are shared by all of the members of a religious sect.'") (citing *Thomas*, 450 U.S. at 715–16).
100 *Id.* at 862 ("[T]he District Court committed a similar error in suggesting that the burden on petitioner's religious exercise was slight because, according to petitioner's testimony, his religion would 'credit' him for attempting to follow his religious beliefs, even if that attempt proved to be unsuccessful. RLUIPA, however, applies to an exercise of religion regardless of whether it is 'compelled.'").
101 *Id.* at 866 (citing *O Centro*, 546 U.S. at 436).
102 *Id.* ("The Department failed to show, in the face of petitioner's evidence, why the vast majority of States and the Federal Government permit inmates to grow ½-inch beards, either for any reason or for religious reasons, but it cannot.").

8 Lower courts and the protection of religion

The jurisprudence spelling out the protections afforded by RFRA and RLUIPA will develop more fully as the Court decides more cases. However, it is not as if the Court will be without input with respect to the issues not already addressed, because lower courts have offered interpretations of RFRA and RLUIPA on a variety of matters that have not yet been before the Court. Further, various states have enacted their own Religious Freedom Restoration Acts, and the way that those have been interpreted *may* help predict how the Court will interpret or apply RFRA and RLUIPA in the future.

That many important issues have been addressed elsewhere does not indicate that there is an emerging consensus. On the contrary, the lower courts have been diverging rather than converging with respect to how various important issues should be resolved, and there are clear costs and benefits associated with the differing approaches as a matter of both constitutional law and public policy. When the Court is asked to resolve some of these thorny issues, it will face the same kinds of difficulties that arose in determining the breadth and depth of free exercise guarantees.

The Court will have numerous options, for example, not only addressing the particular issue before it but at least laying a framework compatible with other solutions to problems that will soon be raised. Regrettably, the free exercise jurisprudence does not provide much basis for optimism—in light of what has been done in the past, the Court seems most likely to adopt one or both of the following two approaches: (1) offer an inconsistent jurisprudence with respect to the formulation or application of the relevant standards, or (2) continue to do what it has already chosen to do with respect to the interpretations of these statutes—refuse to address some of the most difficult issues and let the circuits fend for themselves, resulting in the same statute's affording relatively robust protections in one circuit and relatively lax protections in another.

State and federal protection of religion and the lower courts

Lower courts have been addressing RFRA and RLUIPA requirements in a variety of cases. Regrettably, those courts have reached no consensus about which test to use or how the relevant test should be applied, and the United States Supreme Court has done too little to clarify matters. State courts have attempted to spell out the protections of their respective state Religious Freedom Restoration Act, and the jurisprudence that has developed in some states is not particularly promising. If the way that lower courts have interpreted free exercise guarantees in these statutes reflects how the United States Supreme Court will analyze federal guarantees, then we can expect that the pre-*Smith* inconsistent approaches to free exercise will be incorporated into the interpretation of federal statutory protections, a result that Congress almost certainly neither intended nor desired.

Substantial burdens

Both RFRA and RLUIPA protections are triggered when a substantial burden is imposed on religious exercise. While it is clear that the two statutes use the same standard for what qualifies as a substantial burden,[1] the Court has not spelled out the criteria for determining when a burden qualifies as substantial.[2] This is especially problematic because the definition of substantial burden in RFRA and RLUIPA is determined in accordance with free exercise jurisprudence,[3] and the Court has offered mixed signals about how or whether to define that term in the free exercise context.[4] Because of those mixed signals, the circuit courts have developed differing approaches to determine when religious practice has been substantially burdened under RFRA and RLUIPA.

In *Adkins v. Kaspar*,[5] the Fifth Circuit outlined some of the differing approaches used by the circuit courts to determine whether free exercise has been substantially burdened. The court explained that notwithstanding

> RLUIPA's eschewing the requirement of centrality in the definition of religious exercise, the Eighth Circuit adopted the same definition that it had employed in RFRA cases, requiring the burdensome practice to affect a "central tenet" or fundamental aspect of the religious belief.[6]

In contrast, the Seventh Circuit suggested that a practice "that imposes a substantial burden on religious exercise is one that necessarily bears direct, primary, and fundamental responsibility for rendering religious exercise . . . effectively impracticable."[7] The Ninth Circuit "defined a 'substantial burden' as one that imposes 'a significantly great restriction or onus upon such exercise.'"[8] These approaches might be contrasted with that of the Eleventh Circuit, which "declined to adopt the Seventh Circuit's definition, holding instead that a 'substantial burden' is one that results 'from pressure that tends to force adherents to forego religious precepts or from pressure that mandates religious conduct.'"[9]

The circuits have offered a variety of approaches, varying both in what tests would be applied and in how robustly free exercise interests would be protected. Consider *Civil Liberties for Urban Believers v. City of Chicago*.[10] The Seventh Circuit realized that when interpreting RLUIPA a court might interpret "substantial burden on religious exercise" to mean that the relevant protections will be triggered whenever a regulation has the effect of "'inhibit[ing] or constrain[ing] the use, building, or conversion of real property for the purpose of religious exercise.'"[11] But such an interpretation would be very broad, and holding that "inhibiting or constraining *any* religious exercise" would trigger the applicable test "would render meaningless the word 'substantial.'"[12] Not only would such an interpretation not account for the text, but it would have important implications. "[T]he slightest obstacle to religious exercise incidental to the regulation of land use . . . could then constitute a burden sufficient to trigger RLUIPA's requirement that the regulation advance a compelling governmental interest by the least restrictive means."[13] Such a test is very difficult to meet and, if easily triggered, might frequently impose very burdensome limitations on the state. In part to be truer to the text and in part to reduce the number of times that the test would be triggered, the Seventh Circuit interpreted "substantial burden on religious exercise [a]s one that necessarily bears direct, primary, and fundamental responsibility for rendering religious exercise . . . effectively impracticable."[14]

The Seventh Circuit feared that too deferential a standard would mean that even insubstantial burdens would trigger the relevant test. Other circuits have offered other, apparently more forgiving interpretations of what constitutes a substantial burden. However, some of those more forgiving constructions have resulted in decisions that bring to mind some of the difficulties that plagued the Court's free exercise jurisprudence, namely, the articulated standard is applied in a way that belies its terms.

Consider *Midrash Sephardi, Incorporated v. Town of Surfside*[15] in which the Eleventh Circuit offered a seemingly less demanding standard for a burden to qualify as substantial. The court said that "a 'substantial burden' is akin to significant pressure which directly coerces the religious adherent to conform his or her behavior accordingly."[16]

At issue in *Midrash Sephardi* was whether a synagogue, which leased space in one area of town, could be forced to move to a different location because of a zoning requirement. Because of a religious requirement that individuals walk to services on the Sabbath and holidays, moving the synagogue would make it very difficult for some of the congregants, e.g., the old or infirm, to attend services. This would affect not only the individual congregant's religious exercise, but might also affect the health of the congregation as a whole if enough congregants were dissuaded from attending services. In addition, it was not clear that there was any suitable location for the synagogue within the area zoned for houses of worship.

The Eleventh Circuit noted that under RLUIPA "an individual's exercise of religion is 'substantially burdened' if a regulation completely prevents the individual from engaging in religiously mandated activity."[17] Notwithstanding the difficulties posed by "Floridian heat and humidity [for those aged and infirm who] . . . walk to services, the burden of walking a few extra blocks, made greater by Mother Nature's occasional incorrigibility, is not 'substantial' within the meaning of RLUIPA."[18] The court offered the consolation that "congregants wishing to practice Orthodox Judaism [can] . . . move where [the] synagogues are located."[19] Apparently, the burden imposed by having to acquire a new home or by simply forgoing attending services on the Sabbath did not constitute "significant pressure which directly coerces the religious adherent to conform his or her behavior accordingly."[20]

The Eleventh Circuit's interpretation of what constitutes coercion is difficult to reconcile with the *Sherbert* Court's understanding of that term. Sherbert was coerced because required to choose between observing her Sabbath and keeping her job. The *Midrash Sephardi* congregants, especially if of limited means, would simply be precluded from going to their house of worship to observe their Sabbath. Further, precisely because there seemed to be no available space in the area zoned for religious houses of worship, the regulation at issue would simply force this synagogue out of existence.

While the Eleventh Circuit's substantial burden test seems more forgiving on the face of it, the test as applied was anything but forgiving. But that raises an additional potential difficulty. Where terms are applied in a way that is unexpected, there might be a greater risk of variation in application. Some courts might simply apply the test in accord with the stated terms whereas others might try to apply the unstated rule, which might result in greater inconsistency within the circuit as well as across circuits.

The Ninth Circuit also declines to use the Seventh Circuit standard. In *International Church of Foursquare Gospel v. City of San Leandro*,[21] the Ninth Circuit rejected the applicability of *Civil Liberties for Urban Believers* (which used the Seventh Circuit test)[22] for determining whether a substantial burden had been placed on a religious institution precluded from building a church in the only suitable place in the city. The court remanded the case for a determination of whether the city had used the least restrictive means to promote a compelling interest. In contrast, the *Midrash Sephardi* court simply rejected that a substantial burden had been placed on a religious institution even though there seemed to be no suitable location for the synagogue in the only area where the local zoning law permitted it to go.

It is unsurprising that the circuits have developed differing interpretations of RLUIPA, given the lack of guidance from the Court. Certainly, it is fair to suggest that even when the Court offers a great deal of guidance, circuit decisions will diverge because the Court simply cannot anticipate and address all issues that might arise. Further, divergence among the circuits should be expected even when the circuits agree about the relevant multi-factor test, for example, because some circuits might emphasize certain factors while others might emphasize others. But the circuits' differing tests cannot merely be attributed to contrasting emphases, and the Court has done too little to provide helpful guidance. Indeed, the Court has refused to grant certiorari in several of the cases that apply differing tests, almost guaranteeing that the same federal law will offer protection in some circuits but not in others even where the factual scenarios are relevantly similar.

What is religious?

Not only do the circuits disagree about what constitutes a substantial burden on free exercise, but they disagree about a more basic question, namely, what qualifies as religious. To some extent, they are merely following the example set by the United States Supreme Court when it refused to settle on a particular definition to determine which beliefs and practices qualify as religious. But the lack of criteria has had the foreseeable effect that some of the circuit approaches are much more inclusive than others, which means that the same practice might qualify for *federal* religious protection in one circuit but not in another.

While the United States Supreme Court has not offered definitive criteria for determining what qualifies as religion, it has suggested that a rather forgiving approach should be used. For example, there is no need for an individual to belong to a particular sect or be a member of a particular congregation in order for her beliefs to qualify as religious. Further, while some bizarre beliefs will not be treated as religious, the Court has offered no examples of beliefs that would not count and was willing to include the Ballards' beliefs about their own supernatural powers to cure the incurable to count as religious and thus to receive First Amendment protection. Nonetheless, one approach that has been gaining some acceptance across the circuits seems much more restrictive than the approach implicitly adopted by the Supreme Court.

Malnak v. Yogi, which involved an Establishment Clause challenge to teaching Transcendental Meditation in the public schools, provides the basis for the standard used in some of the circuits in free exercise cases.[23] The court stated some of the salient aspects of the case: Each student needed his or her own personal mantra, a "sound aid used while meditating."[24] The mantra was delivered to the student in a ceremony called a puja, which seemed religious in nature. In addition, the textbook involved religious themes. While the court found that Transcendental Meditation was a religion for Establishment Clause purposes, the reason that *Malnak* has been influential was not its holding but the analysis offered in Judge Arlin Adams's concurring opinion.[25]

Judge Adams noted that there had been "a newer, more expansive reading of 'religion' that has been developed in the last two decades in the context of free exercise and selective service cases," although he believed that *Yoder* represented a retrenchment in the jurisprudence.[26] He described the "modern approach [as] look[ing] to the familiar religions as models in order to ascertain, by comparison, whether the new set of ideas or beliefs is confronting the same concerns, or serving the same purposes, as unquestioned and accepted 'religions.'"[27]

Judge Adams outlined three factors that he believed important to consider:

> (1) [We] must, at least to a degree, examine the content of the supposed religion, not to determine its truth or falsity, or whether it is schismatic or orthodox, but to determine whether the subject matter it comprehends is consistent with the assertion that it is, or is not, a religion.[28]

For example, he approvingly quoted "Dr. Paul Tillich, who expressed his view on the essence of religion in the phrase 'ultimate concern.'"[29] However, Judge Adams cautioned that addressing one very important issue may not suffice, noting that "[c]ertain isolated answers to 'ultimate' questions . . . are not necessarily 'religious' answers, because they lack the element of comprehensiveness, the second of the three indicia."[30]

Judge Adams's qualification that certain answers to ultimate questions may not qualify as religious helps explain the second factor:

> (2) A religion is not generally confined to one question or one moral teaching; it has a broader scope. It lays claim to an ultimate and comprehensive "truth."[31]

Thus, Judge Adams suggested that religion may have to address more than one matter of ultimate concern to assure that the belief system has sufficient scope.

The third category was not content-related but instead focused on the presence of more formal characteristics:

> (3) Courts should examine any formal, external, or surface signs that may be analogized to accepted religions. Such signs might include formal services, ceremonial functions, the existence of clergy, structure and organization, efforts at propagation, observation of holidays and other similar manifestations associated with the traditional religions.[32]

Judge Adams noted that the third factor was not necessary—"a religion may exist without any of these signs."[33] Indeed, he noted that Seeger's beliefs qualified as religious, notwithstanding that those beliefs were not espoused by an institution, much less one associated with several elements of this formal structure.[34] Further, Seeger's beliefs would likely not qualify under Judge Adams's first criterion either, as Adams himself seemed to acknowledge.[35] If Seeger's beliefs did not involve a matter of "ultimate concern" (the first factor), then they also did not involve the "broader scope" involved in the second factor. But this means that Seeger's beliefs likely did not qualify under any of Judge Adams's factors. If the *Seeger* Court had employed Judge Adams's approach, Seeger's beliefs would likely not have been found religious, even though *Seeger* was allegedly one of the very cases upon which Judge Adams's approach was based.

While Judge Adams admitted that no one of the factors had to be met in order for beliefs to qualify as religious,[36] his formulation is at the very least problematic if it does not provide a good account of *Seeger*'s holding.[37] Judge Adams argued that "it is important to have some objective guidelines in order to avoid *ad hoc* justice."[38] While that is correct, it is also important not to use *incorrect* objective guidelines, and Judge Adams's factors do not account well for the Court's jurisprudence.[39]

While the discussion of Tillich and matters of ultimate concern comes from *Seeger*,[40] there are two distinct reasons to believe that the Court was not including matters of ultimate concern in its analysis in the way Judge Adams implied. First, Seeger's beliefs did not seem accurately characterized as involving matters of ultimate concern but, instead, as "largely personal,"[41] and his beliefs nonetheless qualified as religious. Second, and more importantly, the *Seeger* Court shied away from a discussion of content and instead explained that "the beliefs which prompted [Seeger's] objection occupy the same place in his life as the belief in a traditional deity holds in the lives of his friends, the Quakers."[42] By focusing on the role played by the beliefs *rather than* their content, the *Seeger* opinion suggests that Adams's focus on content is misconceived.[43]

An additional point might be made about the contents on which the courts might focus. Judge Adams suggests that the appropriate focus is on matters of "ultimate concern."[44] Yet, ironically, Judge Adams also claimed to have been guided by *Yoder*,[45] and *Yoder*'s focus was not on matters of ultimate concern but on matters "intimately related to daily living."[46] *Yoder* at the very least suggests that the acceptable religious contents are not nearly as limited as Judge Adams implies.[47]

The Third Circuit adopted Judge Adams's analysis in *Africa v. Pennsylvania*, which involved Frank Africa, "a 'Naturalist Minister' for the MOVE organization."[48] He was incarcerated and claimed that "the state government is . . . required, under the religion clauses of the [F]irst [A]mendment, to provide him with a special diet consisting entirely of raw foods."[49] His dietary needs were accommodated at one prison.

MOVE had been founded "by John Africa, who serve[d] as the group's revered 'coordinator' and whose teachings Frank Africa and his fellow 'family' members follow[ed]."[50] Frank Africa testified that MOVE was a religion, although "MOVE members participate in no distinct 'ceremonies' or 'rituals'; instead, every act of life itself is invested with religious meaning and significance."[51] An important element of MOVE teaching was its concept of an "unadulterated existence," which could only be attained through "MOVE's 'religious diet[,]' . . . comprised largely of raw vegetables and fruits."[52] The failure to observe the dietary restrictions "constitutes deviation from the 'direct, straight, and true' and results in 'confusion and disease.'"[53] When asked about the ethical obligations imposed by the religion, Africa responded that it would be impermissible to serve in the military.

A different witness testified that Frank Africa was an ordained naturalist minister. She also testified that "Africa's raw food diet is both a necessary 'part of' and a sincere 'reflection of' his religious commitment."[54]

The district court also heard testimony from Julius T. Cuyler, the Graterford prison superintendent, who testified that it would be very difficult for the prison to accommodate Africa's request any more than it already had, and its being ordered to do so might wreak havoc in the system. The district court rejected that MOVE was a religion, characterizing it instead as "merely a quasi-back-to-nature social movement of limited proportion" that was "concerned solely with 'concepts of health and a return to simplistic living' . . . more akin to a 'social philosophy' than to a religion."[55]

The Third Circuit described its "task [a]s to decide whether the beliefs avowed are (1) sincerely held, and (2) religious in nature, in the claimant's scheme of things."[56] The court did not question Africa's sincerity, which meant that the important issue was whether MOVE constituted a religion. But courts are at a disadvantage when asked to decide which sets of beliefs are religious: "Judges are ill-equipped to examine the breadth and content of an avowed religion; [they] must avoid any predisposition toward conventional religions so that unfamiliar faiths are not branded mere secular beliefs."[57] Such a task is all the more difficult because the "Supreme Court has never announced a comprehensive definition of religion."[58] Nonetheless, the court reasoned that "the modern analysis consists of a 'definition by analogy' approach [which] is at once a refinement and an extension of the 'parallel'-belief course first charged by the Supreme Court in *Seeger*."⁵⁹

The parallel belief approach should have supported Africa's claim that MOVE was a religion. In *Seeger*, the Court was concerned with whether Seeger's beliefs played a role in his life comparable to how religious beliefs played a role in others' lives. Given the testimony that MOVE "encompasses every aspect of MOVE members' lives[,] there is nothing that is left out,"⁶⁰ one might have expected that MOVE would be paradigmatic of what would qualify. Further, the *Yoder* Court had been concerned with aspects of daily living, and MOVE seemed to qualify on that score as well.

Lessons from *Seeger* and *Yoder* notwithstanding, the *Africa* court rejected that MOVE was a religion because of its apparent failure to "satisfy the 'ultimate' ideas criterion."⁶¹ In addition, MOVE "recognize[d] no Supreme Being and refer[red] to no transcendental or all-controlling force,"⁶² even though the Supreme Court has never imposed such a requirement. The *Africa* court concluded that "the concerns addressed by MOVE, even assuming they are 'ultimate' in nature, are more akin to Thoreau's rejection of 'the contemporary secular values accepted by the majority' than to the 'deep religious conviction[s]' of the Amish."⁶³ Of course, MOVE members did not view their own beliefs as secular and, further, their belief system seemed to operate in a way that was at least analogous to the way that beliefs operate in more traditional religions. The Supreme Court's more forgiving approach notwithstanding, the *Africa* court offered an analysis that could easily be used to undermine protections for minority religions.

Even if MOVE were classified as a religion, the prison would not have had to accede to Africa's request if indeed that refusal was narrowly tailored to promote a compelling state interest. However, the *Africa* court was not convinced that it would have been so difficult for the prison to have acceded to Africa's request, given that a different prison had done so.⁶⁴ Rather than require the prison to meet Africa's dietary needs, the court simply said that MOVE did not qualify as a religion.

Perhaps the *Africa* court feared other implications that would have followed were it to have held that MOVE was a religion, either because the State might then have a sharp increase in the number of individuals requesting dietary accommodations or because other avowedly religious groups would seek other kinds of accommodations.⁶⁵ Whatever the court's motivation, the adopted approach does not account for the spirit of what the United States Supreme Court has said and provides a blueprint for marginalizing nontraditional belief systems.

The Tenth Circuit followed a modified form of the *Africa* approach in determining whether a particular set of beliefs qualified as religious.⁶⁶ At issue in *United States v. Meyers* was the prosecution of David Meyers, who

> testified that he is the founder and Reverend of the Church of Marijuana and that it is his sincere belief that his religion commands him to use, possess, grow and distribute marijuana for the good of mankind and the planet earth.⁶⁷

The court examined the protections afforded under the Free Exercise Clause and under the Religious Freedom Restoration Act (RFRA).⁶⁸

The *Meyers* district court held that the definition of religion in RFRA mirrored the definition of religion for First Amendment purposes,⁶⁹ a view endorsed by the Tenth Circuit.⁷⁰ A separate issue is whether that is correct,⁷¹ although that issue need not be addressed here.

The district court considered several elements in its analysis of whether Meyers's beliefs were religious, including whether they (1) involved "Ultimate Ideas"; (2) were "Metaphysical"; (3) involved a "Moral or Ethical System"; and (4) were sufficiently "Comprehensive."[72] In addition, the court considered various "Accoutrements of Religion," which included whether there existed: (a) a founder, prophet or teacher; (b) important writings; (c) an official gathering place; (d) clergy; (e) ceremonies or rituals; (f) a structure or organization; (g) holidays; (h) fast days or days involving special dieting; (i) rules about clothing or appearance; and (j) an attempt to teach the beliefs to nonbelievers.[73] The Tenth Circuit adopted these criteria.[74]

The *Meyers* district court rejected that Meyers's sincere belief that his views were religious established that they in fact were.[75] That is fair enough as a general matter—the *Thomas* Court discussed the possibility of "an asserted claim so bizarre, so clearly nonreligious in motivation, as not to be entitled to protection under the Free Exercise Clause."[76] However, the *Thomas* Court implied that its test was not at all demanding, because a claim would have to be quite "bizarre"[77] to fail to trigger the relevant guarantees, whereas the *Meyers* court employed a test that was much less forgiving.

Meyers's claim was not so bizarre as to be beyond the pale, as the court itself made clear when considering other religious groups' practices involving the sacramental use of illicit drugs. Indeed, the *Meyers* court was forced to engage in careful line-drawing to justify its differentiation between Meyers's allegedly non-religious practices and other drug practices that the court admitted were religious.[78] In certain "religions, such as Native American religions, ancient Mexican religions, and primitive tribal religions, mind-altering plants are sacred."[79] However, those groups use the drugs "to attain a state of religious, spiritual, or revelatory awareness," whereas Meyers's drug use merely "results in a 'peaceful awareness.'"[80] But the difference between revelatory and peaceful awareness simply is not enough to make the former but not the latter sufficiently bizarre to fall outside the reach of free exercise guarantees.

There were other respects in which the Church of Marijuana seemed to qualify as a religion in light of the district court's criteria. The district court noted that Meyers was the founder of the church, and that there were "allegedly ... 800 members and one designated meeting spot."[81] The church had "teachers," although no formal clergy members.[82] Apparently, the court believed that a factor counseling against recognizing the group as religious was that the "church does not attempt to propagate its beliefs in any way, and does not assert that everyone should smoke marijuana," although "part of the 'religion' is to work towards the legalization of marijuana."[83] Yet, individuals or groups can have religious beliefs even if they do not attempt to convert nonbelievers.[84]

An additional factor apparently militating against recognition was that in "response to questioning from the Court about the church's teachings, if any, on 'ultimate ideas' such as life, death, and purpose, Meyers essentially stated that his views on these issues are Christian."[85] The court noted that all members of the church were Christians for whom "the marijuana plant is the center of attention."[86] Yet, Meyers had claimed to have a stand-alone church rather than that his views were essentially Christian with the addition of a particular belief in the importance of marijuana.[87] The court suggested that the Church of Marijuana could not be recognized as a separate religion, although the beliefs would likely have been credited as religious if Meyers had testified that he was a leader of a Christian sect.[88]

One does not know how the district court would in fact have ruled had Meyers claimed to have been the leader of a Christian sect. Perhaps those beliefs would not have qualified as religious either—Meyers was criticized for mentioning that he was a Christian without tying his beliefs in marijuana to Christian theology to the court's satisfaction.[89] The *Meyers* court seemed to require a more consistent doctrinal underpinning before it would recognize beliefs as religious,[90] although such a requirement flies in the face of the *Thomas* Court's warning that "religious beliefs need not be acceptable, logical, consistent, or comprehensible to others in order to merit First Amendment protection."[91]

The *Meyers* district court may simply have believed that Meyers did not have a sincere religious belief, although the court claimed to have "given Meyers the benefit of the doubt by not scrutinizing the sincerity of his beliefs."[92] Yet, a court giving an individual the benefit of the doubt would likely not have expressly stated that the individual was "astute enough to know that by calling his beliefs 'religious,' the First Amendment or RFRA might immunize him from prosecution," or that his "professed beliefs have an ad hoc quality that neatly justify his desire to smoke marijuana."[93]

If the decision were really based on a finding that Meyers's beliefs were not sincerely held,[94] then it would have been better to have said so. The First Amendment does not bar a court from assessing sincerity,[95] so that would have been a permissible basis upon which to deny an exemption.[96] However, the United States Supreme Court has not required individuals to offer theological defenses of their positions.[97] Nor does an individual have to belong to a sect to enjoy free exercise protections—Frazee did not belong to a particular sect[98] and was not a member of an organized church.[99] Further, he did not provide the kind of religious analysis that had been demanded of Meyers.[100]

The *Meyers* court feared that if it were to have

> recognize[d] Meyers' beliefs as religious, it might soon find itself on a slippery slope where anyone who was cured of an ailment by a "medicine" that had pleasant side-effects could claim that they had founded a constitutionally or statutorily protected religion based on the beneficial "medicine."[101]

Yet, even that slippery slope rationale was not particularly persuasive, once the court admitted that Meyers "would have been able to purchase 'religious' status for his beliefs by coattailing on Christianity."[102] Thus, the *Meyers* court held that Meyers's beliefs were not religious but also seemed to provide a blueprint for those wishing to constitutionally immunize their "beneficial 'medicine.'"[103]

The *Ballard* Court was rather deferential with respect to what constituted religion when reviewing the fraud conviction of individuals who claimed to have the power to cure the incurable.[104] Those beliefs might also be thought in the words of the *Meyers* court to have an "ad hoc quality,"[105] because those beliefs in effect immunized the individuals when they sought donations from those afflicted with "diseases which are ordinarily classified by the medical profession as being incurable."[106] Ad hoc nature notwithstanding, the *Ballard* Court accepted that these beliefs were religious, noting that "[r]eligious experiences which are as real as life to some may be incomprehensible to others."[107] While the religious nature of these beliefs was beyond examination, the *Ballard* Court suggested that the trier of fact could examine whether the asserted beliefs were sincerely held.[108]

In his *Meyers* dissent, Judge Wade Brorby rejected that "it is the proper role of the court to establish a factor-driven test to be used to define what a religion is."[109] He noted that the *Yoder* Court "held that religious beliefs are distinct from philosophical and personal choices but failed to provide a test or a definition against which lower courts could hold the religious claims of petitioners to determine whether the claims warrant constitutional protection."[110] Judge Brorby cited the *Thomas* Court's admonition that "religious beliefs need not be acceptable, logical, consistent or comprehensible to others in order to merit First Amendment protection"[111] and, further, the Court's express declaration that "it is no business of courts to say that what is a religious practice or activity for one group is not religion under the protection of the First Amendment."[112] Indeed, the United States Supreme Court seemed to disavow the very approach used by the Tenth Circuit when the Court rejected the inapplicability of First Amendment protections to a group merely because its "religious service [wa]s less ritualistic, more unorthodox, less formal than some."[113] Judge Brorby feared that the *Meyers* majority had "essentially gutted the Free Exercise Clause of its meaning"[114] and had "ignor[ed] the Supreme Court's cautionary words that a person's views can be 'incomprehensible' to the court and still be religious in his or her 'own scheme of things.'"[115]

The *Meyers* court's approach is worrisome for an additional reason if Meyers might indeed have been successful if only his claims had been framed differently. That worry was addressed in *Gillette v. United States* in which the United States Supreme Court was deciding whether individuals with religious objections to the Vietnam War in particular should be accorded conscientious objector status: "There is a danger that as between two would-be objectors, both having the same complaint against a war, that objector would succeed who is more articulate, better educated, or better counseled."[116] The *Meyers* approach is at the very least open to that kind of manipulation.

Consider two individuals or groups seeking exemptions for their (relevantly similar) sincere religious beliefs and practices. One but not the other might succeed because of an ability to offer a more coherent theology or, perhaps, because he is sufficiently prudent to claim to be a sect rather than an independent church. But free exercise guarantees should not only protect those whose arguments are particularly well crafted.[117]

Some circuits have eschewed the factor approach and instead have offered analyses that more closely capture the prevailing Supreme Court jurisprudence. Nonetheless, these approaches also need to be honed.

In *Patrick v. LeFevre*, the Second Circuit noted that "the judiciary is singularly ill-equipped to sit in judgment on the verity of an adherent's religious beliefs."[118] However, rather than follow the Third Circuit's lead and perform the very task that the court has admitted it is ill-equipped to perform, the *Patrick* court instead suggested that the judiciary's focus should be elsewhere, because its "competence properly extends to determining 'whether the beliefs professed by a [claimant] are sincerely held and whether they are, in his own scheme of things, religious.'"[119] The court explained that "[s]incerity analysis seeks to determine an adherent's good faith in the expression of his religious belief."[120] This test can help "differentiat[e] between those beliefs that are held as a matter of conscience and those that are animated by motives of deception and fraud."[121] Thus, the court is permitted to assess whether an individual sincerely holds the beliefs that she claims to hold.

A separate issue is whether the individual's sincerely held beliefs are religious, and the court can "examine[] an individual's inward attitudes towards a particular belief system."[122] The Second Circuit explained that "[i]mpulses prompted by dictates of conscience as well as those engendered by divine commands are therefore safeguarded against secular intervention, so long as the claimant conceives of the beliefs as religious in nature."[123] However, the factfinder must be careful not to permit judgment about either sincerity or religiosity to be based on "the factfinder's perception of what a religion should resemble."[124]

While the Second Circuit avoided some of the pitfalls associated with evaluating the contents of beliefs, the court's requirement that "the claimant conceives of the beliefs as religious in nature"[125] requires further explication. An individual may not categorize her own beliefs as religious if she is using a narrow, conventional definition of religion, even though her beliefs operate in a way that satisfies the Free Exercise Clause's broader definition of religion. The *Welsh* Court explained, "The Court's statement in *Seeger* that a registrant's characterization of his own belief as 'religious' should carry great weight, does not imply that his declaration that his views are nonreligious should be treated similarly."[126] When an individual describes his own beliefs as religious, "that information is highly relevant to the question of the function his beliefs have in his life."[127] However, because an individual may not be "fully aware of the broad scope of the word 'religious,'" a "statement that his beliefs are nonreligious is a highly unreliable guide."[128] Further exploration is required before a conclusion can be reached with respect to whether the beliefs at issue are religious for free exercise purposes, so a court should not reject a claim merely because an individual testified at trial that his beliefs were not religious (in the conventional sense of that term).

The Seventh Circuit explained in *Kaufman v. McCaughtry* that the United States Supreme Court "has adopted a broad definition of 'religion' that includes non-theistic and atheistic beliefs, as well as theistic ones."[129] Kaufman had argued that "his atheist beliefs play[ed] a central role in his life, and the defendants d[id] not dispute that his beliefs [we]re deeply and sincerely held."[130] The Seventh Circuit reasoned that because atheism is "a school of thought that takes a position on religion, the existence and importance of a supreme being, and a code of ethics," it qualified as a religion for First Amendment purposes.[131]

The Seventh Circuit is clearly correct that religions need not incorporate a belief in God.[132] Yet, a "position on religion" need not itself be religious.[133] Further, one need not take a position on God's existence in order for one's beliefs to qualify as religious. For example, Seeger, whose beliefs were characterized as religious, expressly stated that he "preferred to leave the question as to his belief in a Supreme Being open."[134]

The approaches taken in the circuits differ dramatically. Some seek to assess content while others limit their inquiries to assessments of sincerity and whether the beliefs at issue play an appropriate role. The sincerity/role approach is a much closer approximation of what the United States Supreme Court has said than is an approach in which (nonbizarre)[135] content is examined to see whether it is of sufficient religiosity to qualify.

Yet, it should not be thought that the sincerity/role approach is free from difficulty. Sincerity is notoriously difficult to assess.[136] Further, the degree to which the beliefs must play a role in a person's life has not been defined. Individuals may be more or less devout.[137] But those who are less devout still have religious (rather than nonreligious) beliefs,[138] which means that the degree to which beliefs must play an "important" role in an individual's life in order to be classified as religious is itself controversial.

State RFRAs

In response to the *Smith II* Court's narrow reading of free exercise guarantees and the *Boerne* Court's striking down RFRA as applied to the states, various state legislatures passed state religious freedom restoration acts.[139] While the acts vary in language,[140] they are all designed to correct *Smith*'s alleged undermining of free exercise protections.[141] Yet, the state RFRAs have proven to be less protective than might originally have been thought,[142] and it is helpful to consider a few of the state cases litigated under the state RFRAs to understand why that is so.

Florida has had substantial litigation[143] under its state RFRA,[144] and it may be helpful to understand how that statute has been interpreted. Consider *Freeman v. Department of Highway Safety and Motor Vehicles*,[145] which involved a challenge to a denial of a driver's license because Sultaana Lakiana Myke Freeman "refused to have her picture taken without her veil."[146] Freeman was permitted to wear her veil when she was photographed for her Illinois driver's license,[147] but Florida law requires a "'fullface' photograph of the license holder."[148] She was informed that she could not get a license unless she were willing to have a photograph taken without a veil,[149] which she testified was simply not an option.[150]

An expert for the state testified that "where the Department had accommodated the belief by having a female photographer and no males present, a Muslim woman could have her license photograph taken."[151] An expert for Freeman testified that "Muslim women must veil themselves and that ... the doctrine of necessity, found in Islamic law, [could not be] applied to [permit] removing the veil to take a driver's license photograph."[152]

While accepting that Freeman's beliefs were sincere,[153] the Florida appellate court rejected that a substantial burden had been placed on Freeman's religious exercise.[154] Because there had been testimony that it was "[c]onsistent with Islamic law [for] women ... [to be] required to unveil for medical needs and for certain photo ID cards,"[155] and because "the Department's existing procedure would accommodate Freeman's veiling beliefs by using a female photographer with no other person present,"[156] this meant that "[h]er veiling practice is 'merely inconvenienc[ed]' by the photograph requirement [and that] ... she failed to demonstrate a substantial burden."[157] While the *Freeman* court "recognize[d] the tension created as a result of choosing between following the dictates of one's religion and the mandates of secular law,"[158] it reasoned that "as long as the laws are neutral and generally applicable to the citizenry, they must be obeyed,"[159] citing *Braunfeld* in support.[160]

The *Freeman* court readily admitted that the "protection afforded to the free exercise of religiously motivated activity under the FRFRA [Florida Religious Freedom Restoration Act] is broader than that afforded by the decisions of the United States Supreme Court."[161] However, it rejected that the substantial burden test under the Florida act had been met[162] and thus had no need to determine whether the state could meet its "heavy dual burden of demonstrating a compelling interest and that the regulation is the least restrictive means to meet that interest."[163]

If *Thomas* is any guide,[164] then the mere fact that others of the faith may have different views about what the religion permits does not undermine an individual's claim that a restriction imposes a substantial burden on her free exercise rights.[165] That said, at least two points might be made.

First, whether federal constitutional guarantees are violated by the Florida requirement that those receiving a Florida driver's license be photographed without a veil is not the focus of this discussion—such a determination might depend on whether this is a neutral, generally applicable law and on whether there are very important interests justifying such a law. Second, a separate question is whether the Florida court's interpretation of what constitutes a substantial burden for purposes of the statute was itself too restrictive—it may be that the Florida Supreme Court's "narrow definition of substantial burden" was not meant to be this narrow.[166] In any event, the interpretation of the Florida Religious Freedom Restoration Act offered in *Freeman* is clearly not as robust as might have been expected under the *Sherbert-Thomas* line of cases.[167]

At issue in a different Florida case—*Christian Romany Church Ministries, Incorporated v. Broward County*—was whether the county would be permitted to condemn and remove a church through use of its eminent domain power.[168] While the county's doing so served a public purpose,[169] the church nonetheless claimed that its condemnation would violate Florida's Religious Freedom Restoration Act[170] because the church had nowhere else to go.[171]

Condemnation and destruction of the church might result in the congregation's being unable to hold worship services, which would seem to be a paradigmatic example of burdening free exercise.[172] Yet, the court rejected that the challenged action would impose such a burden for purposes of the state's Religious Freedom Protection Act, because condemnation could not be construed as either compelling or forbidding religious conduct.[173] Because there was "nothing about this location that is unique or integral to the conduct of the religion,"[174] the court held that "the condemnation does not substantially burden the exercise of religion."[175]

Perhaps the Florida appellate court is correct that condemnation does not qualify as imposing a substantial burden on religion for purposes of the state RFRA. Absent some evidence of "bad faith or gross abuse of discretion,"[176] it may be that state law did not prevent the church from being forced to move. But it can hardly be thought that Florida's Religious Freedom Restoration Act provides robust protection if a church can be condemned (for an admittedly legitimate purpose), even when that condemnation and destruction would make it impossible for the congregation to worship.[177]

Other states have their own Religious Freedom Restoration Acts. Idaho's protections had to be applied in *Idaho v. Cordingley*,[178] where it was claimed that Cordingley's possession of marijuana and drug paraphernalia was protected under the Idaho Free Exercise of Religion Protected Act (FERPA).[179] Cordingley had founded the "Church of Cognitive Therapy (COCT), established specifically for the use of marijuana as a 'sacrament,'"[180] and he argued that his religious exercise was substantially burdened by Idaho law.

The Idaho appellate court explained that the

> legislative history of the FERPA makes it clear that in adopting the statute, the Idaho legislature intended to adopt the "compelling interest test" contained in its federal counterpart, the Religious Freedom Restoration Act (RFRA), which the United States Supreme Court held in *City of Boerne v. Flores* . . . was invalid as it applied to states.[181]

The plaintiff had to show that he was engaging in a religious exercise and that the challenged state law substantially burdened that exercise.[182]

At issue was not whether Cordingley's beliefs were sincere or even whether the Idaho law substantially burdened the activity associated with those beliefs.[183] Instead, the issue was whether the beliefs at issue were "religious" for purposes of the Idaho statute when Cordingley had admitted that "the Church of Cognitive Therapy is not so much a religion as it is a companion to religion."[184] As such, it provided a way for people to "become spiritual or enlightened, but it [did] not have a comprehensive belief system with the trappings of a religion."[185]

When analyzing whether the burdened practices qualified as religious, the court cited *Ballard* and *Thomas*, but also cited *Yoder*'s attempt to distinguish between the religious and the merely personal and philosophical.[186] The Idaho court denied that it was trying to be extremely restrictive with respect to what constituted a religion, instead suggesting that should there be "any doubt about whether a particular set of beliefs constitutes a religion, the court will err on the side of freedom and find the beliefs are a religion."[187]

To determine whether the beliefs at issue constituted religious beliefs, the court used a multifactor test.

> Under this test, to help determine whether a particular set of beliefs qualifies as "religious" under the RFRA or its state equivalent, a court examines the extent to which

a party's asserted 'religion' (1) addresses "deeper and more imponderable questions" of the meaning of life, man's role in the universe, moral issues of right and wrong, and other "ultimate concerns"; (2) contains an "element of comprehensiveness"; and (3) the "formal, external, or surface signs that may be analogized to accepted religions."[188]

The court found that the church met the relevant criteria to some extent.[189] However, because some of the factors were not met and because "COCT is singularly focused on the use of marijuana to a degree that has consistently been found not to be indicative of statutorily recognized religious practice,"[190] the Idaho appellate court found that the practices at issue were not religious and thus did not qualify for enhanced protection under the Idaho statute.

Yet, it is difficult to reconcile this approach with the approach taken in *Ballard*, where the beliefs of the "I Am movement" were not examined with respect to whether they incorporated "ultimate ideas" or constituted a "moral or ethical belief structure" or even whether the "comprehensiveness of beliefs" entitled the group to be designated as religious. The *Ballard* Court noted that "[r]eligious experiences which are as real as life to some may be incomprehensible to others,"[191] and that the fact that certain experiences are "beyond the ken of mortals does not mean that they can be made suspect before the law."[192] Further, a set of beliefs that is described by the adherents as a "companion to religion"[193] would seem to be religious even if not providing many desired metaphysical answers, precisely because it was to be understood in light of other beliefs or belief systems.

That said, it was fair for the *Cordingley* court to point out that the United States Supreme Court has not always espoused deference to the claim that particular views are religious.[194] The *Yoder* Court suggested that it is permissible to distinguish between the religious and the philosophical,[195] although the Court provided no guidance about how to perform that task beyond saying that Thoreau's views were not religious.[196] The failure to say more was regrettable, if only because many of such analyses will be subject to one of the dangers mentioned by the *Ballard* Court—permitting the trier-of-fact to decide whether a particular set of beliefs is religious or, perhaps, sufficiently profound or comprehensive opens the door to a potentially unsympathetic trier-of-fact subjecting a set of avowedly religious beliefs to very critical examination.[197] While *Yoder* might have been trying to protect the diversity of religious belief,[198] it has been used to exclude belief systems from qualifying as religious.

Conclusion

The United States Supreme Court has not decided many cases involving RFRA or RLUIPA. However, it is reasonable to expect that many more will come before the Court, especially if the Court does not overrule *Smith II*'s rather forgiving approach towards neutral and generally applicable statutes that impose incidental burdens on religion. Many individuals claiming that state or federal statutes, policies, or practices impose too great a burden on religious practice will now challenge under federal statute or state (constitutional or statutory) law rather than under First Amendment guarantees.

This shift away from an emphasis on First Amendment protections may seem beneficial. Where the protections afforded by federal statute are at issue, less might seem to be at stake when the Court issues a decision if only because a bad decision can be legislatively overruled—it will not be necessary to pass a constitutional amendment in order for an allegedly mistaken Court interpretation to be corrected. Yet, merely because Congress would have the power to correct a bad decision about legislative intent would not mean that a very dysfunctional

Congress would be able to reach a consensus about how the statute at issue should be amended.

Some of the difficulties that arose in the context of interpreting free exercise guarantees are again arising in the context of interpreting federal statutory protections. The circuits have offered very different interpretations of the protections afforded under RFRA and RLUIPA, and the Court has done little to clarify the applicable standard. Yet, the difficulty is not merely that the Court is refusing to give direction. Some of the direction given by the Court is being ignored, although the Court seems not to notice.

The Court has been relatively forgiving with respect to what constitutes religious practice and relatively forgiving with respect to what constitutes a substantial burden on religion. But the Court (unlike the circuit courts) does not seem to have appreciated the implications of such an approach when either RFRA or RLUIPA has been triggered. Basically, a relaxed approach towards both what counts as a religious practice and what counts as a substantial burden will mean that the state will have a very difficult time justifying its imposing even incidental burdens on religious practice. But if that is so, then there will be many instances in which state and federal laws will have to be struck down or, at least, interpreted as incorporating religious exemptions, especially if the state can only justify its law by showing why permitting *this particular individual* to engage in the contested practice would be very burdensome for the state.

When discussing how it would interpret RFRA's requirement that the Government "demonstrate[ ] that application of the burden *to the person*"[199] passes strict scrutiny, the *Hobby Lobby* Court suggested that it would use a "What if everyone did that?" approach to tax challenges, just as it had in *United States v. Lee*.[200] The Court seemed not to notice that *Lee* was not using an "application of the burden to the person" test. In *Lee*, for example, it would not have been very burdensome for the state to have exempted Amish employers from paying into Social Security for their Amish employees, which in fact is what Congress later allowed by statute. But this failure to attend to the applicable standard suggests that the Court may well import an inconsistent and unprincipled free exercise approach when interpreting federal statutory protections of religious practice.

If *Hobby Lobby* and *Holt* are any guide, the Court is going to continue being deferential about what constitutes religious exercise and what constitutes a substantial burden on religion. The circuit courts are going to use a tougher standard because they will be unwilling to countenance a great number of successful challenges to zoning or prison regulations, and also will likely be much less sympathetic to those seeking exemptions under federal law.

At some point, the Court will be asked to clarify the jurisprudence, but it will not want to put courts in the position of judging what counts as religious or what constitutes a substantial burden. But this will force the Court to offer ad hoc rationalizations and interpretations, just as it did in the free exercise jurisprudence. Or, the Court will simply refuse to address the underlying difficulties because there seems to be no consistent or principled way to resolve the issues at hand.

The Court has made matters in this area more confusing rather than less, which does not inspire confidence that the Court will offer a helpful way out of the mess that it has had a hand in creating. In short, the current unsustainable approach is likely to become even more confusing and confused, and neither Congress nor the federal courts will likely be able to offer an approach that provides reasonable protections to both the religious and the non-religious. No one should be pleased about the recent turn in the jurisprudence, which almost guarantees unequal application, the imposition of undeserved burdens, even greater confusion in the courts, and further balkanization in the country.

Notes

1 See *Holt v. Hobbs*, 135 S. Ct. 853, 860 (2015) ("Section 3 [of RLUIPA] mirrors RFRA and provides that '[n]o government shall impose a substantial burden on the religious exercise of a person residing in or confined to an institution . . . even if the burden results from a rule of general applicability.'" (quoting 42 *United States Code* § 2000cc-1(a))).
2 *Patel v. United States Bureau of Prisons*, 515 F.3d 807, 813–14 (8th Cir. 2008) ("When the significance of a religious belief is not at issue, the same definition of 'substantial burden' applies under the Free Exercise Clause, RFRA and RLUIPA." (citing *Murphy v. Missouri Department of Corrections*, 372 F.3d 979, 988 (8th Cir. 2004))).
3 See *Vision Church v. Village of Long Grove*, 468 F.3d 975, 996–97 (7th Cir. 2006) ("RLUIPA's legislative history indicates that the term 'substantial burden' was intended to be interpreted by reference to First Amendment jurisprudence[.]" (citing 146 *Congressional Record* S7774–01 (daily ed. July 27, 2000) (joint statement of Senator Hatch and Senator Kennedy))).
4 *Washington v. Klem*, 497 F.3d 272, 278 (3d Cir. 2007) ("Supreme Court precedent with respect to the definition of 'substantial burden' in the Free Exercise Clause context has not always been consistent.").
5 *Adkins v. Kaspar*, 393 F.3d 559 (5th Cir. 2004).
6 *Id.* at 568 (citing *Murphy v. Missouri Department of Corrections*, 372 F.3d 979, 988 (8th Cir. 2004), certiorari denied, 543 U.S. 991 (2004)).
7 *Id.* (citing *Civil Liberties for Urban Believers v. City of Chicago*, 342 F.3d 752, 761 (7th Cir. 2003), certiorari denied, 541 U.S. 1096 (2004)).
8 *Id.* (citing *San Jose Christian College v. City of Morgan Hill*, 360 F.3d 1024, 1034 (9th Cir. 2004)).
9 *Id.* at 568–69 (citing *Midrash Sephardi, Incorporated v. Town of Surfside*, 366 F.3d 1214, 1227 (11th Cir. 2004), certiorari denied, 543 U.S. 1146 (2005)).
10 342 F.3d 752.
11 *Id.* at 761 (citing *Mack v. O'Leary*, 80 F.3d 1175, 1179 (7th Cir. 1996)).
12 *Id.*
13 *Id.*
14 *Id.*
15 *Midrash Sephardi, Incorporated v. Town of Surfside*, 366 F.3d 1214 (11th Cir. 2004).
16 *Id.* at 1227.
17 *Id.* (citing *Cheffer v. Reno*, 55 F.3d 1517, 1522 (11th Cir. 1995)).
18 *Id.* at 1228.
19 *Id.*
20 *Id.* at 1227.
21 *International Church of Foursquare Gospel v. City of San Leandro*, 673 F.3d 1059, 1069 (9th Cir. 2011) ("This higher standard [used in *Civil Liberties for Urban Believers*] has been rejected in this circuit." (citing *Guru Nanak Sikh Soc. of Yuba City v. County of Sutter*, 456 F.3d 978, 989 n. 12 (9th Cir. 2006))).
22 See *id.* at 1068–69.
23 *Malnak v. Yogi*, 592 F.2d 197, 197–98 (3d Cir. 1979).
24 *Id.* at 198.
25 Cf. David Young, "The Meaning of 'Religion' in the First Amendment: Lexicography and Constitutional Policy, *University of Missouri-Kansas City Law Review* 56:313–41 (1988), p. 326 ("In the past ten years, few jurists have given such systematic thought to the definition of 'religion' as Judge Adams of the Third Circuit.").
26 *Malnak*, 592 F.2d at 200, 204 (Adams, J., concurring) ("[There is] some indication that the Court has, to some degree, drawn back from the broadest possible reading of these cases." (citing *Wisconsin v. Yoder*, 406 U.S. 205, 216 (1972))).
27 *Id.* at 207.
28 *Id.* at 208.
29 *Id.* (quoting Paul Tillich, *Dynamics of Faith* 1–2 (1958)).
30 *Id.* at 208–09.
31 *Id.* at 209.
32 *Id.*
33 *Id.*

34 See *id.* at 209 n. 43.
35 See *id.* at 209 n. 43. ("[P]urely personal ideas, even if sincere, may not rise to a religious level." (citing *Wisconsin v. Yoder*, 406 U.S. 205, 216 (1972))).
36 *Malnak*, 592 F.2d at 210 (Adams, J., concurring) ("Although these indicia will be helpful, they should not be thought of as a final 'test' for religion.").
37 Craig A. Mason, "'Secular Humanism' and the Definition of Religion: Extending a Modified 'Ultimate Concern' Test to *Mozert v. Hawkins County Public Schools* and *Smith v. Board of School Commissioners*," *Washington Law Review* 63:445–68 (1988), pp. 450–51 ("Judge Adams' formulation illustrates the problems inherent in an analogical method of definition. This approach explicitly prefers 'traditional' religions, to the exclusion of less conventional beliefs. Additionally, Judge Adams' method grants preference to religions which have incubated in a leisured elite long enough to become 'comprehensive' in a systematic sense; in contrast to the less intellectually systematized passions . . . and of lower classes everywhere. Finally, the analogical method's views of 'fundamental' and 'ultimate' questions are severely ethnocentric."); Young (1988), p. 327 ("Adams' approach is subject to a number of criticisms.").
38 *Malnak*, 592 F.2d at 210 (Adams, J., concurring).
39 Arlin M. Adams and Charles J. Emmerich, "A Heritage of Religious Liberty," *University of Pennsylvania Law Review* 137:1559–671 (1989), p. 1665 ("The Supreme Court has not defined religion for constitutional purposes, but decisions in other contexts reveal the steady expansion of the term 'religion' to meet needs arising in an increasingly complex and pluralistic society.").
40 See *United States v. Seeger*, 380 U.S. 163, 180, 187 (1965).
41 See *Malnak*, 592 F.2d at 209 n. 43 (Adams, J., concurring).
42 *Seeger*, 380 U.S. at 187.
43 See "Developments in the Law—Religion and the State," *Harvard Law Review* 100:1612–39 (1987), p. 1625 ("Although neither *Seeger* nor *Welsh* directly addressed the meaning of 'religion' as used in the [F]irst [A]mendment, these cases indirectly support a subjective, functionalist approach to the definition of religion.").
44 See *Malnak*, 592 F.2d at 208 (Adams, J., concurring) (agreeing with Dr. Paul Tillich's view of ultimate concern, which means religion is intimately connected to concepts "that are of the greatest depth and utmost importance").
45 *See id.* at 204 n. 20 (discussing *Yoder*'s "apparent retrenchment").
46 *Wisconsin v. Yoder*, 406 U.S 205, 216 (1972).
47 *See* Young (1988), pp. 332–33 (explaining that Judge Adams's approach in defining religion is more restrictive than the approach incorporated by the Court in *Yoder*).
48 *Africa v. Pennsylvania*, 662 F.2d 1025, 1025 (3d Cir. 1981); see also "Developments in the Law—Religion and the State," *Harvard Law Review* 100:1612–39, p. 1626 (1987) (stating that the court's opinion in *Africa* focused on whether the belief was "religious in nature" and citing to Judge Adams's opinion in *Seeger*).
49 *Africa*, 662 F.2d at 1025.
50 *Id.* at 1026.
51 *Id.* at 1027.
52 *Id.*
53 *Id.* at 1028.
54 *Id.*
55 *Id.* at 1029 ("Africa had failed to establish that MOVE is 'a religion within the purview and definition of the [F]irst [A]mendment.'").
56 *Id.* at 1030 (citing *Seeger*, 380 U.S. at 185).
57 *Id.* at 1031.
58 *Id.*
59 *Id.* at 1032.
60 *Id.* at 1028.
61 *Id.* at 1033.
62 *Id.*
63 *Id.* at 1035 (alteration in original); see also Binkley (2010), p. 209 ("In sum, MOVE did not resemble Judge Adams's paradigm of religion closely enough to qualify as a religion under

the First Amendment."); Erez Reuveni, "On Boy Scouts and Anti-Discrimination Law: The Associational Rights of Quasi-Religious Organizations," *Boston University Law Review* 86:109–71 (2006), p. 147 ("The court applied a three-part analysis, holding that MOVE was not concerned with religious principles, failed to embody a comprehensive, multi-faceted theology, and lacked the defining structural characteristics of a traditional religion.").

64 *Africa*, 662 F.2d at 1037 ("Especially in light of the apparent willingness of Graterford officials to accede to the dietary requirements of other prisoners, both for religious and for medical reasons, it is not clear from the record why special accommodations cannot be made in this instance for a prisoner who obviously cares deeply about what food he eats.").

65 John S. Hilbert, "God in a Cage: Religion, Intent, and Criminal Law," *Buffalo Law Review* 36:701–42 (1987), p. 717 ("The answer may well be based less on the court's assurance as to its competency to identify religion as on its concerns as to the possible consequences of so deciding. The prison superintendent had testified that recognizing MOVE as a religion would possibly lead to 'a proliferation of other groups' requesting special diets and MOVE attracting new 'sympathizers.'" (quoting *Africa*, 662 F.2d at 1028)).

66 See *United States v. Meyers*, 95 F.3d 1475, 1483 (10th Cir. 1996) (citing *Africa* when affirming the factors used by the district court in denying that the belief system qualified as religious); see also Donna D. Page, "Veganism and Sincerely Held 'Religious' Beliefs in the Workplace: No Protection Without Definition, *University of Pennsylvania Journal of Labor & Employment Law* 7:363–408 (2005), p. 382 ("In *United States v. Meyers*, the Tenth Circuit developed an approach for defining religion similar to Judge Adams's three-indicia approach.").

67 *Meyers*, 95 F.3d at 1479.

68 See *id.* at 1481–84 ("Meyers' challenge to his convictions under the Free Exercise Clause must fail. . . . [W]e hold that Meyers' challenge fails for the same reasons as the respondents challenge in *Smith* failed, i.e., the right to free exercise of religion under the Free Exercise Clause of the First Amendment does not relieve an individual of the obligation to comply with a valid and neutral law of general applicability on the ground that the law incidentally affects religious practice.").

69 See *United States v. Meyers*, 906 F. Supp. 1494, 1499 (D. Wyoming 1995), affirmed, 95 F.3d 1475 (10th Cir. 1996) ("'[R]eligion' under RFRA is the same as 'religion' under the First Amendment.").

70 See *Meyers*, 95 F.3d at 1484 ("We agree with the district court. Under the district court's thorough analysis of the indicia of religion, which we adopt, we hold that Meyers' beliefs more accurately espouse a philosophy and/or way of life rather than a 'religion.'").

71 It may be that religion itself is broader under RFRA than under the Free Exercise Clause, or it may be that the exercise of religion is broader under RFRA than under the Free Exercise Clause. Cf. *Burwell v. Hobby Lobby Stores, Incorporated*, 134 S. Ct. 2751, 2772 (2014) ("It is simply not possible to read these provisions as restricting the concept of the 'exercise of religion' to those practices specifically addressed in our pre-*Smith* decisions.").

72 *Meyers*, 95 F.3d at 1483; see also *Meyers*, 906 F. Supp. at 1502 (citing *Africa v. Pennsylvania*, 662 F.2d 1025, 1035 (3d Cir. 1981)).

73 *Meyers*, 95 F.3d at 1483–84; see also *Meyers*, 906 F. Supp. at 1502–03.

74 See *Meyers*, 95 F.3d at 1484 ("[W]e agree with . . . the district court's thorough analysis of the indicia of religion."). Professor Beschle writes, "*Meyers* shows that courts have been able to reject some free exercise claims as nonreligious, despite the broad language of the Supreme Court draft cases." Donald L. Beschle, "Does a Broad Free Exercise Right Require a Narrow Definition of 'Religion'?," *Hastings Constitutional Law Quarterly* 39:357–90 (2011), p. 376. However, Professor Beschle does not seem to appreciate that the *Meyers* court was not applying the test suggested by the U.S. Supreme Court. See *Meyers*, 95 F.3d at 1491 (Brorby, J., dissenting) ("By applying a broad factor-driven test as advocated by the majority opinion, the subjective perceptions of the court are necessarily invoked in evaluating whether what the individual claims to be religious is indeed religious. It also requires the court to judge the practices of the individual to see if they are indeed 'religious.' This test clearly violates the spirit, if not the intent, of the First Amendment.").

75 See *Meyers*, 95 F.3d at 1484 (majority opinion) ("If he thinks that his beliefs are a religion, then so be it. No one can restrict his beliefs, and no one should begrudge him those beliefs. None of this, however, changes the fact that his beliefs do not constitute a 'religion' as that term is uneasily defined by law." (quoting *Meyers*, 906 F Supp. at 1508)).

Lower courts and protection of religion 143

76 *Thomas v. Review Board*, 450 U.S. 707, 715 (1981).
77 *Id.*
78 *See Meyers*, 906 F. Supp. at 1506.
79 *Id.*
80 *Id.*
81 *Id.* at 1504 ("Meyers founded the 'Church of Marijuana' in 1973.").
82 *Id.* ("The church does not have a formal clergy, but does have approximately 20 'teachers.'").
83 *Meyers*, 906 F. Supp. at 1504.
84 See Ruti Teitel, "When Separate Is Equal: Why Organized Religious Exercises, Unlike Chess, Do Not Belong in the Public Schools," *Northwestern University Law Review* 81:174–89 (1986), p. 178; Matthew L. Sandgren, "Extending Religious Freedoms Abroad: Difficulties Experienced by Minority Religions," *Tulsa Journal of Comparative & International Law* 9:251–84 (2001), p. 254 ("[S]ome religions do not feel it necessary to proselytize.").
85 *Meyers*, 906 F. Supp. at 1504.
86 *Id.* at 1505 ("Meyers said that all church members are Christians.").
87 *Id.* at 1508 ("Meyers presented the Church of Marijuana as a 'stand alone' religion. . . . He did not claim that any of his beliefs were based on Christianity, or that any of his beliefs were related to Christianity.").
88 *Id.* ("Had Meyers asserted that the Church of Marijuana was a Christian sect, and that his beliefs were related to Christianity, this Court probably would have been compelled to conclude that his beliefs were religious.").
89 *Id.* ("[H]e mentioned that he was a Christian. After asserting that other church members also were Christians and that they believed in God, Meyers never mentioned Christianity again. He did not claim that any of his beliefs were based on Christianity, or that any of his beliefs were related to Christianity.").
90 *Id.* at 1509 ("Meyers did not cite any Christian texts, refer to any Christian doctrines, or discuss any Christian teachings in support of his beliefs. The Court cannot, therefore, conclude that his marijuana smoking is rooted, let alone 'deeply rooted,' in Christian religious belief." (quoting *Teterud v. Burns*, 522 F.2d 357, 360 (8th Cir. 1975))).
91 *Thomas*, 450 U.S. at 714.
92 *Meyers*, 906 F. Supp. at 1509.
93 *Id.* The Circuit Court might also have suspected that Meyers did not sincerely hold the religious beliefs that he claimed to have. See *United States v. Meyers*, 95 F.3d 1475, 1484 (10th Cir. 1996) (expressly noting the district court's observation that Meyers's beliefs had an "ad hoc quality" that justified the desire to smoke marijuana).
94 See, e.g., David Garrett, "Vine of the Dead: Reviving Equal Protection Rites for Religious Drug Use," *American Indian Law Review* 31:143–62 (2007), pp. 160–61 (suggesting that Meyers did not have a sincere religious belief concerning marijuana use).
95 See *United States v. Ballard*, 322 U.S. 78, 86–87 (1944).
96 See *Luckette v. Lewis*, 883 F. Supp. 471, 478 (D. Arizona 1995) ("Courts must be able to sort out the insincere and illegitimate prisoner Free Exercise claims from the legitimate ones."); see also *Society of Separationists, Incorporated v. Herman*, 939 F.2d 1207, 1219 (5th Cir. 1991), affirmed on rehearing, 959 F.2d 1283 (5th Cir. 1992) ("Beliefs may be rejected only if they are patently insincere, bizarre, or not related to the free exercise of religion.").
97 See *Thomas*, 450 U.S. at 714.
98 *Frazee v. Illinois Department of Employment Security*, 489 U.S. 829, 834 (1989) ("Frazee asserted that he was a Christian, but did not claim to be a member of a particular Christian sect.").
99 *Id.* at 831 ("Frazee was not a member of an established religious sect or church.").
100 *Id.* ("[N]or did he claim that his refusal to work resulted from a 'tenet, belief or teaching of an established religious body.'" (quoting *Frazee v. Department of Employment Security*, 512 N.E.2d 789, 791 (Illinois Appellate Court 1987))).
101 *Meyers*, 906 F. Supp. at 1508.
102 *Id.*
103 *Id.*

104 United States v. Ballard, 322 U.S. 78, 80 (1944).
105 *Meyers*, 906 F. Supp. at 1509.
106 *Ballard*, 322 U.S. at 80.
107 *Id.* at 86.
108 *Id.* at 81, 88 ("The court . . . confined the issues on this phase of the case to the question of the good faith of respondents . . . . [T]he District Court ruled properly when it withheld from the jury all questions concerning the truth or falsity of the religious beliefs or doctrines of respondents.").
109 *Meyers*, 95 F.3d at 1489 (Brorby, J., dissenting).
110 *Id.* (Brorby, J., dissenting).
111 *Id.* at 1491 (Brorby, J., dissenting) (quoting *Thomas*, 450 U.S. at 714).
112 *Id.* (Brorby, J., dissenting) (quoting *Fowler v. Rhode Island*, 345 U.S. 67, 70 (1953)).
113 *Fowler*, 345 U.S. at 69.
114 *Meyers*, 95 F.3d at 1490 (Brorby, J., dissenting).
115 *Id.* (Brorby, J., dissenting) (quoting *Seeger*, 380 U.S. at 185).
116 *Gillette v. United States*, 401 U.S. 437, 457 (1971).
117 But see Stephen M. Feldman, "Religious Minorities and the First Amendment: The History, the Doctrine, and the Future," *University of Pennsylvania Journal of Constitutional Law* 6:222–77 (2003), p. 259 ("Religion Clause litigants obviously would be wise to frame their claims, whenever possible, as establishment rather than free exercise issues.").
118 Patrick v. LeFevre, 745 F.2d 153, 157 (2d Cir. 1984).
119 *Id.* (alteration in original) (quoting *Seeger*, 380 U.S. at 185); see also *United States v. Ward*, 989 F.2d 1015, 1018 (9th Cir. 1992) ("In determining whether Ward's own peculiar notions are protected as religious beliefs, '[the] task is to decide whether the beliefs professed . . . are sincerely held and whether they are, in [Ward's] own scheme of things, religious.'" (alteration in original) (quoting *Seeger*, 380 U.S. at 185)).
120 *Patrick*, 745 F.2d at 157 (citing *International Society for Krishna Consciousness, Incorporated v. Barber*, 650 F.2d 430, 441 (2d Cir. 1981)).
121 *Id.*
122 *Id.* (citing *Thomas*, 450 U.S. at 713–15).
123 *Id.* at 158.
124 *Id.* at 157.
125 *Id.* at 158.
126 *Welsh v. United States*, 398 U.S. 333, 341 (1970) (citing *Seeger*, 380 U.S. at 184).
127 *Id.*
128 *Id.*
129 *Kaufman v. McCaughtry*, 419 F.3d 678, 682 (7th Cir. 2005).
130 *Id.*
131 *Id.* ("[W]e are satisfied that it qualifies as Kaufman's religion for purposes of the First Amendment claims he is attempting to raise.").
132 See *Torcaso v. Watkins*, 367 U.S. 488, 495 n. 11 (1961).
133 Cf. Leslie Griffin, "'We Do Not Preach. We Teach.' Religion Professors and the First Amendment," *Quinnipiac Law Review* 19:1–65 (2000), p. 9 ("[R]eligious studies is teaching about religion; theology is teaching of religion.").
134 *Seeger*, 380 U.S. at 166, 187 ("Seeger professed 'religious belief' and 'religious faith.'").
135 While the *Thomas* Court noted that bizarre beliefs are beyond the reach of free exercise protections, see *Thomas*, 450 U.S. at 715–16, the Court nowhere specified a criterion for determining which beliefs are so bizarre as to fall outside of free exercise protection. For example, the beliefs at issue in *Ballard*, namely, that the Ballards had the power to cure any and all diseases, were not so bizarre as to be unprotected.
136 See *United States v. Nugent*, 346 U.S. 1, 10 (1953) ("It is always difficult to devise procedures which will be adequate to do justice in cases where the sincerity of another's religious convictions is the ultimate factual issue."); Kevin L. Brady, "Religious Sincerity and Imperfection: Can Lapsing Prisoners Recover Under RFRA and RLUIPA?" *University of Chicago Law Review* 78:1431–64 (2011), p. 1451 ("[R]eligious sincerity is difficult to prove.").

137 Cf. Gregory C. Sisk et al., "Searching for the Soul of Judicial Decisionmaking: An Empirical Study of Religious Freedom Decisions, " *Ohio State Law Journal* 65:491–614 (2004), p. 579 (comparing the voting patterns of those who are more devout with those who are less devout).
138 Cf. Eric C. Freed, "Secular Humanism, the Establishment Clause, and Public Education," *New York University Law Review* 61:1149–85 (1986), p. 1166 ("A belief should not be able to escape establishment clause strictures merely because its adherents place other concerns above their religion, or even because the adherents have doubts about the truth of their belief.").
139 See John D. Inazu, "The Four Freedoms and the Future of Religious Liberty," *North Carolina Law Review* 92:787–853 (2014), p. 820 n. 165 ("In response to *Smith* and *City of Boerne*, a number of post-*Smith* state legislative acts or constitutional amendments provided increased protections for religious freedom.").
140 See Christopher C. Lund, "Religious Liberty after *Gonzales*: A Look at State RFRAs," *South Dakota Law Review* 55:466–97 (2010), pp. 478–79 (discussing some of the differences among the state RFRAs).
141 See *id.* at 466 ("*Smith*, as everyone knows, dramatically narrowed the scope of the Free Exercise Clause.").
142 *Id.* at 467 ("In most jurisdictions, plaintiffs have not won a single state RFRA case litigated to judgment. To be sure, some states have seen significant state RFRA litigation and there have been some very important victories. But in many states, state RFRAs seem to exist almost entirely on the books.").
143 *Id.* at 481 ("Florida passed its RFRA early; it has seen substantial litigation. Yet of all the claims asserted over the years, only a single state Florida RFRA claim litigated to judgment has won.").
144 See *Florida Statutes Annotated* § 761.03: "(1) The government shall not substantially burden a person's exercise of religion, even if the burden results from a rule of general applicability, except that government may substantially burden a person's exercise of religion only if it demonstrates that application of the burden to the person:
(a) Is in furtherance of a compelling governmental interest; and
(b) Is the least restrictive means of furthering that compelling governmental interest.
(2) A person whose religious exercise has been burdened in violation of this section may assert that violation as a claim or defense in a judicial proceeding and obtain appropriate relief."
145 *Freeman v. Department of Highway Safety & Motor Vehicles*, 924 So. 2d 48 (Florida Appellate 2006).
146 *Id.* at 50.
147 See *id.* at 51.
148 *Id.*
149 See *id.* at 52.
150 See *id.*
151 *Id.*
152 *Id.*
153 See *id.* at 54.
154 *Id.* ("[T]here is no substantial burden on Freeman's exercise of religion.").
155 *Id.* at 56.
156 *Id.*
157 *Id.* at 57.
158 *Id.*
159 *Id.*
160 *Id.*
161 *Id.* at 55 (citing *Warner v. City of Boca Raton*, 887 So. 2d 1023, 1032 (Florida 2004)).
162 *Id.* at 54.
163 *Id.* at 56.
164 See *Thomas*, 450 U.S. 707.
165 Lund (2010), at 488 ("The court essentially says that because other Muslim women in other countries remove the veil for photographs, Freeman should consider herself free to do

so as well. But . . . [i]ndividuals have a right to religious accommodation even on matters where they differ from their co-religionists.").
166 See *Freeman*, 924 So. 2d at 56 ("The narrow definition of substantial burden adopted by the supreme court tempers the act's strict scrutiny requirement. A plaintiff must meet a high standard to show a substantial burden on religious freedom.").
167 See *Sherbert v. Verner*, 374 U.S. 398 (1963); see *Thomas*, 450 U.S. at 707.
168 *Christian Romany Church Ministries, Inc. v. Broward County*, 980 So. 2d 1164, 1165 (Florida Appellate 2008).
169 *Id.* ("[T]he church does not dispute that the taking would serve a public purpose.").
170 *Id.* ("[The church] asserts that the county has failed to show a reasonable necessity for the taking and is in violation of the Florida Religious Freedom Restoration Act (FRFRA).").
171 *Id.* at 1166 ("The pastor testified that he did not know where they will go if the church is taken, and he has no other place for holding religious education.").
172 See *id.* at 1168 ("[The] church's insistence that a specific church building for holding worship services is fundamental to religious exercise.").
173 See *id.* ("Our supreme court expressly rejected any definition of substantial burden other than that compelling conduct or that forbidding conduct. By no stretch does an otherwise valid condemnation fall within these limits.").
174 *Id.*
175 *Id.*
176 *Id.* at 1167.
177 Cf. *Guru Nanak Sikh Society of Yuba City v. County of Sutter*, 456 F.3d 978, 981 (9th Cir. 2006) ("We find that the County imposed a substantial burden on Appellee Guru Nanak Sikh Society of Yuba City's . . . religious exercise under RLUIPA because the stated reasons and history behind the denial at issue, and a previous denial of Guru Nanak's application to build a temple on a parcel of land zoned 'residential,' to a significantly great extent lessened the possibility of Guru Nanak constructing a temple in the future.").
178 *Idaho v. Cordingley*, 302 P.3d 730 (Idaho Appellate 2013).
179 *Id.* at 731 ("Levon Fred Cordingley appeals from the district court's intermediate appellate decision affirming the magistrate's denial of his motion to dismiss the possession of marijuana and paraphernalia charges against him on the basis his right to religious freedom under the Idaho Free Exercise of Religion Protected Act (FERPA).").
180 *Id.* at 732.
181 *Id.* at 733.
182 See *id.* ("To establish a prima facie RFRA claim, a plaintiff must present evidence sufficient to allow a trier of fact rationally to find the existence of two elements. First, the activities the plaintiff claims are burdened by the government action must be an 'exercise of religion.' Second, the government action must 'substantially burden' the plaintiff's exercise of religion.") (quoting *Navajo Nation v. United States Forest Service*, 535 F.3d 1058, 1068 (9th Cir. 2008) (internal citations omitted)).
183 *Cordingley*, 302 P.3d. at 734 ("[I]t was undisputed that Cordingley's beliefs were both sincerely held and substantially burdened by the applicable controlled substances statutes.").
184 *Id.* (citing the district court opinion).
185 *Id.* (citing the district court opinion).
186 *Id.* at 736.
187 *Id.* (citing *Meyers*, 906 F. Supp. at 1499).
188 *Id.* (citing *Malnak*, 592 F.2d at 208–09) (Adams, J., concurring).
189 *Id.* at 744 ("to some degree the COCT is comprised of a structure containing some of the 'accoutrements of religion'").
190 *Id.* at 745.
191 *Ballard*, 322 U.S. at 86.
192 *Id.* at 87.
193 *Cordingley*, 154 P.3d at 734.
194 See *id.* at 736 (discussing *Yoder*, 406 U.S. at 215–16).
195 See *Yoder*, 406 U.S. at 216.
196 *Id.*

197 Cf. *Ballard*, 322 U.S. at 87 ("The miracles of the New Testament, the Divinity of Christ, life after death, the power of prayer are deep in the religious convictions of many. If one could be sent to jail because a jury in a hostile environment found those teachings false, little indeed would be left of religious freedom.").
198 See *Yoder*, 406 U.S. at 220–21.
199 Religious Freedom Restoration Act (RFRA) of 1993, 42 *United States Code* § 2000bb-3(b) (2012) (emphasis added).
200 See *Hobby Lobby*, 134 S. Ct. at 2784 (citing *Lee*, 455 U.S. at 260).

Bibliography

Federal courts

Supreme Court cases

Ballard, United States v., 322 U.S. 78 (1944)
Ballard v. United States, 329 U.S. 187 (1946)
Barrentine v. Arkansas-Best Freight System, Incorporated, 450 U.S. 728 (1981)
Bland, United States v., 283 U.S. 636 (1931), overruled in part by *Girouard v. United States*, 328 U.S. 61 (1946)
Bob Jones University v. United States, 461 U.S. 574 (1983)
Bouldin v. Alexander, 82 U.S. 131 (1872)
Bowen v. Roy, 476 U.S. 693 (1986)
Braunfeld v. Brown, 366 U.S. 599 (1961)
Burwell v. Hobby Lobby Stores, Incorporated, 134 S. Ct. 2751 (2014)
Cantwell v. Connecticut, 310 U.S. 296 (1940)
Chaplinsky v. New Hampshire, 315 U.S. 568 (1942)
Church of the Lukumi Babalu Aye, Incorporated v. City of Hialeah, 508 U.S. 520 (1993)
City of Boerne v. Flores, 521 U.S. 507 (1997)
Coale v. Pearson, 290 U.S. 597 (1933)
Corporation of Presiding Bishop of Church of Jesus Christ of Latter-Day Saints v. Amos, 483 U.S. 327 (1987)
County of Allegheny v. American Civil Liberties Union Greater Pittsburgh Chapter, 492 U.S. 573 (1989)
Cox v. New Hampshire, 312 U.S. 569 (1941)
Cutter v. Wilkinson, 544 U.S. 709 (2005)
Davis v. Beason, 133 U.S. 333 (1890)
Day-Brite Lighting, Incorporated v. Missouri, 342 U.S. 421 (1952)
Department of Health & Human Services v. Gilardi, 134 S. Ct. 2902 (2014)
Employment Division, Department of Human Resources of Oregon v. Smith (Smith I), 485 U.S. 660 (1988)
Employment Division, Department of Human Resources of Oregon v. Smith (Smith II), 494 U.S. 872 (1990)
Engel v. Vitale, 370 U.S. 421 (1962)
Epperson v. Arkansas, 393 U.S. 97 (1968)
Estate of Thornton v. Caldor, Incorporated, 472 U.S. 703 (1985)
Everson v. Board of Education of Ewing, 330 U.S. 1 (1947)
Fowler v. Rhode Island, 345 U.S. 67 (1953)
Frazee v. Illinois Department of Employment Security, 489 U.S. 829 (1989)
Gallagher v. Crown Kosher Super Market of Massachusetts, Incorporated, 366 U.S. 617 (1961)
Geneva College v. Burwell, 136 S. Ct. 445 (2015)

Gilardi v. Department of Health & Human Services, 134 S. Ct. 2902 (2014)
Gillette v. United States, 401 U.S. 437 (1971)
Girouard v. United States, 328 U.S. 61 (1946)
Gonzales v. O Centro Espirita Beneficente Uniao de Vegeta, 546 U.S. 418 (2006)
Gonzalez v. Roman Catholic Archbishop of Manila, 280 U.S. 1 (1929)
Hamilton v. Regents of the University of California, 293 U.S. 245 (1934)
Hobbie v. Unemployment Appeals Commission of Florida, 480 U.S. 136 (1987)
Holt v. Hobbs, 135 S. Ct. 853 (2015)
Hosanna-Tabor Evangelical Lutheran Church & School v. Equal Employment Opportunity Commission, 565 U.S. 171 (2012)
Jimmy Swaggart Ministries v. Board of Equalization of California, 493 U.S. 378 (1990)
Johnson v. Robison, 415 U.S. 361 (1974)
Jones v. Wolf, 443 U.S. 595 (1979)
Kedroff v. St. Nicholas Cathedral of Russian Orthodox Church in North America, 344 U.S. 94 (1952)
Lawrence v. Texas, 539 U.S. 558 (2003)
Lee, United States v., 455 U.S. 252 (1982)
Lyng v. Northwest Indian Cemetery Protective Association, 485 U.S. 439 (1988)
McCreary County, Kentucky v. American Civil Liberties Union of Kentucky, 545 U.S. 844 (2005)
McGowan v. Maryland, 366 U.S. 420 (1961)
Macintosh, United States v., 283 U.S. 605 (1931), overruled in part by *Girouard v. United States*, 328 U.S. 61 (1946)
Marbury v. Madison, 5 U.S. 137 (1803)
Meyer v. Nebraska, 262 U.S. 390 (1923)
Mitchell v. Helms, 530 U.S. 793 (2000)
Murdock v. Pennsylvania, 319 U.S. 105 (1943)
Nugent, United States v., 346 U.S. 1 (1953)
Obergefell v. Hodges, 135 S. Ct. 2584 (2015)
Pierce v. Society of Sisters, 268 U.S. 510 (1925)
Presbyterian Church in the United States v. Mary Elizabeth Blue Hull Memorial Presbyterian Church, 393 U.S. 440 (1969)
Prince v. Massachusetts, 321 U.S. 158 (1944)
Reynolds v. United States, 98 U.S. 145 (1878)
Romer v. Evans, 517 U.S. 620 (1996)
Rowland v. California Men's Colony, Unit II Men's Advisory Council, 506 U.S. 194 (1993)
Saia v. New York, 334 U.S. 558 (1948)
Schneider v. New Jersey, 308 U.S. 147 (1938)
School District of Abington Township v. Schempp, 374 U.S. 203 (1963)
Schwimmer, United States v., 279 U.S. 644 (1929), overruled in part by *Girouard v. United States*, 328 U.S. 61 (1946)
Seeger, United States v., 380 U.S. 163 (1965)
Serbian Eastern Orthodox Diocese for United States of America and Canada v. Milivojevich 426 U.S. 696 (1976)
Sherbert v. Verner, 374 U.S. 398 (1963)
Sicurella v. United States, 348 U.S. 385 (1955)
Sisson v. United States, 399 U.S. 267 (1970)
Sossamon v. Texas, 563 U.S. 277 (2011)
Thomas v. Review Board of the Indiana Employment Security Division, 450 U.S. 707 (1981)
Tony & Susan Alamo Foundation v. Secretary of Labor, 471 U.S. 290 (1985)
Torcaso v. Watkins, 367 U.S. 488 (1961)
Town of Greece, New York v. Galloway, 134 S. Ct. 1811 (2014)
Trans World Airlines, Incorporated v. Hardison, 432 U.S. 63 (1977)

Union Naval Stores Company v. United States, 240 U.S. 286 (1916)
United States v. _____ (see opposing party)
Walz v. Tax Commission of City of New York, 397 U.S. 664 (1970)
Watson v. Jones, 80 U.S. 679 (1871)
Welsh v. United States, 398 U.S. 333 (1970)
West Virginia Board of Education v. Barnette, 319 U.S. 624 (1943)
Wheaton College v. Burwell, 134 S. Ct. 2806 (2014)
Williamson v. Lee Optical of Oklahoma, Incorporated, 348 U.S. 483 (1955)
Wisconsin v. Yoder, 406 U.S. 205 (1972)
Zorach v. Clauson, 343 U.S. 396 (1952)
Zubik v. Burwell, 136 S. Ct. 444 (2015)

Courts of appeal

Adkins v. Kaspar, 393 F.3d 559 (5th Cir. 2004)
Africa v. Pennsylvania, 662 F.2d 1025, 1025 (3rd Cir. 1981)
Bob Jones University v. United States, 639 F.2d 147 (4th 1980)
Cheffer v. Reno, 55 F.3d 1517 (11th Cir. 1995)
Civil Liberties for Urban Believers v. City of Chicago, 342 F.3d 752 (7th Cir. 2003)
Geneva College v. Secretary United States Department of Health & Human Services, 778 F.3d 422 (3rd Cir. 2015), certiorari granted in part sub nomine *Zubik v. Burwell*, 136 S. Ct. 444 (2015) and certiorari granted sub nomine *Geneva College v. Burwell*, 136 S. Ct. 445 (2015)
Gilardi v. United States Department of Health & Human Services, 733 F.3d 1208 (District of Columbia Cir. 2013), certiorari granted, judgment vacated sub nomine *Gilardi v. Department of Health & Human Services*, 134 S. Ct. 2902 (2014) and certiorari denied sub nomine *Department of Health & Human Services v. Gilardi*, 134 S. Ct. 2902 (2014)
Grove v. Mead School District Number 354, 753 F.2d 1528 (9th Cir. 1985)
Guru Nanak Sikh Soc. of Yuba City v. County of Sutter, 456 F.3d 978 (9th Cir. 2006)
Hobby Lobby Stores, Incorporated v. Sebelius, 723 F.3d 1114 (10th Cir. 2013)
International Church of Foursquare Gospel v. City of San Leandro, 673 F.3d 1059 (9th Cir. 2011)
International Society for Krishna Consciousness, Incorporated v. Barber, 650 F.2d 430 (2nd Cir. 1981)
Kalka v. Hawk, 215 F.3d 90 (District of Columbia Cir. 2000)
Kaufman v. McCaughtry, 419 F.3d 678 (7th Cir. 2005)
Kauten, United States v., 133 F.2d 703 (2nd Cir. 1943)
Korte v. Sebelius, 735 F.3d 654 (7th Cir. 2013)
Mack v. O'Leary, 80 F.3d 1175 (7th Cir. 1996)
Malnak v. Yogi, 592 F.2d 197, 197–98 (3rd Cir. 1979)
Meyers, United States v., 95 F.3d 1475 (10th Cir. 1996)
Midrash Sephardi, Incorporated v. Town of Surfside, 366 F.3d 1214 (11th Cir. 2004)
Murphy v. Missouri Department of Corrections, 372 F.3d 979 (8th Cir. 2004)
Navajo Nation v. United States Forest Service, 535 F.3d 1058 (9th Cir. 2008)
Patel v. United States Bureau of Prisons, 515 F.3d 807 (8th Cir. 2008)
Patrick v. LeFevre, 745 F.2d 153 (2nd Cir. 1984)
San Jose Christian College v. City of Morgan Hill, 360 F.3d 1024 (9th Cir. 2004)
Smith v. Board of School Commissioners of Mobile County, 827 F.2d 684 (11th Cir. 1987)
Society of Separationists, Incorporated v. Herman, 939 F.2d 1207 (5th Cir. 1991), affirmed on rehearing, 959 F.2d 1283 (5th Cir. 1992)
Teterud v. Burns, 522 F.2d 357 (8th Cir. 1975)
United States v. _____ (see opposing party)
Vision Church v. Village of Long Grove, 468 F.3d 975 (7th Cir. 2006)

Ward, United States v., 989 F.2d 1015 (9th Cir. 1992)
Washington v. Klem, 497 F.3d 272 (3rd Cir. 2007)

District courts

Donovan v. Tony & Susan Alamo Foundation, 567 F. Supp. 556 (W.D. Arkansas 1982)
Geneva College v. Sebelius, 988 F. Supp. 2d 511 (W.D. Pennsylvania 2013), reversed sub nomine *Geneva College v. Secretary United States Department of Health & Human Services*, 778 F.3d 422 (3rd Cir. 2015), certiorari granted in part sub nomine *Zubik v. Burwell*, 136 S. Ct. 444 (2015) and certiorari granted sub nomine *Geneva College v. Burwell*, 136 S. Ct. 445 (2015)
Gilardi v. Sebelius, 926 F. Supp. 2d 273 (D. District of Columbia) affirmed in part, reversed in part sub nomine *Gilardi v. United States Department of Health & Human Services*, 733 F.3d 1208 (District of Columbia Cir. 2013), certiorari granted, judgment vacated sub nomine *Gilardi v. Department of Health & Human Services*, 134 S. Ct. 2902 (2014) and certiorari denied sub nomine *Department of Health & Human Services v. Gilardi*, 134 S. Ct. 2902 (2014)
Luckette v. Lewis, 883 F. Supp. 471 (D. Arizona 1995)
Meyers, United States v., 906 F. Supp. 1494 (D. Wyoming 1995), affirmed 95 F.3d 1475 (10th Cir. 1996)
Roy v. Cohen, 590 F. Supp. 600 (M.D. Pennsylvania 1984)
Sisson, United States v., 297 F. Supp. 902 (D. Massachusetts)
Smith v. Board of School Commissioners of Mobile County, 655 F. Supp. 939 (S.D. Alabama), reversed, 827 F.2d 684 (11th Cir. 1987)
United States v. _____ (see opposing party)

State courts

Christian Romany Church Ministries, Inc. v. Broward County, 980 So. 2d 1164 (Florida Appellate 2008)
Fellowship of Humanity v. County of Alameda, 315 P.2d 394 (California Appellate 1957)
Frazee v. Department of Employment Security, 512 N.E.2d 789 (Illinois Appellate 1987), reversed 489 U.S. 829 (1989)
Freeman v. Department of Highway Safety & Motor Vehicles, 924 So. 2d 48 (Florida Appellate 2006)
Gerhardt v. Heid, 267 N.W. 127 (North Dakota 1936)
Idaho v. Cordingley, 302 P.3d 730 (Idaho Appellate 2013)
Pearson v. Coale, 167 A. 54 (Maryland 1933)
People ex rel. Ring v. Board of Education of District 24, 92 N.E. 251 (Illinois 1910)
Sherbert v. Verner, 125 S.E.2d 737 (South Carolina 1962), reversed 374 U.S. 398 (1963)
Smith v. Employment Division, 763 P.2d 146 (Oregon 1988), reversed 494 U.S. 872 (1990)
Thomas v. Review Board of the Indiana Employment Security Division, 391 N.E.2d 1127 (Indiana 1979), reversed 450 U.S. 707 (1981)
Warner v. City of Boca Raton, 887 So. 2d 1023 (Florida 2004)

Cited secondary literature

Adams, Arlin M. & Charles J. Emmerich, ""A Heritage of Religious Liberty," *University of Pennsylvania Law Review* 137:1559–671 (1989)
Austin, Andrew W., "Faith and the Constitutional Definition of Religion," *Cumberland Law Review* 22:1–47 (1992)
Baron, Noah Butsch, "'There Can Be No Assumption . . .': Taking Seriously Challenges to Polygamy Bans in Light of Developments in Religious Freedom Jurisprudence," *Georgetown Journal of Gender & Law* 16:323–46 (2015)

Bernstein, David E., "Sex Discrimination Laws Versus Civil Liberties," *University of Chicago Legal Forum* 1999:133–95 (1999)

Beschle, Donald L., "Does a Broad Free Exercise Right Require a Narrow Definition of 'Religion'?" *Hastings Constitutional Law Quarterly* 39:357–90 (2011)

Bieber, Aaron D., "Constitutional Law—the Supreme Court Can't Have It Both Ways Under RFRA: The Tale of Two Compelling Interest Tests," *Wyoming Law Review* 7:225–57 (2007)

Binkley, Mason Blake, "A Loss for Words: 'Religion' in the First Amendment," *University of Detroit Mercy Law Review* 88:185–234 (2010)

Blatnik, Edward J.W., "No RFRAF Allowed: The Status of the Religious Freedom Restoration Act's Federal Application in the Wake of *City of Boerne v. Flores*," *Columbia Law Review* 98:1410–60 (1998)

Book Note, "Religion and *Roe*: The Politics of Exclusion," *Harvard Law Review* 108:495–500 (1994)

Brady, Kevin L., "Religious Sincerity and Imperfection: Can Lapsing Prisoners Recover Under RFRA and RLUIPA?" *University of Chicago Law Review* 78:1431–64 (2011)

Chopko, Mark E., "Continuing the Lord's Work and Healing His People: A Reply to Professors Lupu and Tuttle," 2004 *Brigham Young University Law Review* 2004:1897–920 (2004)

Chopko, Mark E. and Michael F. Moses, "Freedom to Be a Church: Confronting Challenges to the Right of Church Autonomy," *Georgetown Journal of Law & Public Policy* 3:387–452 (2005)

Comment, "Zoning Ordinances Affecting Churches: A Proposal for Expanded Free Exercise Protection," *University of Pennsylvania Law Review* 132:1131–62 (1984)

Cowan, Charles, "Creationism's Public and Private Fronts: The Protection and Restriction of Religious Freedom," *Mississippi Law Journal* 82:223–56 (2013)

Cushman, Barry, "The Secret Lives of the Four Horsemen," *Virginia Law Review* 83:559–84 (1997)

Davidson, Michael J., "War and the Doubtful Soldier," *Notre Dame Journal of Law, Ethics & Public Policy* 19:91–161 (2005)

Dehn, Max, "How It Works: Sobriety Sentencing, the Constitution, and Alcoholics Anonymous," *Michigan State University Journal of Medicine & Law* 10:255–98 (2006)

"Developments in the Law—Religion and the State," *Harvard Law Review* 100:1612–39 (1987)

DiPippa, John M.A., "God and Guns: The Free Exercise of Religion Problems of Regulating Guns in Churches and Other Houses of Worship," *Marquette Law Review* 98:1103–46 (2015)

Doernberg, Donald L., "Pass in Review: Due Process and Judicial Scrutiny of Classification Decisions of the Selective Service System," *Hastings Law Journal* 33:871–902 (1982)

Drabble, William, "Righteous Torts: *Pleasant Glade Assembly of God v. Schubert* and the Free Exercise Defense in Texas," *Baylor Law Review* 62:267–89 (2010)

Dugan, Conor B., ""Religious Liberty in Spain and the United States: A Comparative Study," *Notre Dame Law Review* 78:1675–730 (2003)

Eberle, Edward J., "Roger Williams' Gift: Religious Freedom in America," *Roger Williams University Law Review* 4:425–86 (1999)

Falk, Donald, "*Lyng v. Northwest Indian Cemetery Protective Association*: Bulldozing First Amendment Protection of Indian Sacred Lands," *Ecology Law Quarterly* 16:515–70 (1989)

Feldman, Stephen M., "Religious Minorities and the First Amendment: The History, the Doctrine, and the Future," *University of Pennsylvania Journal of Constitutional Law* 6:222–77 (2003)

Flanders, Chad, "The Possibility of a Secular First Amendment," *Quinnipiac Law Review* 26:257–303 (2008)

Freed, Eric C., "Secular Humanism, the Establishment Clause, and Public Education," *New York University Law Review* 61:1149–85 (1986)

Freeman III, George C., "The Misguided Search for the Constitutional Definition of 'Religion,'" *Georgetown Law Journal* 71:1519–65 (1983)

French, Rebekah J., "Free Exercise of Religion on the Public Lands," *Public Land Law Review* 11:197–209 (1990)

Galligan, Michael William, "Judicial Resolution of Intrachurch Disputes," *Columbia Law Review* 83:2007–38 (1983)

Garrett, David, "Vine of the Dead: Reviving Equal Protection Rites for Religious Drug Use," *American Indian Law Review* 31:143–62 (2007)

Gordon, III, James D., "Free Exercise on the Mountaintop," *California Law Review* 79:91–116 (1991)

Greenawalt, Kent, "Religion as a Concept in Constitutional Law," *California Law Review* 72:753–816 (1984)

Griffin, Leslie, "'We Do Not Preach. We Teach.' Religion Professors and the First Amendment," 19 *Quinnipiac Law Review* 19:1–65 (2000)

Hilbert, John S., "God in a Cage: Religion, Intent, and Criminal Law," *Buffalo Law Review* 36:701–42 (1987)

Inazu, John D., "More Is More: Strengthening Free Exercise, Speech, and Association," *Minnesota Law Review* 99:485–534 (2014)

Inazu, John D., "The Four Freedoms and the Future of Religious Liberty," *North Carolina Law Review* 92:787–853 (2014)

Jackson, Bruce B., "Secularization by Incorporation: Religious Organizations and Corporate Identity," *First Amendment Law Review* 11:90–147 (2012)

Kellett, Christine Hunter, "Draft Registration and the Conscientious Objector: A Proposal to Accommodate Constitutional Values," *Columbia Human Rights Law Review* 15:167–81 (1984)

Kelty, Lisa J., "Malicki v. Doe: The Constitutionality of Negligent Hiring and Supervision Claims," *Brooklyn Law Review* 69:1121–57 (2004)

Kenney, Elaine Gareri, "For the Sake of Your Health: ERISA's Preemption Provisions, HMO Accountability, and Consumer Access to State Law Remedies," *University of San Francisco Law Review* 38:361–89 (2004)

Kmiec, Douglas W., "The Original Understanding of the Free Exercise Clause and Religious Diversity," *University of Missouri Kansas City Law Review* 59:591–609 (1991)

Laycock, Douglas & Steven T. Collis, "Generally Applicable Law and the Free Exercise of Religion," *Nebraska Law Review* 95:1–27 (2016)

Lund, Christopher C., "Religious Liberty after *Gonzales*: A Look at State RFRAs," *South Dakota Law Review* 55:466–97 (2010)

Lund, Christopher C., "In Defense of the Ministerial Exception," *North Carolina Law Review* 90:1–72 (2011)

McConnell, Michael W., "Free Exercise Revisionism and the *Smith* Decision," *University of Chicago Law Review* 57:1109–53 (1990)

Marshall, Lawrence C., "The Religion Clauses and Compelled Religious Divorces: A Study in Marital and Constitutional Separations," *Northwestern University Law Review* 80:204–58 (1985)

Marshall, William P., "In Defense of *Smith* and Free Exercise Revisionism," *University of Chicago Law Review* 58:308–27 (1991)

Marshall, William P., "In Defense of the Search for Truth as a First Amendment Justification," *Georgia Law Review* 30:1–39 (1995)

Mason, Craig A., "'Secular Humanism' and the Definition of Religion: Extending a Modified 'Ultimate Concern' Test to *Mozert v. Hawkins County Public Schools* and *Smith v. Board of School Commissioners*," *Washington Law Review* 63:445–68 (1988)

Mason, III, James R., "*Smith*'s Free-Exercise 'Hybrids' Rooted in Non-Free-Exercise Soil," *Regent University Law Review* 6:201–59 (1995)

Muzzey, David Saville, *Ethics as a Religion*. New York: Simon & Schuster, 1951Note, "Conscientious Objectors: Recent Developments and a New Appraisal," *Columbia Law Review* 70:1426–41 (1970)

Note, "Toward a Constitutional Definition of Religion," *Harvard Law Review* 91:1056–89 (1978)

Nugent, Nicholas, "Toward a RFRA That Works," *Vanderbilt Law Review* 61:1027–66 (2008)

O'Connor, Michelle, "The Religious Freedom Restoration Act: Exactly What Rights Does It "Restore" in the Federal Tax Context?" *Arizona State Law Journal* 36:321–402 (2004)

Olree, Andy G., "The Continuing Threshold Test for Free Exercise Claims," *William & Mary Bill of Rights Journal* 17:103–56 (2008)

Page, Donna D., "Veganism and Sincerely Held 'Religious' Beliefs in the Workplace: No Protection Without Definition," *University of Pennsylvania Journal of Labor & Employment Law* 7:363–408 (2005)

Paulsen, Michael S., "A RFRA Runs Through It: Religious Freedom and the U.S. Code," *Montana Law Review* 56:249–94 (1995)

Peñalver, Eduardo, "The Concept of Religion," *Yale Law Journal* 107:791–822 (1997)

Reuveni, Erez, "On Boy Scouts and Anti-Discrimination Law: The Associational Rights of Quasi-Religious Organizations," *Boston University Law Review* 86:109–71 (2006)

Rhea, Michael, "Denying and Defining Religion under the First Amendment: Waldorf Education as a Lens for Advocating a Broad Definitional Approach," *Louisiana Law Review* 72:1095–127 (2012)

Rosato, Steven M., "Saving Oklahoma's 'Save Our State' Amendment: Sharia Law in the West and Suggestions to Protect Similar State Legislation from Constitutional Attack," *Seton Hall Law Review* 44:659–93 (2014)

Rosenzweig, Sidney A., "Restoring Religious Freedom to the Workplace: Title VII, RFRA and Religious Accommodation," *University of Pennsylvania Law Review* 144:2513–35 (1996)

Rutledge, Thomas E., "A Corporation Has No Soul—the Business Entity Law Response to Challenges to the PPACA Contraceptive Mandate," *William & Mary Business Law Review* 5:1–53 (2014)

Sandgren, Matthew L., "Extending Religious Freedoms Abroad: Difficulties Experienced by Minority Religions," *Tulsa Journal of Comparative & International Law* 9:251–84 (2001)

Shah, Amit, "The Impact of *Gonzales v. O Centro Espirita Beneficente Uniao Do Vegetal*, 546 U.S. 418 (2006)," *Rutgers Journal of Law & Religion* 10:4–29 (2008)

Shulman, Jeffrey, "The Parent as (Mere) Educational Trustee: Whose Education Is It, Anyway?" *Nebraska Law Review* 89:290–357 (2010)

Siegel, Neil S. & Reva B. Siegel, "Compelling Interests and Contraception," *Connecticut Law Review* 47:1025–43 (2015)

Sisk, Gregory C., Michael Heise, & Andrew P. Morriss, "Searching for the Soul of Judicial Decisionmaking: An Empirical Study of Religious Freedom Decisions," *Ohio State Law Journal* 65:491–614 (2004)

Strang, Lee J., "The Meaning of 'Religion' in the First Amendment," *Duquesne Law Review* 40:181–240 (2002)

Tan, Jonathan T., "Nonprofit Organizations, For-Profit Corporations, and the HHS Mandate: Why the Mandate Does Not Satisfy RFRA's Requirements," *University of Richmond Law Review* 47:1301–70 (2013)

Teitel, Ruti, "When Separate Is Equal: Why Organized Religious Exercises, Unlike Chess, Do Not Belong in the Public Schools," *Northwestern University Law Review* 81:174–89 (1986)

Tillich, Paul, *Systematic Theology*, Vol. II. Chicago: University of Chicago Press, 1957

Tillich, Paul, *Dynamics of Faith*, New York: Harper Torchbook, 1958

White, Michael J., "The First Amendment's Religion Clauses: 'Freedom of Conscience' versus Institutional Accommodation," *San Diego Law Review* 47:1075–105 (2010)

Whitehead, John W., "The Conservative Supreme Court and the Demise of the Free Exercise of Religion," *Temple Political & Civil Rights Law Review* 7:1–139 (1997)

Young, David, "The Meaning of 'Religion' in the First Amendment: Lexicography and Constitutional Policy, *University of Missouri-Kansas City Law Review* 56:313–41 (1988)

Index

accommodation 61, 73–4, 100, 119, 131
Adams, Judge Arlin 128–30
Adkins v. Kaspar 126
Affordable Care Act (ACA) 106–07, 116–17
Africa v. Pennsylvania 130–31
Aid to Families with Dependent Children (AFDC) 78
alcohol 6, 112
Americans with Disabilities Act (ADA) 34
animus 96
arbitrariness 28–9, 33–4
assisted reproductive technologies (ART) 114–15

Ballard, United States v. 11–13, 19–20, 128, 133, 137–38
Bible, 14–15, 85, 117
bizarre 17, 19–21, 128, 132, 135
Bland, United States v. 43
Bob Jones University v. United States 117–18
Bouldin v. Alexander 28
Bowen v. Roy 78–82, 95, 115, 118
Braunfeld v. Brown 60–8, 72, 74–7, 81, 91, 101, 109, 116–20, 136
Brennan, Justice William 15, 62
Brorby, Judge Wade 133–34
burden: direct 61, 64, 91–2; indirect 61, 63, 75, 91–2
Burger, Chief Justice Warren 82
Burwell v. Hobby Lobby Stores, Incorporated 106–20, 139

Cantwell v. Connecticut 9–12, 57–9, 68, 93
Cardozo, Justice Benjamin 44
child labor laws 59–60, 93
Christian Romany Church Ministries, Incorporated v. Broward County 136–37
Church of the Lukumi Babalu Aye, Incorporated v. City of Hialeah 96–7
City of Boerne v. Flores 97–100, 135, 137
Civil Liberties for Urban Believers v. City of Chicago 126–27
clergy 3, 20, 30, 33, 35, 37, 129, 132

coercion 14–15, 127
collusion 28, 33–5
communion 6, 100
competence 5, 26–7, 31–7, 134
conscientious objector 3, 40–4, 57, 68, 81, 134; who qualifies 45–53
contraception 107, 110–13, 116
convert 82, 132
corporations: for profit 107–10, 115–17; non-profit 107–10, 115–17
criminal 6–12, 21, 48, 76, 80, 91–5
Cutter v. Wilkinson 100–01

Davis v. Beason 7–9, 11
Day-Brite Lighting Incorporated v. Missouri 61
divorce 114

Employee Retirement Income Security Act (ERISA) 114
Employment Division, Department of Human Resources of Oregon v. Smith (Smith I) 91–2
Employment Division, Department of Human Resources of Oregon v. Smith (Smith II) 2–4, 90, 92–7, 101–02, 106, 117–20, 125, 135, 138
Engel v. Vitale 14
Equal Employment Opportunity Commission (EEOC) 35
Establishment Clause 8, 13–14, 45–7, 78, 99–100, 111, 128
Estate of Thornton v. Caldor, Incorporated 78
Everson v. Board of Education 13

Fair Labor Standards Act (FLSA) 76–7, 109, 118
falsity 11–13, 21, 129
Family Medical Leave Act (FMLA) 114
fines 112
Food and Drug Administration (FDA) 116
fornication 8
Frankfurter, Justice Felix 46

fraud 10–13, 28, 33–5, 78, 133–34
Frazee v. Illinois Department of Employment Security 17–18, 20, 84, 90, 93, 133
Freeman v. Department of Highway Safety and Motor Vehicles 135–36

Gallagher v. Crown Kosher Super Market of Massachusetts, Incorporated 63, 68, 72, 75–6, 117–20
generally applicable 57, 74, 80, 84–5, 93–8, 136, 138
Gillette v. United States 20, 48–52, 66, 81, 134
Girouard v. United States 43–4
Gonzales v. O Centro Espirita Beneficente Uniao de Vegeta 100
Gonzalez v. Roman Catholic Archbishop of Manila 28–9, 33

Hamilton v. Regents of the University of California 43–4
Hand, Judge Augustus 46
Harlan, Justice John 47, 78
Health and Human Services (HHS) 106–07, 109–12, 116
heresy 11
hierarchical 26–33
hoasca 100–01
Hobbie v. Unemployment Appeals Commission of Florida 82, 84
Holt v. Hobbs 119, 139
Hosanna-Tabor Evangelical Lutheran Church & School v. Equal Employment Opportunity Commission 34–38
hostility 15
Hughes, Chief Justice Charles 42–3
human sacrifice 6–7, 9

Idaho v. Cordingley 137–38
independent church 27–8, 134
infringement: direct 73; indirect 75
Internal Revenue Service (IRS) 118
International Church of Foursquare Gospel v. City of Leandro 127

Jackson, Justice Robert 12–13
Jimmy Swaggart Ministries v. Board of Equalization of California 84–5, 90
Johnson v. Robison 51–2, 67
Jones v. Wolf 31, 33

Kaufman v. McCaughtry 135
Kauten, United States v. 46
Kedroff v. St. Nicholas Cathedral of Russian Orthodox Church in North America 29–30, 35
kosher 63, 96, 117–18

land use 4, 99, 120, 126–28, 136–37, 139
Lee, United States v. 72–6, 79, 81, 85, 90, 101, 116–20, 139
logic 17, 19, 77, 133–34
Lyng v. New Indian Cemetery Protective Association 82–4

Macintosh, United States v. 42–4
Malnak v. Yogi 128–30
marijuana 131–33, 137–38
Meyer v. Nebraska 66
Meyers, United States v. 131–34
Midrash Sephardi, Incorporated v. Town of Surfside 127–28
Mitchell v. Helms 111
Murdock v. Pennsylvania 10–11

neutrality 2, 28, 30–5, 37, 49, 80–2, 93–8, 136, 138

O'Connor, Justice Sandra Day 78, 93, 95, 111

parental rights 59–60, 65–8, 93
Patrick v. LeFevre 134
persons: artificial 107–08; natural 107–08
peyote 90–2, 94
philosophy 16–17, 19, 45, 51, 65 133, 137–38
Pierce v. Society of Sisters 66
polygamy 6–8, 10–13
prayer 14
preaching 10, 36, 59, 96
Presbyterian Church in the United States v. Mary Elizabeth Blue Hull Memorial Presbyterian Church 30–1
Prince v. Massachusetts 50–60, 68, 72, 93

Religious Freedom Restoration Act (RFRA): federal 4, 120, 125–56, 131 133, 139; and the Constitution 97–101, and corporations 106–10; and substantial burdens 111–19; state 135–39
Religious Land Use and Institutionalized Person Act (RLUIPA) 4, 90, 100–01, 106, 119–20, 138–39; and lower court interpretations 125–28
religious test 13–14
Reynolds v. United States 6–7, 9, 11
Romer v. Evans 95

same-sex marriage 114
School District of Abington Township v. Schempp 14–15
Schwimmer, United States v. 41–4
sectarian 15, 111
Seeger, United States v. 45–7, 65, 129–31, 135

Serbian Eastern Orthodox Diocese for United States of America and Canada v. Milivojevich 33–4
Sherbert v. Verner 63–8, 72, 75, 78–80, 84; and *Smith* 90–5; and RFRA 97, 101, 117; and coercion 127; and state RFRA 136
Sicurella v. United States 45, 49
Sisson v. United States 47–8
social security 66, 72–6, 79, 101, 116, 139; and numbers 78–9, 81, 83, 117
special treatment 5–7, 13–14, 19
Stevens, Justice John Paul 74
Stone, Chief Justice Harlan 12
substantial deviation 28, 31–2
Sunday closing laws 60–3, 116, 119

tax 11, 13, 44, 52, 114–15, 139; social security 66, 72–4; sales and use 84–5; exempt 117–18
Thomas v. Review Board of the Indiana Employment Security Division 68, 72, 75–6, 79–80, 84, 137; and doctrinal understandings 16–17, 19, 67, 77, 132–33, 136

Thoreau, Henry David 16, 131, 138
Tillich, Paul 129
Tony and Susan Alamo Foundation v. Secretary of Labor 76–8, 109, 118
Torcaso v. Watkins 13–15
Transcendental Meditation 128
truth 11–12, 21, 129

ultimate concern 19, 129–30, 138
unemployment compensation 16, 63, 67, 75, 78–82, 84–5, 90–5, 101
United States v. _____ (*see* opposing party)

Vietnam War 47–50, 134

Watson v. Jones 6, 27–31
Welsh v. United States 47, 51, 135
Williamson v. Lee Optical of Oklahoma, Incorporated 61–2
Wisconsin v. Yoder 15–16, 20, 65–8, 73, 81, 93, 97, 130–31, 137–38
worship 9–10, 15, 27, 64, 96, 127, 137

zoning *see* land use